Among
Schoolchildren

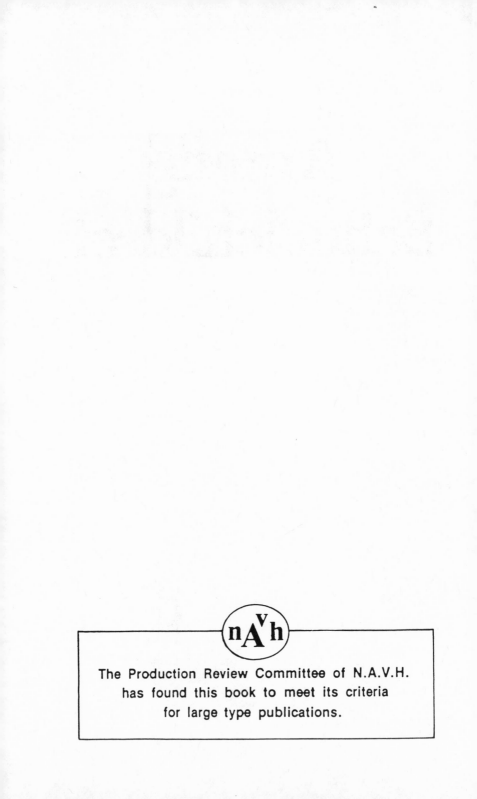

Among Schoolchildren

Tracy Kidder

Thorndike Press • Thorndike, Maine

Library of Congress Cataloging in Publication Data:

Kidder, Tracy.
    Among schoolchildren / Tracy Kidder. -- Large print ed.
    p. cm.
    "A Richard Todd Book."
    Includes bibliographical references.
    ISBN 0-89621-967-4 (alk. paper : lg. print)
    1. Elementary school teaching--United States--Case stud-
ies. 2. Fifth grade (Education)--United States--Case studies.
3. Large type books. I. Title.
[LB1776.K48   1989b]   89-49559
372.11'02--dc20   CIP

Author's Note: This is a work of nonfiction. I have changed
the names of the children and of the student teacher;
Eduardo is also a pseudonym.

Thorndike Press Large Print editon published in 1990 by
arrangement with Houghton Mifflin Company.

Cover design by Wendell Minor.

**The trees indicium is a trade mark of Thorndike
Press.**

This book is printed on acid-free, high opacity paper. ∞

For Reine Marie Melanie Kidder
Syosset High School English Department,
1960–1981

September

Mrs. Zajac wasn't born yesterday. She knows you didn't do your best work on this paper, Clarence. Don't you remember Mrs. Zajac saying that if you didn't do your best, she'd make you do it over? As for you, Claude, God forbid that you should ever need brain surgery. But Mrs. Zajac hopes that if you do, the doctor won't open up your head and walk off saying he's almost done, as you just said when Mrs. Zajac asked you for your penmanship, which, by the way, looks like who did it and ran. Felipe, the reason you have hiccups is, your mouth is always open and the wind rushes in. You're in fifth grade now. So, Felipe, put a lock on it. Zip it up. Then go get a drink of water. Mrs. Zajac means business, Robert. The sooner you realize she never said everybody in the room has to do the work except for Robert, *the sooner you'll get along with her. And . . . Clarence. Mrs. Zajac knows you didn't try. You don't just hand in junk to Mrs. Zajac. She's been teaching an awful lot of years. She*

9

didn't fall off the turnip cart yesterday. She told you she was an old-lady teacher.

She was thirty-four. She wore a white skirt and yellow sweater and a thin gold necklace, which she held in her fingers, as if holding her own reins, while waiting for children to answer. Her hair was black with a hint of Irish red. It was cut short to the tops of her ears, and swept back like a pair of folded wings. She had a delicately cleft chin, and she was short – the children's chairs would have fit her. Although her voice sounded conversational, it had projection. She had never acted. She had found this voice in classrooms.

Mrs. Zajac seemed to have a frightening amount of energy. She strode across the room, her arms swinging high and her hands in small fists. Taking her stand in front of the green chalkboard, discussing the rules with her new class, she repeated sentences, and her lips held the shapes of certain words, such as "homework," after she had said them. Her hands kept very busy. They sliced the air and made karate chops to mark off boundaries. They extended straight out like a traffic cop's, halting illegal maneuvers yet to be perpetrated. When they rested momentarily on her hips, her hands looked as if they were in holsters. She told the children, "One thing Mrs. Zajac expects from

10

each of you is that you do *your* best." She said, "Mrs. Zajac gives homework. I'm sure you've all heard. The only meanie gives homework." *Mrs. Zajac.* It was in part a role. She worked her way into it every September.

At home on late summer days like these, Chris Zajac wore shorts or blue jeans. Although there was no dress code for teachers here at Kelly School, she always went to work in skirts or dresses. She dressed as if she were applying for a job, and hoped in the back of her mind that someday, heading for job interviews, her students would remember her example. Outside school, she wept easily over small and large catastrophes and at sentimental movies, but she never cried in front of students, except once a few years ago when the news came over the intercom that the Space Shuttle had exploded and Christa McAuliffe had died – and then she saw in her students' faces that the sight of Mrs. Zajac crying had frightened them, and she made herself stop and then explained.

At home, Chris laughed at the antics of her infant daughter and egged the child on. She and her first-grade son would sneak up to the radio when her husband wasn't looking and change the station from classical to rock-and-roll music. "You're regressing, Chris," her husband would say. But especially on the first few

11

days of school, she didn't let her students get away with much. She was not amused when, for instance, on the first day, two of the boys started dueling with their rulers. On nights before the school year started, Chris used to have bad dreams: her principal would come to observe her, and her students would choose that moment to climb up on their desks and give her the finger, or they would simply wander out the door. But a child in her classroom would never know that Mrs. Zajac had the slightest doubt that students would obey her.

The first day, after going over all the school rules, Chris spoke to them about effort. "If you put your name on a paper, you should be proud of it," she said. "You should think, This is the best I can do and I'm proud of it and I want to hand this in." Then she asked, "If it isn't your best, what's Mrs. Zajac going to do?"

Many voices, most of them female, answered softly in unison, "Make us do it over."

"Make you do it over," Chris repeated. It sounded like a chant.

"Does anyone know anything about Lisette?" she asked when no one answered to that name.

Felipe — small, with glossy black hair — threw up his hand.

"Felipe?"

"She isn't here!" said Felipe. He wasn't being

12

fresh. On those first few days of school, whenever Mrs. Zajac put the sound of a question in her voice, and sometimes before she got the question out, Felipe's hand shot up.

In contrast, there was the very chubby girl who sat nearly motionless at her desk, covering the lower half of her face with her hands. As usual, most of their voices sounded timid the first day, and came out of hiding gradually. There were twenty children. About half were Puerto Rican. Almost two-thirds of the twenty needed the forms to obtain free lunches. There was a lot of long and curly hair. Some boys wore little rattails. The eyes the children lifted up to her as she went over the rules – a few eyes were blue and many more were brown – looked so solemn and so wide that Chris felt like dropping all pretense and laughing. Their faces ranged from dark brown to gold, to pink, to pasty white, the color that Chris associated with sunless tenements and too much TV. The boys wore polo shirts and T-shirts and new white sneakers with the ends of the laces untied and tucked behind the tongues. Some girls wore lacy ribbons in their hair, and some wore pants and others skirts, a rough but not infallible indication of religion – the daughters of Jehovah's Witnesses and Pentecostals do not wear pants. There was a lot of prettiness in the room, and all of the children looked cute to Chris.

So did the student teacher, Miss Hunt, a very young woman in a dress with a bow at the throat who sat at a table in the back of the room. Miss Hunt had a sweet smile, which she turned on the children, hunching her shoulders when they looked at her. At times the first days, while watching Chris in action, Miss Hunt seemed to gulp. Sometimes she looked as frightened as the children. For Chris, looking at Miss Hunt was like looking at herself fourteen years ago.

The smell of construction paper, slightly sweet and forest-like, mingled with the fading, acrid smell of roach and rodent spray. The squawk box on the wall above the closets, beside the clock with its jerky minute hand, erupted almost constantly, adult voices paging adults by their surnames and reminding staff of deadlines for the census forms, attendance calendars, and United Way contributions. Other teachers poked their heads inside the door to say hello to Chris or to ask advice about how to fill out forms or to confer with her on schedules for math and reading. In between interruptions, amid the usual commotion of the first day, Chris taught short lessons, assigned the children seat work, and attended to paperwork at her large gray metal desk over by the window.

For moments then, the room was still. From the bilingual class next door to the south came the baritone of the teacher Victor Guevara, singing to his students in Spanish. Through the small casement windows behind Chris came sounds of the city – Holyoke, Massachusetts – trailer truck brakes releasing giant sighs now and then, occasional screeches of freight trains, and, always in the background, the mechanical hum of ventilators from the school and from Dinn Bros. Trophies and Autron, from Leduc Corp. Metal Fabricators and Laminated Papers. It was so quiet inside the room during those moments that little sounds were loud: the rustle of a book's pages being turned and the tiny clanks of metal-legged chairs being shifted slightly. Bending over forms and the children's records, Chris watched the class from the corner of her eye. The first day she kept an especially close eye on the boy called Clarence.

Clarence was a small, lithe, brown-skinned boy with large eyes and deep dimples. Chris watched his journeys to the pencil sharpener. They were frequent. Clarence took the longest possible route around the room, walking heel-to-toe and brushing the back of one leg with the shin of the other at every step – a cheerful little dance across the blue carpet, around the perimeter of desks, and along the back wall, passing under the American flag, which didn't quite brush his head. Reaching the sharpener, Clarence would turn his pencil into a stunt plane, which did several loop-the-loops before plunging in the hole.

The first morning, Chris didn't catch one of the intercom announcements. She asked aloud if anyone had heard the message. Clarence, who seemed to stutter at the start of sentences when he was in a hurry to speak, piped up right away, "He he say to put the extra desks in the hall." Clarence noticed things. He paid close attention to the intercom. His eyes darted to the door the moment a visitor appeared. But he paid almost no attention to her lessons and his work. It seemed as if every time that she glanced at Clarence he wasn't working.

"Take a look at Clarence," Chris whispered to Miss Hunt. She had called Miss Hunt up to her desk for a chat. "Is he doing anything?"

The other children were working. Clarence was just then glancing over his shoulder, checking on the clock. Miss Hunt hunched her shoulders and laughed without making a sound. "He has such huge eyes!" she said.

"And they're looking right through me," said Chris, who lifted her voice and called, "Clarence, the pencil's moving, right?" Then Chris smiled at Miss Hunt, and said in a half whisper, "I can see that Clarence and I will have a little chat out in the hall, one of these days."

Miss Hunt smiled, gulped, and nodded, all at once.

Chris had received the children's "cumulative" records, which were stuffed inside salmon-colored folders known as "cumes." For now she checked only addresses and phone numbers, and resisted looking into histories. It was usually better at first to let her own opinions form. But she couldn't help noticing the thickness of some cumes. "The thicker the cume, the more trouble," she told Miss Hunt. "If it looks like *War and Peace* . . ." Clarence's cume was about as thick as the Boston phone book. And Chris couldn't help having heard what some colleagues had insisted on telling her about Clarence. One teacher whom Chris trusted had described him as probably the most difficult child in all of last year's fourth-grade classes. Chris wished she hadn't heard that, nor the rumors about Clarence. She'd heard confident but unsubstantiated assertions that he was a beaten child. These days many people applied the word "abused" to any apparently troubled student. She had no good reason to believe the rumors, but she couldn't help thinking, "What if they're true?" She wished she hadn't heard anything about Clarence's past at this early moment. She found it hard enough after thirteen years to believe that all fifth graders' futures lay before them out of sight, and not in plain view behind.

She'd try to ignore what she had heard and deal with problems as they came. Clarence's were surfacing quickly. He came to school the second morning without having done his homework. He had not done any work at all so far, except for one math assignment, and for that he'd just written down some numbers at random. She'd try to nip this in the bud. "No work, no recess," she told Clarence late the second morning. He had quit even pretending to work about half an hour before.

Just a little later, she saw Clarence heading for the pencil sharpener again. He paused near Felipe's desk. Clarence glanced back at her. She could see that he thought she wasn't looking.

Clarence set his jaw. He made a quick, sharp kick at Felipe's leg under the desk. Then he stalked, glancing backward at Chris, to the pencil sharpener. Felipe didn't complain.

Maybe Felipe had provoked the kick. Or maybe this was Clarence's way of getting even with her for threatening to keep him in from recess. It wasn't a pleasant thought. She let the incident pass. She'd have to watch Clarence carefully, though.

The afternoon of that second day of class,

Chris warned Clarence several times that she would keep him after school if he didn't get to work. Detention seemed like a masochistic exercise. Sometimes it worked. It was a tool she'd found most useful at the beginning of a year and after vacations. In her experience, most children responded well to clearly prescribed rules and consequences, and she really didn't have many other tangible weapons. The idea was to get most of the unpleasantness, the scoldings and detentions, out of the way early. And, of course, if she threatened to keep Clarence after school, she had to keep her word. Maybe he would do some work, and she could have a quiet talk with him. She didn't plan to keep him long.

The other children went home, and so did Miss Hunt. Chris sat at her desk, a warm late-summer breeze coming through the little casement window behind her. She worked on her plans for next week, and from under cover of her bowed head, she watched Clarence. The children's chairs, the plastic backs and seats of which came in primary colors, like a bag full of party balloons, were placed upside down on the tops of their desks. Clarence sat alone at his desk, surrounded by upended chairs. He had his arms folded on his chest and was glaring at her. The picture of defiance. He would show her. She felt like laughing for a moment. His stubbornness was impressive. Nearly an hour passed, and the boy did no work at all.

Chris sighed, got up, and walked over to Clarence.

He turned his face away as she approached.

Chris sat in a child's chair and, resting her chin on her hand, leaned her face close to Clarence's.

He turned his farther away.

"What's the problem?"

He didn't answer. His eyelashes began to flutter.

"Do you understand the work in fifth grade?"

He didn't answer.

"I hear you're a very smart boy. Don't you want to have a good year? Don't you want to take your work home and tell your mom, 'Look what I did'?"

The fluorescent lights in the ceiling were pale and bright. One was flickering. Tears came rolling out of Clarence's eyes. They streaked his brown cheeks.

Chris gazed at him, and in a while said, "Okay, I'll make a deal with you. You go home and do your work, and come in tomorrow with all your work done, and I'll pretend these two days never happened. We'll have a new Clarence tomorrow. Okay?"

Clarence still had not looked at her or answered.

"A new Clarence," Chris said. "Promise?"

Clarence made the suggestion of a nod, a slight concession to her, she figured, now that it was clear she would let him leave.

Her face was very close to his. Her eyes almost touched his tear-stained cheeks. She gazed. She knew she wasn't going to see a new Clarence tomorrow. It would be naive to think a boy with a cume that thick was going to change overnight. But she'd heard the words in her mind anyway. She had to keep alive the little voice that says, Well, you never know. What was the alternative? To decide an eleven-year-old was going to go on failing, and there was nothing anyone could do about it, so why try? Besides, this was just the start of a campaign. She was trying to tell him, "You don't have to have another bad year. Your life in school can begin to change." If she could talk him into believing that, maybe by June there *would* be a new Clarence.

"We always keep our promises?" Chris said.

He seemed to make a little nod.

"I bet everyone will be surprised. We'll have a new Clarence," Chris said, and then she let him go.

2

When Chris had first walked into her room –
Room 205 – back in late August, it felt like an
attic. The chalkboards and bulletin boards were
covered up with newspaper, and the bright
colors of the plastic chairs seemed calculated to
force cheerfulness upon her. On the side of one
of the empty children's desks there was a faded
sticker that read, OFFICIAL PACE CAR. A
child from some other year must have put it
there; he'd moved on, but she'd come back to
the same place. There was always something a
little mournful about coming back to an empty
classroom at the end of summer, a childhood
feeling, like being put to bed when it is light
outside.

She spent her summer days with children,
her own and those of friends. While her daughter splashed around in the wading pool and her
son and his six-year-old buddies climbed the
wooden fort her husband had built in their
back yard, she sat at the picnic table and there
was time to read – this summer, a few popular
novels and then, as August wore on, a book
called *The Art of Teaching Writing*, which she
read with a marking pencil in hand, underlin-
ing the tips that seemed most useful. There
was time for adult conversation, around the

swimming pool at her best friend's house, while their children swam. In August she left Holyoke and spent a couple of weeks near the ocean with her husband and children, on Cape Cod. She liked the pace of summer, and of all the parts of summer she liked the mornings best, the unhurried, slowly unfolding mornings, which once again this year went by much too fast.

Chris looked around her empty classroom. It was fairly small as classrooms go, about twenty-five by thirty-six feet. The room repossessed her. She said to herself, "I can't believe the summer's over. I feel like I never left this place." And then she got to work.

She put up her bulletin board displays, scouted up pencils and many kinds of paper – crayons hadn't yet arrived; she'd borrow some of her son's – made a red paper apple for her door, and moved the desks around into the layout she had settled on in her first years of teaching. She didn't use the truly ancient arrangement, with the teacher's desk up front and the children's in even rows before it. Her desk was already where she wanted it, in a corner by the window. She had to be on her feet and moving in order to teach. Over there in the corner, her desk wouldn't get in her way. And she could retire to it in between lessons, at a little distance from the children, and still see down the hallway between her door and the boys' room – a strategic piece of real estate – and also keep an eye on all the children at their desks. She pushed most of the children's small, beige-topped desks side by side, in a continuous perimeter describing three-quarters of a square, open at the front. She put four desks in the middle of the square, so that each of those four had space between it and any other desk. These were Chris's "middleperson desks," where it was especially hard to hide, although even the back row of the perimeter was more exposed than back rows usually are.

When the room was arranged to her liking, she went home to the last days of summer.

Chris let the children choose their own desks the first day. On the morning of the second, she announced, "I'm going to make a few changes in seats right now. Some of you are too short for where you are. There's nothing wrong with being short. Mrs. Zajac's short." She directed traffic as, without audible protests but with a lot of clanging of metal, the children pushed their chairs like vendor's carts across the blue carpet. Shortness had little to do with where she placed them, but it was too soon to tell them most of the real reasons.

She knew all of their names by that second

morning. She wasn't any better than most people at remembering names, but in a classroom that knack is a necessity and naturally acquired. Confronting a new class isn't like meeting strangers at a party. Inside her room, Chris didn't have to think as much about how she looked to the children as how they looked to her.

Here they were, and they were, as always, compelling. Four years ago these children were still learning to dress themselves. Four years from now these cute little ten- and eleven-year-olds would be able — but not disposed, she hoped — to produce children of their own. Some of their voices hadn't changed yet, but they were only pausing here on their way to adolescence.

One boy, Julio, had the beginnings of a mustache. Julio was repeating fifth grade. He wrote in one of his first essays:

Yesterday my mother and my father unchul cusint me we all went to springfield to see the brudishduldog and rode piper ricky stemdout ladey is fight for the lult

She put Julio in one of the middle-person desks. ("He's sort of a special project, and I also know he's got to be pushed. He's very quiet. He doesn't bother anyone. That was the problem last year, I'm told. He didn't bother anyone. He just didn't *do* anything.")

Kimberly, whom Chris had noticed squinting yesterday and who confessed she'd lost her glasses, got a seat on a wing of the perimeter, up near the board.

Chris moved Claude to the wing farthest from her desk. ("Because he seems to be the type who would be up at my desk every minute, and if he's going to drive me crazy, he's going to do it over there.") Claude was a pale boy with elfin ears. He had spent most of the first day picking at his lip and making it bleed. When Chris took the globe out of her closet and carried it up to the front table, Claude piped up, "My uncle got a big globe like that. It cost about, let's see, a hundred and ninety-two dollars. It stood up this high."

"Oh, my," said Chris. She smiled.

She had caught Courtney not paying attention several times yesterday. Courtney was small and doll-like, with a mobile, rubbery face — she had a way, when worried, of making her mouth an O and moving it over to one side. Courtney wore what looked like long underwear, clinging to her skinny frame. ("I look at Courtney and I think, 'I hope she stays in school. If school doesn't become important for her, and she doesn't do better at it, she'll have a boyfriend at fourteen and a baby at sixteen. But, you never know.") Courtney got a middle-person spot.

Chris put Robert in another of the hot seats. Robert was a burly child with a cume almost as thick as Clarence's.

She sent handsome, enthusiastic Felipe to a spot between Margaret and Alice. Felipe seemed to be very talkative and excitable. He was probably used to being the center of attention. Chris guessed, "He's easily influenced by the people around him. If he sits between twits, he'll be a twit." Placed between two obviously well-mannered children, Felipe might be an asset. ("People think that teachers want a room full of girls with their hands folded in their laps. I don't! You like a lively room.")

Alice and Margaret, both from what was called the upperclass Highlands, were obviously friends. But to Chris, it seemed as though Margaret hovered near Alice, aware of Alice when Alice didn't seem to be aware of Margaret. Margaret would need to learn some independence. Felipe would be a buffer between the two girls. ("I want to separate Margaret from Alice, but not too far.")

Several children seemed quick academically, especially Alice and Judith, a Puerto Rican girl with long, dark, curly hair and penetrating eyes. Judith was easy to spot. On the second day, Chris organized an exploratory math game called Around the World, a game like Musical Chairs, in which the players advance around the room on the strength of their right answers. In Chris's experience, one child rarely beat everyone. Yet Judith did, not once but twice. In victory, Judith walked quickly back to her desk, a little unsteadily on medium high heels, which emphasized the sway of her hips, and with her head laid against one shoulder, as if she were trying to hide her face. Every child clapped for Judith. Felipe cheered loudly. So Judith was popular, too, Chris thought. Also curiously reserved. The girl didn't even smile at the applause.

Chris moved Judith next to Alice. ("Judith's exceptional, and I want Alice to get to know an Hispanic kid who's at her level.") Maybe Judith and Alice would become friends. At any rate, they made a comely picture, the silky-haired and pink-cheeked Alice with freckles around her nose, from the Highlands by way of Ireland long ago, and the pale-skinned and dark-eyed Judith, from the Flats by way of Juncos on the island of enchantment (as Puerto Rican license plates say), sitting side by side.

Chris put Clarence in the remaining middle-person desk.

On the third day of school, a Friday, several

children including Clarence came in without homework, and Chris told them that they were in for recess. Holding midday detention would cost her half her lunch break, but what mattered now, it seemed to her, was that they realize that she cared whether they did their work. Clarence objected to the news about being in for recess. He threw an eraser at one classmate and punched another. Chris didn't see him do that; she'd left the room for a moment. A couple of the children told on him. Chris thought, "I have to put a stop to this now."

So much, she thought, for her talk yesterday about a new Clarence today. She called him to her desk. He came, but he stood sideways to her, chin lifted, face averted. She told him, in a matter-of-fact voice that wasn't very stern, that he could put someone's eye out by throwing things, and that he could not hit anyone. He didn't say a word. He just stared away, chin raised, as if to say, "I'm not listening to you."

Chris had to move Felipe's desk again that day, to a spot nearer hers. Felipe was chattering too much.

"Good," hissed Clarence when Felipe pushed his desk to its new spot.

"Why is that good, Clarence?" Chris asked.

He didn't answer.

But it was obvious to her. Clarence felt

wronged. He felt glad that someone else was getting punished, too.

All of the children kept in for recess worked hard, except for Clarence. She had put up lists of the work that children owed on the upper right hand corner of the board, and "Clarence" appeared on every list. He did a little work after lunch, but he came to a full stop when, late in the day, she asked the class to write a paragraph and draw some pictures to describe their visions of the lives of Native Americans. She told them that later, after they'd learned all about Native Americans, they'd look back at these paragraphs and pictures and probably have a good laugh. All the other children got to work, quite happily, it seemed. Clarence said he didn't understand the assignment. She explained it again, twice. Finally, she told him that she'd have to keep him after school again today if he didn't get to work on the paragraph. She called him to her desk and said, "Clarence, you are making a choice between going home with your friends and staying here after school. You're a bright boy. Why don't you just pick up your pencil and write?" She hoped he would. She didn't want to stay after school on a Friday.

She watched Clarence. He sauntered back to his desk. On the way, with an angry swipe, Clarence brushed all the books and papers off Robert's desk. Then he sat down and glared at her.

Chris turned for another whispered conference with Miss Hunt, about scheduling. The other children bent their heads over their papers, working out their impressions about Indians. Chris saw Clarence take out his ruler and put it on top of his pencil. Grinning, he tapped the ruler with his finger. It spun like a helicopter blade.

Chris watched the ruler spin. She understood this as defiance. The lines were being drawn.

The intercom called the last bus. The children who lived near the school — "the walkers" — lined up at the door. Clarence headed for the closet and took out his brown vinyl aviator jacket. It was new and had epaulets. It was a little big for him, and made him look even younger than he was.

"Where do you think you're going, Clarence? I don't know why you think you need your coat." She never liked to hear that ironic sound in her voice, but she felt annoyed. Because this boy would not work, she had to stay after school.

Clarence threw himself into his chair. He sat with his jacket in his lap and watched the other children file out the door.

It was just like yesterday. Chris sat at her desk and did some paperwork while watching

31

Clarence. Now and then she said, without looking up, "The pencil's moving. Right, Clarence?" She could see that it wasn't, but her voice was not ironic. It carried the same sort of message as yesterday's: "Let's assume that you are going to do the work."

Clarence's paper lay on his desk. He hadn't written anything on it. He didn't even look at it. He gazed, mouth slightly ajar, at nothing. Then he glared at her, then stared off. From her desk, his face appeared as if suspended in the forest of inverted chairs.

Children get dealt grossly unequal hands, but that is all the more reason to treat them equally in school, Chris thought. "I think the cruelest form of prejudice is . . . if I ever said, 'Clarence is poor, so I'll expect less of him than Alice.' Maybe he won't do what Alice does. But I want his best." She knew that precept wasn't as simple as it sounded. Treating children equally often means treating them very differently. But it also means bringing the same moral force to bear on all of them, saying, in effect, to Clarence that you matter as much as Alice and won't get away with not working, and to Alice that you won't be allowed to stay where you are either. She wanted Clarence to realize that he would pay a price for not doing his best and for misbehaving. If she was consistent, Clarence might begin to reason that he could make school a lot easier by trying to do his work. If she got him to try, she could help him succeed, and maybe even help him to like school and schoolwork someday.

But this was Friday. Chris never stayed after school on Friday. She felt worn out. The first few days always made her yearn for a sofa and some pillows. Her feet ached. She had earned her Friday afternoon away from here and Clarence. Why had she put herself in this position? On a Friday!

Clarence's teacher last year had said that Clarence cried a lot. The teacher was no fool, but Chris just bet that she, and the teachers before her, had too often relented at the sight of Clarence's tears, just as Chris had yesterday when she'd asked for a new Clarence. She would not relent again. She looked across the room at Clarence and flexed the muscles in her jaw. She felt testy. Just then, it seemed like the best way to feel: *All right, buster. What you need is what I've got.* Chris took a deep breath and let it out. Then she got up and strode across the room, her hands in fists.

Clarence jerked his head away as she approached.

"Are we going to go through this every day, Clarence?"

She grabbed a chair and sat down beside him, leaning her head forward and a little to one side to get it close to his. He turned his farther away. "I can wait you out as much as you can wait me out. If this is not done Monday" – she tapped the blank paper on his desk – "plus all the other work you owe me, you won't have recess. And you'll be after school. You are *going* to do it."

Tears began to streak his cheeks again.

"Secondly," Chris began, and she let her voice rise. It was all right to let it rise; this offense was more severe. "If you're mad at Mrs. Zajac, you deal with me. You don't take it out on others! You raise a hand again to anybody and you're out of here. Do you under*stand?*"

He had turned his face all the way around, so that she was looking at the back of his head.

Chris's voice came down. "I tried yesterday to be nice to you, and said, 'Let's start over.' But you don't want that. Now, Monday, this work is going to be done. Do you understand?"

He didn't speak.

"Now, go," she said.

Clarence jumped up and ran out the door. From the hallway, echoing back up the stairs, came his voice. There were tears in it. It was a sharp little cry. "I *hate* Mrs. Zajac!"

Chris sat for a while in the child's chair that she'd pulled up to Clarence's desk. She sat there, looking out the door, until the worst of her defeated feeling passed. It was the sort of feeling that follows domestic quarrels. You feel that you have every right to speak angrily to your child or your parents, and when you do and a wound appears, you suddenly see the situation altogether differently. She hadn't been able to sympathize fully with Clarence until now, when she had hurt him.

She couldn't help getting angry sometimes, and sometimes getting angry worked. Usually, the sort of child who got her angry was the sort of child who got angry back. They could wrangle openly. Together, they could clear the air. But Clarence wasn't that child, and mistaking anger for reason was always dangerous. Clarence needed firmness, but she wondered if he hadn't seen too much anger from adults already.

I hate Mrs. Zajac! Once she heard the cry, she could imagine any number of gentler words she could have used on him, and all of them seemed better than the ones she'd chosen. By yelling it on the stairs, he let her know she'd wounded him and didn't give her a chance to make repairs. He won that skirmish.

There were a lot of stories about Clarence around. One school department psychologist remembered him as a kindergartner and remembered being struck by the eagerness with which he climbed into her lap. There seemed to be a desperate quality about Clarence's search for love. Chris would have felt better if she could have told herself that Clarence really did dislike her. But, of course, that wasn't what he meant. He *hated* her. Had he attached himself that strongly to her already? This was only the third day of school. If things went on this way with Clarence, it was going to be an exhausting year.

Chris got up and walked over to her desk. She stared out the window. It was one long, rectangular sheet of smoky, slightly scratched plexiglass flanked by two small casements. The windows opened onto the playground below: a field of grass with a baseball diamond and a concrete basketball court in one corner and a few scrawny young trees on the edges along the chain link fence. The playground ended at a line of warehouses and factories. One factory building was old, of dingy brick, with its ground-floor windows covered in plywood. Another, Laminated Papers, had pale green walls the color of hospital corridors. The factory roofs hid all views of the wide, brown Connecticut River, rushing down from the huge falls, which once powered all of industrial Holyoke. Under a string of high-tension wires, a lumpy horizon of trees, the only full-grown trees in sight, rose from the Chicopee bank of the river. Chris stared out at the hospital-green walls of the

Laminated Papers building. Clarence is an angry child, she thought. Angry at the whole world. Worst of all was that stony, averted face he wore when she tried to talk to him. How could she ever get close enough to reason with a child who put up a barrier like that?

Anger wouldn't work, obviously, nor would endless sessions of detention — they would simply make her feel resentful, too. Maybe she should simply warn him that he was getting F's. No, that wouldn't work either. On his first report card he'd flunk everything, and that would tell him the same old news, that he didn't have to do the work because he couldn't.

3

After spending most of six hours alone with children in one room, a teacher needs to talk to another adult, if only to remind herself that she still is an adult. Chris needed to talk more than most people. She couldn't sort out her thoughts until she had turned them loose into the air. She hated, not solitude, but the silences that cover up emotions. This evening especially she would have to talk.

When she got home her husband, Billy, was there already. Billy was about six feet, with prematurely gray hair and an open, youthful face. He was a good listener. The first year or so of their marriage, she would bring home teacher stories and halfway through would pause to check. She'd say accusingly, "You weren't listening, Billy."

"Yes, I was," Billy would reply. "You were telling me that so-and-so was throwing snots around the room."

Actually, it had turned out that Billy remembered the names of her difficult pupils years after she had managed to forget them herself.

Billy understood how badly Chris needed to talk. The few times when he felt truly angry at Chris, he would break off the argument and simply walk away from her. Chris would then chase Billy around the house. She wouldn't be able to help herself. She had to keep on talking at those times. Otherwise, the argument would fester.

Chris found Billy in the kitchen and told him all about this day: Clarence's tears, Clarence's stoniness, Clarence's exit. "I don't know, Billy. Every year you get one, and every year it's the same. But it's discouraging."

She went on: "I wasn't trained for this. I was trained to teach, not to deal with kids like this. And they stick them in your room, and you're supposed to perform miracles. Plus teach all the others."

Poor Billy. She talked about Clarence all weekend. "Guilt," she said. "Guilt plays a large part in my life." She might as well have brought Clarence home for those two days. She kept seeing the big eyes exuding tears, and hearing the sharp, wounded voice saying, "I *hate* Mrs. Zajac!" She was angry at herself about her timing, too. You never scold a child on Friday afternoon and give yourself two days to brood about it. She knew better than to do that.

On Monday morning, Chris told Pam Hunt, the student teacher, "This week I'm going to kill him with kindness. But if he lays a hand on another kid, I'm going to step on him. I'm not going to have a child afraid to come to school because Clarence is going to hit him. I'm not going to let him out of doing his work, but this week I'm just going to keep putting his name on the board and reminding him, and try that for a week."

Pam pursed her lips and nodded.

When Clarence ambled in, walking heel-to-toe as if to music only he could hear, Chris said, "Good morning, Clarence! How are you this morning?"

It seemed as though Friday had never happened. Clarence grinned at her. Chris smiled over her blotter at the after-image. Those dimples of his were so deep she could see them from behind.

Clarence did a 360-degree turn, a pirouette with arms outstretched, and like an airplane coming in for a landing, dropped his books on his desk. Then he took his coat to the closet. Now he was gazing at the week's luncheon menus that were taped up on the closet door. He rubbed his little belly, his hand moving in a circle over it. "Mmmm! Applesauce!" he said.

He really was extraordinarily cute, Chris thought. But in a moment, she would have to ask him for the work he hadn't done last week.

Awakenings

At the beginning of the first social studies lesson of the year, Chris asked the class, "What's the name of our country?" She made her voice sound puzzled. She didn't want to shame the ones who didn't know the answer. About half of the class fell into that category.

"Holyoke?" Courtney ventured to guess.

"No-oh," said Chris. "Holyoke is our city. Our *country*." She called on Arnie.

"Massachusetts?" said Arnie.

"No. That's the name of our state," said Chris. "Dick?"

"North America?" said Dick.

"That's our continent," said Chris. "It's even bigger than our country."

Chris carried in her mind a fifth-grade curriculum guide. It conformed roughly to the twenty-year-old official guide, which she kept in her desk and never consulted anymore. If she could help it, her students would not leave this room in June without improving their penmanship and spelling, without acquiring some new skills in math, reading, and writing, and without discovering some American history and science. At about ten of eight in the morning, before the children arrived, she stood at the chalkboard, coffee cup in her right hand, a piece of chalk in her left. One of her own grade school teachers had slapped Chris's sinister hand when she'd used it, but Chris remained a lefty. The chalk rattled, never squeaked, as she wrote down the word of the day in penmanship under the lists of children who owed her work. Her own handwriting was indeed exemplary, slanted to the right and curvaceous. Sometimes she chose a word to suit her own mood ("fancy") or the weather ("puddles"). Other days she wrote the names of historical figures whom she wanted to discuss ("Benjamin Franklin," "Martin Luther King") and once in a while a word that the children would not know ("eugenics") — she hoped thereby to train them to use the dictionary.

At eight, a high-pitched beep from the intercom announced math, which lasted an hour. Some children left her room for math, replaced by some children from the room next door. For math and reading, children were "levelized," which means the opposite of "leveled" — they were grouped by abilities. Her lower math group began the year with a review of the times tables and her top group with decimals. She would take each group as far as she could, but every child had to improve in problem solving, every member of the low group had to master long division at least, and all of the top group should get at least to the brink of geometry.

A half hour of spelling followed math. For fifteen minutes, Chris would talk to them about their spelling words. Responses were unpredictable.

"What's a cyclone? Arabella?"

"Like a ride?"

"What does 'abroad' mean? Anyone? Robert?"

"A woman," said Robert.

Then came fifteen minutes of study, during which teams of two children quizzed each other. Chris paired up good spellers with poor ones. She also made spelling an exercise in socialization, by putting together children who did not seem predisposed to like each other. She hoped that some would learn to get along with classmates they didn't think they liked. At least they'd be more apt to do some work than if she paired them up with friends. Her guesses were good. Alice raised her eyes to the fluorescent-lit ceiling at the news that she had Claude for a spelling partner. Later she wrote, "Today is the worst day of my life." Clarence scowled at the news that he had Ashley, who was shy and chubby and who didn't look happy either. A little smile collected in one corner of Chris's mouth as she observed the reactions. "Now, you're not permanently attached to that person for the rest of your life," she said to the class.

She'd tell them they could take out their snacks, often adding, "Don't you think you could bring something nutritious? An apple?" One child or another would say "Ugh!" Then, as a rule, she left the spelling partners quizzing each other, and carried her coffee cup to the Teachers' Room, where she sat down for a few minutes, the first minutes of rest for her feet since penmanship. Then she hurried back to her classroom in time to supervise the comings and goings of students for reading.

She had three different reading groups, composed of children from various fifth-grade homerooms. Two of her groups were lodged in the third-grade-level and one in the fourth-grade-level "basal" readers. The school had brand new basals. They were more than reading books. They were mountains of equipment: big charts for teaching what were called "skill lessons," and big metal frames to hold those charts erect, and workbooks for the children to practice those skills, and readers full of articles and stories that did not fairly represent the best of children's literature, and, for each grade level, a fat teacher's manual that went so far as to print out in boldface type the very words that Chris, or any other teacher anywhere, should say to her pupils, so as to *make* them learn to read. Chris didn't teach reading by the numbers, right out of the manual. She made up her own lessons from the basal's offerings.

She spoke with each of her groups for twenty-five minutes every day about skills and stories. Most of the time her reading students enjoyed those conversations, and many enjoyed the twenty-five minutes each group spent in reading whatever they liked to themselves – she let them lie on the floor if they wanted during that time. But almost every child hated the twenty-five minutes spent in the basal's workbooks. Judith, a most proficient reader, who went to another room for that period, said, "I love to read, but I hate reading-reading." Chris had many disaffected readers, and the workbooks were not improving their attitudes. They slumped over those workbooks, and some looked around for other things to do. She could make them behave, but from many she couldn't get more than halfhearted efforts. Her two lower groups weren't making up the ground between them and grade level. She couldn't quit the basal altogether, but she knew she ought to make the children see that there is more to reading than workbooks. She planned to give them breaks from the basal. She'd have them read some novels. Maybe they'd prefer that. She'd have to get Debbie, the director of the reading program, to find her multiple copies of some novels.

Chris wished she could vary the morning's timetable now and then, so that she could linger over certain lessons. But the movement of students among homerooms for math and reading meant that, in the morning, she had to quit every subject when the clock commanded, and, on occasion, had to leave some children puzzled until the next day. As her reading groups left and her homeroom reassembled, the hallway and room full of high-pitched chatter, Chris would stand in her doorway, keeping an eye on the returning Clarence, trying to read his current mood in his face.

She almost always stayed on her feet for the next hour, which belonged to social studies. After the first day they all knew the names of their city, state, and country, and could find them on the map that she pulled down like a window shade, over by the door and the social studies bulletin board. The official curriculum guide expected her to cover all of U.S. history. She had never yet gotten past Reconstruction by June, and did not expect to go further this year. She began with the pre-Columbian Indians, whom she was careful to call Native Americans. She defined the term "stereotype" for the children — that fall a visiting politician helped inadvertently by handing out to the sixth graders paper headdresses that identified the wearers as "Big Chief Friend of Congressman Conte."

Eleven-thirty was lunchtime. She ate in the Teachers' Room, a small, grubby sanctuary with three tables and a couple of orange vinyl sofas and a coffee machine. She usually sat with her best school friend, Mary Ann, and they talked about wakes and weddings, sales and husbands, and only rarely about students and lessons. Afternoon brought some freedom from the clock. She read aloud for fifteen minutes to the children, who usually came back from their recess with flushed faces. Her voice calmed them. She read novels, their favorite that fall about a boy whose toy cowboy comes to life and has adventures. Many times when she closed the book and said, "We'll find out what happens tomorrow," children would groan. "Read some more, please, Mrs. Zajac?" As often as not, she obliged them.

When she closed the novel once and for all, and said, "Okay, take out your journals, please," several children would again groan. She said, day after day, "Oh, come on. I know you have lots of interesting things to write about." They could write about anything, she told them. If they wanted, they could write that they hated Mrs. Zajac. But they must write. The fifteen minutes or so with their journals was to warm them up for an hour of more formal creative writing. They could write stories on any topic they chose. On her own Chris had read up on the so-called "process" technique of teaching writing. Most of the gurus on that subject advised that children pick their own topics, but in her experience some children would not write at all if she did not offer them freedom from complete freedom. She'd turn off the lights and pass around the room a children's book full of spooky illustrations, or she'd say they could write stories imagining how they got on the cover of *Time* magazine.

Every month the children wrote a book report, a science report, a social studies report, and several drafts of a story. They jotted down story ideas for a day or two. They composed rough drafts, which they read aloud to a couple of classmates, who were supposed to give them advice. They wrote second drafts and read those aloud to Mrs. Zajac, who gave more advice. When most had finished their final drafts, Chris would examine the stories and pick out a couple of frequent grammatical errors, and then for a week would teach formal grammar lessons — on the possessive, on verb tenses, on exclamations.

She left science for last. For several other subjects she used textbooks, but only as outlines. She taught science right out of the book; this was one of those texts that takes pains with the obvious and gives the complex short shrift. Chris didn't know much science and didn't usually enjoy teaching it. Sometimes she let creative writing encroach on science's time. About one day in ten she canceled science altogether and announced – to cheers, Felipe's the loudest – an informal art lesson. She often felt guilty about science.

A box of tissues always sat on a corner of Chris's desk – her classes went through about twenty boxes a year. All day long stacks of papers and books accumulated on the corners of her desk, on the front table, on the counter under the window. She handled about 150 pieces of paper each day – the attendance sheet, the free lunch forms, the students' many assignments. The room looked disorderly, but every category of paper had its proper place. Within a couple of weeks, the children had mastered the routines, and only rarely did Chris lose anything, except for the key to her classroom closet, which she misplaced almost daily, the only visible manifestation of the strain on her memory. Counting all her math and reading and homeroom students, she dealt with fifty children. Every morning she brought a new list of special chores, mainly concerning children who needed individual tutoring in a subject. Four or five times a day, the intercom erupted in the middle of her lessons, usually paging staff – usually the guidance counselor – and three or four times another teacher would appear in the doorway with a question or request. After many lessons – and always after ones that had gone badly – Chris paused to perform what she called a "self-evaluation," saying inwardly, "I was boring myself. I've got to think of a way to jazz that up next time."

According to one famous piece of research, a classroom teacher must manage, in a predictable enough way to make the children feel secure, about two hundred unpredictable "personal interactions" an hour. Some interactions are more difficult than others, of course. Chris managed an average of thirty disciplinary incidents during each six-hour day. Some lasted only seconds and required from her just a dark look or a snap of her fingers. Others, mostly incidents involving Clarence, went on for minutes, and some of those led to further incidents – some, in effect, lasted all day.

Some days ended in haste. The intercom would announce, "Bus one," and Chris would still be assigning homework. She wrote the assignments on the narrow chalkboard between the closets in the back of the room, and always explained three times what she expected them to do for tomorrow.

The leaves had begun to turn on the distant trees on the Chicopee bank of the invisible river. The days had grown cooler. Out on the playground, along with the usual incidental trash blowing around in the fall winds, were many small pieces of what must have been a huge jigsaw puzzle mixed in with the grass. The puzzle pieces had lain there since school started and were now soggy bits of brown cardboard. Maybe a frustrated child had dumped the puzzle last summer. Out on the playground, a boy from another homeroom cavorted around on a dirt bike, doing wheelies. He was playing hooky, but evidently couldn't stay away. He waved and shouted whenever he saw a child's face in the windows.

Inside, math was in progress. Clarence went to the room next door for math, but Chris kept Robert, her second most difficult student, and she received from the homeroom next door lanky, mischievous Manny. Math was almost always lively. Chris sat at the spindly-legged table at the front of the room. The top math group, five girls and only three boys, but a nearly equal mixture of white and Puerto Rican children and one Filipino, also from next door, sat at desks on the side of the room by the window, wrestling with word problems in bright morning sunlight. That top group's heads were bowed over open textbooks, their lips bunched up in great concentration. The low math group looked different. Children from next door made up half of this group, too. The low group surrounded Mrs. Zajac: three fidgety children at the table, before her and beside her; Felipe a little behind her on the right; three children standing at the board, working on multiplication problems; and the rest of the fifteen in the low group at desks on the doorway side of the room, behind Mrs. Zajac's back. Some eyes in the low group were darting and furtive. There were always whispers among them, also grins, and a few stifled yawns.

This year's low math group wasn't like last year's, which was entirely remedial. It contained a gang of five boys, who, whenever she turned her back, threw snots and erasers and made armpit farts at the children who were trying to work, and among them was the boy – this was one of her favorite teacher stories – who decided one day to start barking in class. Not, Chris knew, because of Tourette Syndrome, some of whose victims bark involuntarily. This boy barked in order to get suspended, so he'd have a holiday. She thought, "No way, buster. I can wait you out." The boy yipped. She ordered him to stop. He growled. She tried to embarrass him by describing what he was doing. He laid his head back and bayed. So she decided to ignore him, and went on teaching: "Ten times five is what?" "Ruff ruff." "And carry the five." "Aroooo!" Afterward Chris and her math aide found an empty room off the principal's office, went inside, and laughed for a good five minutes. Tears flowed down their cheeks.

Now from the group of low math students behind Chris came the sound of muffled, tuneless singing: "Cha, cha, cha. Cha, cha, cha."

"Robert, would you like to sing for the class?" said Chris, glancing over her shoulder at the burly child. "No? Then why don't you get busy. You still owe me yesterday's math."

The singing stopped.

She held up a flash card, aiming the question "4 × 6 =" backward over her shoulder, for Felipe, who still hadn't learned his times tables, while with her left hand Chris corrected Jorge's paper, then paused and, leaning farther left, examined sleepy Jimmy's work, which wasn't going well. "How much is seven times seven, Jimmy?"

"Forty. Forty-nine."

"And what do you carry?"

"Forty-nine?"

"No. Think, Jimmy." She turned back to

Jorge's paper. "Excellent, Jorge!" Then back to Jimmy. "And carry the what?" That question left hanging, another flash card held aloft for Felipe, she looked toward the children who stood at the board. "Very good, Mariposa. Margaret, look at the problem. See if you can figure out where you went wrong."

"The nine?" said Jimmy at her side.

"No, Jimmy. *Think.*" More noise from the low group behind her. Without turning around, she extended her left hand back, snapped her fingers, and, leaving her index finger extended, said, "Manny. Henrietta. Settle down."

"Diablo!"

That was Manny's voice. Sometimes when he said that, Chris would bop Manny on his gorgeously curly black-haired head with a sheaf of papers, and Manny would leer up at her, and she'd try not to laugh. Sometimes from behind her she'd hear muffled sounds of an argument. Once, she turned to Manny and Henrietta, a tall black girl from the homeroom next door, and said, "Why do you two have to bicker?" A little smile slid over to one side of Chris's mouth. "If you tease each other, it must mean you *like* each other." "Like," to the children of Kelly School, implied matrimony.

Henrietta gasped.

"Diablo!" said Manny.

"No, it don't!" said Henrietta. "I'd rather die than like him!"

"Oh, yes, it does!" sang Chris. "When I was in school, if a boy and girl were always bickering, it meant they liked each other." That shut Manny up, but only for a while.

Chris turned her eyes to the children solving problems on the board. "Very good, Margaret. Do you understand it now?" There was more whispering behind her. Again, her left hand shot back. "Horace, your own work." Another flash card for Felipe while she called over her other shoulder, "Henrietta, come on up here." Then she turned her head all the way around, toward the low math scholars at their desks behind her. "Horace, are you all done?"

"No."

"Then why are you talking to Jorge?"

She turned back around and said to Felipe and Jimmy, "What's the matter with you two? The minute I turn my head, you have to talk? What number do you carry, Jimmy?"

"The four."

"Very good. Got it now? Okay, Jimmy, you can go back to your desk."

"Ocho," said a voice behind Chris, unmistakably Manny's hoarse whiskey voice. Manny was trying to whisper to one of his buddies, but he just couldn't do it quietly.

Chris turned. "Why don't you try Chinese,

Manny? You can say it in Swahili, Manny. I still know you're giving him the answer." Chris liked them to help each other, but today she wanted to find out just how each one was faring in multiplication, so she kept saying, "Your own work."

"Diablo!"

"You keep it up, Manny, and I'll show you what a *diablo* I can be."

Henrietta, who just a moment ago was sticking out her long, pink tongue at Manny, sat down in Jimmy's place, on Mrs. Zajac's left.

"Okay, Henrietta, let's see what you've done," said Chris.

"I wanta quit. It's too hard."

Mrs. Zajac stopped everything else, and looked the girl in the eye. "Wouldn't it be great, Henrietta, if I turned around and said, 'Manny doesn't get multiplication, so I quit'?"

Henrietta nodded in perverse agreement.

"No, Henrietta. You can't quit. You have to keep trying. You can't just quit in life, Henrietta. Believe me, there are times when I'd like to."

Sometimes, at such moments, feeling altogether calm, Chris would think, "In my next life, I'm coming back as an air-traffic controller." But there was always a child somewhere in the room who waited for her. If, in the afternoon during writing time, she sat at the table, bright red fingertips applied to her temples, trying to help Pedro or Julio put his ideas for a story into unscrambled English, Felipe might get jealous, even though she gave him ten minutes just ten minutes ago. Felipe would come up and stand at her side, holding his own story, saying, "Mrs. Zajac, Mrs. Zajac." She'd stick out her arm at him, the traffic cop gesture, and say, still gazing at Pedro's tangled story, "Felipe, I'm with Pedro now." Felipe would travel back to his desk looking like a little storm, and say to his neighbor Irene, "See, she hates me. I told you." Others waited more quietly. Judith always finished assignments early. She killed time by working on her novel, a feminist tale called *Shana and the Warriors,* or she read a published novel — Judith favored stories of teenage romance. Sometimes Judith stopped reading or writing, and lifted her eyes toward the narrow, train-like windows, and she thought about boys — handsome, religious, serious, chivalrous boys she hadn't met yet.

Chris felt them waiting around her. She thought how much fun it would be to sit for a long time with Judith and discuss her novel. She glanced at the clock, up on the wall above the closets. Its minute hand stood still. She had a few minutes before science. But the minute hand was one of those which stored up time and then sprang the news on her all at once. It leaped. She absolutely had to help poor Pedro. "Slow learner" was the kindly term for many of these children. It implied what she knew to be true, that they *could* learn, but she also knew that in this time-bound world, a slow learner might not learn at all if she didn't hurry up. And if she didn't hurry, she wouldn't get to keep her promise to Arabella, who was waiting patiently for Chris to help her fix up her story about becoming a hairdresser someday.

Usually, Chris could manage to keep most of them busy, but that was pure engineering. They always had time on their hands, and she never had much to spare.

This is an era of blossoming research in techniques for teaching math. The new wisdom was supposed to arrive at Kelly School in the person of a representative of the publisher of the new math textbooks. He gave the teachers a lecture in a classroom after school one fall day, the representative at a slide projector and the teachers in chairs made for children. The change in perspective seemed to inspire in the teachers a form of revenge. There was a lot of whispering in the audience. Talking fast and nervously, the representative allowed that the new math texts contained "objectives" that had been "correlated" to "a computer management program." "And we've correlated them to specific objectives. So that the management guide, ad nauseam, I'm going to get this point across, it correlates the specific objectives. . . . Subject integration is whereby math is integrated with other subjects. . . . We do it through means of verbiage and through the actual algorithm itself."

Chris sighed.

"When you see 'Think,' that's for the above average youngster."

"Well, I have *two* of those," murmured Chris to Bob, a sixth-grade teacher.

"These are minimum assignment guides, so please follow them. . . . We have masters for chapter readiness. Testing. We have three forms of tests. . . . Computational error analysis. It not only diagnoses. It offers some remediation."

Bob whispered to Chris, "It slices and it dices."

The teachers didn't ask many questions. The representative seemed disappointed but not surprised. "We're not saying that this is the end-all or know-all," he said.

Chris and Candy, another teacher friend, giggled behind their hands.

Chris felt she could use some help. For the low math group especially, solving the simplest word problems seemed insuperable. She'd had trouble with math herself in school, but she'd been good at reading, and most of her low group weren't good readers. She taught them what she called "clue words." She made stacks of books to illustrate the meanings of those words, of "more than" and "less than" and "equal to." To make word problems palpable, she dumped change on their desks, along with the cookie crumbs that her daughter had dropped in her purse during Chris's last expedition to the grocery store. At the first marking period, Chris had noticed that another fifth-grade teacher's math students had made much better grades than hers in problem solving. She had gone to that teacher and asked how she did it. But the method mainly consisted of the teacher's solving the first two-thirds of the problems herself.

Chris faced a bigger problem, one that looked impossibly far beyond her control. One Monday morning Chris asked Jimmy what time he went to bed last night. Jimmy, whose eyes looked glassy, with little bags beneath them, said he didn't know. Well, said Chris, what time did the last show he watched on TV begin?

Jimmy said eleven-thirty.

"Eleven-thirty?" she cried.

Yeah, said Jimmy, but it was a special, a

really good movie called *Cobra.*

Mrs. Zajac had just started in on her usual speech about bedtimes, the I-don't-care-what-show-it-was-eleven-thirty's-too-late-even-Mrs.-Zajac-can't-stay-up-*that*-late lecture, when from the class rose several other voices.

"I saw that!"

"Yeah, bro, that was fresh!"

"Remember that part where the guy . . ."

"This is what I'm up against," said Chris, slowly turning her head from one child to the other to make sure each got to see her stupefied look, and finally letting her gaze fall on Judith, who smiled back and shook her head.

Maybe the worst thing about TV is not violence or licentiousness but the fact that some children stay up until around midnight to watch it. About half of Chris's class did, at one time or another, and came to school with fewer than six hours of sleep.

It was a Wednesday morning, the dead middle of a week in late fall. Bracing air came in the cracked-open casement behind Chris's desk, the sort of air that ought to make children frisky. The clock read a little past eight. She stood in front of her low math group. As planned, she had begun to go over last night's homework, but Felipe had no idea how many pumpkins *in all* were bought if two people had bought fourteen pumpkins each; Horace said he'd forgotten his book; Manny and Henrietta admitted they hadn't done the homework; Robert just shrugged when she asked where his was; and Alan, of all people, a schoolteacher's son, had a note from his mother saying that he'd lost the assignment. "I think that you think your mother fell off the turnip cart yesterday, too," Chris said to Alan. Then she came to a dead stop.

The day was overcast. Jimmy's skin looked gray under fluorescent light. He lay with his head down on his desk, shifting his stick-like forearms around under his cheek as if rearranging a pillow. The usually high-spirited Manny gazed open-mouthed toward the window. Felipe had slid halfway down the back of his chair and scowled at his lap. "You can't make me do it. I'm not going to do anything unless you give me more attention," Felipe seemed to be saying to her. It would feel good and constructive to spank him, but that would have to wait for the pretext of his birthday. Robert was dismantling another pen. Soon he'd have ink all over his hands and his pants. His mother could worry about that. Horace was trying to do his homework now, by copying from Margaret's. At least he seemed awake. Jorge's eyes were shut, literally shut. Jorge was staying back. He had told his homeroom teacher, who had told the story in the Teachers' Room, that he'd get even by not doing any work this year, and she couldn't make him, because his mother didn't care. He wore the same set of clothes as on the first days of school.

Chris had seen progress in this group. They would start long division fairly soon. But today even the well-behaved ones, such as Margaret, looked sleepy. Bring back Clarence from the room next door. Clarence, at least, never looked sleepy.

Chris considered telling them she couldn't teach *celery*, but the eyes that were open and looking at her seemed to say that they didn't want to hear it all from her again: they'd need to know this if they wanted to move on to something new; if they didn't want to get cheated at the grocery store; if they wanted to learn how to design cars and rocket ships. They did not want to hear that Mrs. Zajac couldn't drill holes in their heads and pour in information, that they had to help, which meant, first of all, paying attention. Jimmy yawned. He didn't even bother to cover his mouth. A paper fell off a child's desk and floated down, gently arcing back and forth like a kite without a tail. She'd try something different. An old trick might work.

Chris turned and wrote on the board:

$$296$$
$$\times 78$$

"All right, Jimmy, you go to the board."

Jimmy arose slowly, twisting his mouth. He slouched up to the green board and stared at the problem.

Chris sat down in Jimmy's seat. "I want you to pretend you're the teacher, and you're going to show me how to multiply, and I don't know how." So saying, and in one abandoned movement, Chris collapsed on Jimmy's desk, one cheek landing flat on the pale brown plastic top and her arms hanging lifelessly over the sides.

A child giggled.

"Gonna get my attention first, Jimmy?" called Mrs. Zajac.

Several children giggled. Jorge's eyes opened, and he grinned. All around the little room, heads lifted. Chris's mouth sagged open. Her tongue protruded. Her head lay on the desk top. Up at the board, Jimmy made a low, monotonic sound, which was his laugh.

Abruptly, Chris sat up. "Okay, Jimmy," she called. "I'm awake now. What do I do first? Seven times six is . . ."

Jimmy was shaking his head.

"No? Why can't I multiply seven times six first?" she said, and she pouted.

There was a lot more light in the room now. It came from smiles. The top group had all lifted their eyes from their papers. Judith smiled at Mrs. Zajac from across the room.

Jimmy got through the first step, and Chris turned around in Jimmy's chair and said to Manny, "You're next. You're a teacher, too."

"Diablo!" Manny looked up toward the ceiling.

Chris climbed into Manny's seat as he sauntered to the board.

"I'm gonna give you a hard time, like you give me," Chris called at Manny's back. She looked around at the other children. They were all looking at her. "When you sit in this seat, see, you've got to sit like this." She let her shoulders and her jaw droop, and she stared at the window.

"Look out in space!" declared Felipe.

"Look out in space," she agreed.

The clock over the closets jumped and rested, jumped and rested. The smell of pencil shavings was thick in the air. Giggles came from all sides.

"Boy, do I have a lot of friends helping me out! Now who wants to teach Mrs. Zajac?"

"Me!" cried most of the class in unison.

Crying "No!" and "No way!" at Chris's wrong answers and "Yes!" when the child at the board corrected her and she turned to the others to ask if the correction was right, the low group found their way to the end of the problem. Arising from the last child's chair she had occupied, her black hair slightly infused with the new redness in her cheeks, her skirt rustling, she turned back into Mrs. Zajac. "Okay, thank you. Now that I know how to do it, I hope you know how to do it. I'm going to put examples on the board," she said. "You are going to work on them."

3

Alphonse Laudato, the principal, arrived first in the morning and did not leave until long after most teachers went home. During the day, Al roamed the hallways, a short man in an oxford shirt with a clip-on necktie and, though in his forties, very trim. He had gone to college to play baseball and football, he said, and had drifted into education. He looked like an athlete. He rarely stayed still.

Al belonged to Kelly School, and Kelly School belonged to Al. He once said, "I'm responsible for every teacher who walks in this door. Not that I'm in charge of everybody, the only one in charge. But I'm responsible. Come in, talk, and I'll decide if we're gonna do it."

The building Al ruled is a complex place with more architectural flourish than most public schools have. A spacious library occupies the center of the classroom wing. Eleven classrooms surround the library on the first floor — Al had assigned most of those rooms to the fourth grade. The ceiling, which has a gray plexiglass dome, stands three open stories above the library. At the second-story level, a rectangle of balcony corridors leads past sixteen more full-sized classrooms, Room 205 among them. Al liked to lean on the balcony railing and gaze down at his library. He'd talk about the money he'd finagled for buying more books. "When this library's done, it's gonna be something. You see what I'm saying?" He'd look around that amphitheater-like space and declare, "This is a gorgeous school, okay?"

Olive carpeting covered the hallways of the classroom wing. The carpeting suppressed some noise, but the architect had made the walls between rooms collapsible and very thin. Teachers could take some solace from that. They could hear from their own rooms that colleagues had trouble getting work from their pupils and lost their tempers, too. The adjacent administrative wing had air conditioning, and the classroom wing didn't. No one who worked there knew why. Over in the administrative wing, near the school office, there were two kindergarten rooms and a huge chamber called the "cafetorium" — it served as both auditorium and cafeteria. When Chris arrived in the morning, the first person she saw was Al, standing watch over the children who waited in line for free breakfast at the cafetorium door. Al would lean slightly backward, arms folded on his chest, and bark at the first signs of mischief. "Hey, you! Yeah, you! Excuse me! Stay in line with your mouth shut!" When Chris saw Al in that stance, she thought of pictures she had seen of the Colossus of Rhodes. Al was a diminutive colossus.

Teachers' unions had made "grieve" a transitive verb, and at Kelly School its direct object was usually Al. For example: "I'm going to grieve Al. See, Al's wife is a friend of that teacher's, and that teacher has a much better class than I do." That was the gist of the first grieving that fall. Chris thought it largely nonsense, and didn't want to get involved.

Al dragged out meetings. Sometimes he gave his teachers printed handouts and then read the contents to them. At the first faculty meeting this year, proscribing the act of one teacher getting another to watch her kids for detention, Al formed a T with lifted hands, emitted a quick referee's whistle, and said, "Time out." He often said, "Which is fine," about something that wasn't. About the new institution of the two-day-a-week "late bus," he told his teachers, "This is a home run for us, it really is."

"Page ten," Al read at that first faculty meeting. "When you're ready and you have your weekly schedule, you're to block this off. When do I have math, when do I have reading, when do I have health, when do I have art."

Out in the audience, a teacher near Chris muttered, "When do I have coffee?" Chris smiled.

Al often ended meetings by saying — the logic wasn't always clear — "But. We're doin' a good job."

When Al said that, Chris worried that he might at last be on the verge of denying the real problems all around them in the school. Almost no one involved in education says the outrageously wrong thing. Plenty do it. But Chris thought Al was almost an opposite case. On really important matters, he usually did what was best for the students. Somehow he always seemed to find the money for new books or materials or field trips. She thought Kelly's classes remained small partly because of Al's clever budgeting. She gathered that Al sometimes fell out of favor on Suffolk Street, school administration headquarters, but she thought it significant that during the first crucial year of desegregation, Suffolk Street had sent Al to Kelly, to soothe the white parents who had demanded proof that their children would be safe down in the Flats. Al, with a great deal of help from the chief secretary, Lil, kept the school running smoothly. The office of the Director of Bilingual Education for the city was situated in Al's school. At least once a year Al would pick a fight with that department over some small administrative matter. The director insisted, though, that he could easily forgive Al because of the way Al ran Kelly School.

These were a couple of the ways in which Al described himself: "One of the better skills I have is organization: How." "One thing you're gonna learn about me, I'm not gonna change." He could be brusque, even with Chris, who was one of his favorites. Chris attributed most of Al's mannerisms, the ones that irritated her, to his being short, a condition that she understood. If in the morning he walked right past her hello, he would show up in her room later on, ostensibly to chat about something of small importance, and this was, Chris realized, Al's way of apologizing. He was teasable. She found him coming out of his office one morning, jingling his huge bunch of keys. "The more keys, the more power," she said.

"Not at all," Al answered, implying what he often said directly about his job, which was:

"This isn't easy, hey."

Al could be gracious. He'd sent thank you notes to her and the other teachers who had come in before school started to prepare their rooms. Chris appreciated the gesture; she didn't get many thank you notes. Al wasn't fastidious about every little rule. He wasn't one of those principals who made a hard job harder. And she was glad that he wasn't a "Mr. Mealy Mouth." Around Kelly School the threat of a trip to the principal's office had weight. When she sent a child there, Al almost always took some action. Unlike some principals she'd heard about, he never declared that he was off duty. Some teachers disliked Al, but Chris would stand behind him, if a little off to one side.

Al was Chris's government, all the government she knew. But Al did not imagine himself expert in instructional theory and practice. Mostly he visited the classrooms of new teachers who needed help in keeping order. This year he'd observe only one lesson taught by each of his veteran teachers. After watching Chris in action, he'd say little more than that she was doing a good job. Chris appreciated Al's restraint, but she thought she'd like more advice.

She didn't get much advice of any sort from her students' parents. Research shows that, typically, teachers in affluent school districts complain of too much parental interference, while those in poor districts, such as Holyoke, complain that parents don't get involved enough. These days, Chris always had a hard time persuading some of her students' parents to visit her, even for the scheduled biannual conferences. This year she would receive just one note from a parent that contained a request about her teaching. The note came from the upper-class Highlands, from Alice's mother. It read: "Alice seems to be having trouble with her math homework. Would you please go over her work with her in class."

Chris felt grateful for the message. "I'd like to have one year of parents pushing me," she said. "Just one year."

She had always pushed herself. Over the years she had volunteered for almost all of the extra training that the school system occasionally offered. She had a reputation, not to all minds flattering, for signing up to serve on committees – the School Improvement Council and the Language Arts Curriculum Committee were her current ones. In the past, Chris had gotten some push from other teachers, swapping ideas and tips about instruction. Once in a while, she had taught classes jointly with other teachers. The opportunities for that kind of collegiality always arose by accident, when like-minded teachers were placed in the same grade as she and had similar schedules. The arrangements were always informal. They seemed precious because they resembled acts of free will, and because in her experience they were relatively rare.

Some evenings that fall Chris called up teacher friends – Candy or Mary Ann or Debbie – to discuss ways of handling Clarence. In between lessons during the day, she often conferred with Debbie about strategies for teaching reading. But the faculty did not routinely discuss academic matters when groups of them on the same schedules met over coffee and lunch in the Teachers' Room. In there, banter and complaints were more common than shop talk. Snatches of Teachers' Room conversation suggested that a few might have lost their enthusiasm for the job, but Teachers' Room conversation proved nothing. The real test of a teacher was her conduct in class, and Chris had never seen most of her colleagues at work in their classrooms. One lunchtime, the conversation drifted onto the dangerous subject of troublesome students. One teacher, new to the school, remarked, "I think you have to be patient with children." And another, a veteran, replied from the side of her mouth, "*Some* you don't have to bother with." Chris wondered if she shouldn't stick up for the new teacher, but Chris held her tongue. "If I worry about what everyone else is doing around here, I'll go out of my mind," she told herself as she headed back for the lonely but safe and sealed-off domain of her own classroom.

Teaching is an anomalous profession. Unlike doctors or lawyers, teachers do not share rules and obligations that they set for themselves. They are hirelings of communities, which have frequently conceived of them as servants and have not always treated them well.

Take, for instance, the plight of the female teacher in not very distant times. As the number of public schools burgeoned in the late nineteenth century, teaching became overwhelmingly a female occupation. The dream of universal education required lots of teachers, and women could be hired much more cheaply than men. Nature, educationists reasoned, fitted women nicely to the role of surrogate mothers. If they became actual mothers, they weren't allowed to continue teaching in many districts. That fact alone guaranteed that many teachers would soon quit. Those who stayed on were apt to be subjected to extreme isolation. The classic sociological study of teaching — written by one Willard Waller and published in 1932 — contains the terms of a contract that female teachers in "a certain southern community" had to sign in the early 1930s. The contract obligated the teacher to engage in "all phases of Sunday-school work," to get at least eight hours of sleep while maintaining a healthy diet, and to consider herself "at all times the willing servant of the school board and the townspeople." She had to promise not to go out dancing, not to "dress immodestly," not to be in the company of "any young man" outside Sunday school, and not to "encourage or tolerate the least familiarity from her male pupils." The contract also contained this provision:

I promise not to fall in love, to become engaged or secretly married.

Even for its time, that contract was extraordinary, but it was not atypical in spirit. In general, America has invested an enormous amount of faith in the idea of education, but not much in teachers. Today, teachers get four years of college and better occupational training than they did in the first half of the century (which is to say that they get *some* training). Tenure has alleviated one major source of insecurity — and has also removed one major tool of quality control; in many places it is virtually impossible to fire a teacher who hasn't committed a criminal offense. And nowadays teachers are allowed to fall in love. Their social status has not improved immensely, though. Male teachers and perhaps increasingly female ones, who now have other options, are still regarded by many people as belonging to what Waller in the 1930s called the "failure belt." People teach, this theory goes, because they can't do anything else. There is a modern stereotype — it has not been quantified, but every teacher knows about it — that depicts teachers as numbskulls who work short hours, get long vacations, do lousy jobs, and then walk picket lines, whining about how badly they are treated.

Teachers' salaries have increased some in the 1980s, but generally remain low. Al got paid $37,597 a year. Chris had reached the top of the local salary scale and was being paid $25,532 this year. Pay scales vary from district to district, but the national average places teachers lowest on all lists of presumed professionals. As a sociologist named Dan Lortie puts it, America has always chosen to secure an adequate number of teachers, not with money or status, but by making it easy to become a teacher. America has never really tried to make teaching an attractive lifetime occupation.

Like everyone else, teachers learn through experience, but they learn without much guidance. One problem, of course, is that experience, especially the kind that is both repetitious and disappointing, can easily harden into narrow pedagogical theories. Most schools have a teacher with a theory built on grudges. This teacher knows that there is just one way to conduct a lesson; she blames the children and their parents if the children don't catch on; she has a list of types and makes her students fit them; and she prides herself on her realism – most children come to school, she knows, to give her a hard time. Current research holds that most teachers get set in their ways, both their good and bad ones, after about four years of learning by experience. Many teachers don't last that long.

Studies suggest that many of the best teachers quit soonest. If they stay in education, they tend to move on to administrative jobs, which represent the only real form of professional advancement in this profession. Not surprisingly, public education has always suffered from high turnover in faculties, rates as high as 50 percent, in some schools, in some eras. Lortie speculates that this flux led long ago to what he calls "cellular structure in schools. A complex and collegial arrangement – teachers sharing many duties – would not have accommodated a large turnover in faculties. So instead, schools have traditionally been arranged in modular fashion: each teacher to her own room and her own duties. The arrangement makes teachers conveniently interchangeable in the administrative sense, and also gives an institution a ready-made system of damage control – watertight bulkheads, as it were. When problems arise, they are isolated from the start in individual rooms. The doors to the rooms of incompetent and inadequately trained teachers can always be closed.

Almost two and a half million people teach in public schools. Many of them work in curiously insular circumstances. Most teachers have little control over school policy or curriculum or choice of texts or special placement of students, but most have a great deal of autonomy inside their classrooms. To a degree shared by only a few other occupations, such as police work, public education rests precariously on the skill and virtue of the people at the bottom of the institutional pyramid. Chris had nearly absolute autonomy inside her room. In that narrow, complicated place, she was the only arbiter of her own conduct. Sometimes she felt very lonely. "The worst thing about it," she once said, "is you don't even know if you're doing something wrong."

Al sympathized with his teachers, in his own way. "I always tell people if you want to see *anything,* come here. We got it. Because a lot of schools don't have the little curly-haired white kid. You have it all here, the doctor's, the lawyer's. Then you get your middle-of-the-road kid, and then your poverty kid. You get Hispanic kids dressed to a T. The parents own a grocery. Chris has to deal with it all. Alcoholic parents, you name it." Al went on: "Kids come in at seven-thirty and ask for a Band-Aid. They just came from home and they had the cut already, but they have to get the Band-Aid here. It's tough, it really is. I say to everybody on the staff, Do the best you can. But remember, you're not the lawyer, you're not the psychologist, you're not the social worker, you're not the doctor."

But to be a teacher implies parts of most of those roles and of some others, too. Decades of research and reform have not altered the fundamental facts of teaching. The task of universal, public, elementary education is still usually being conducted by a woman alone in a little room, presiding over a youthful distillate of a town or city. If she is willing, she tries to cultivate the minds of children both in good and desperate shape. Some of them have problems that she hasn't been trained even to identify. She feels her way. She has no choice.

Homework

At the end of the day, after the intercom had announced, "We have some birthdays," and had named the birthday children and then had sent everyone home, first the ones who went on buses and then the walkers, Chris would gather up her own homework and go to the door. She'd look back one last time, to ask of Room 205 if she'd forgotten something, and shut off the lights. She'd head down the hallway, past half a dozen doors like her own. She'd shove her keys in her mailbox in the office, and often she would stop a moment to exchange pleasantries with the chief secretary, Lil, who would be standing behind the long, motel-like reception desk.

Grandmotherly, white-haired Lil was the only person in the school whom *everybody* liked. Her admirers included the children who chronically ended up sitting in the bad-boy chairs — these children were mostly boys — outside the principal's office. While they sat there waiting to get yelled at by Al, Lil would talk to them. "I'm *very* disappointed with you." They'd smile sheepishly. In the middle of one day that fall, Chris came through the office and found Lil leading a group of tough-looking boys in song. She had them singing "My Bonnie Lies over the Ocean." It was a most improbable scene, Lil behind the counter wearing a small smile, and the tough-looking boys in their muscle T-shirts sitting there with heads thrown back, belting out that song. Sometimes at the end of the day, Chris would find Lil dealing calmly with the typical sort of unpredictable problem, as on the afternoon that fall when, around two o'clock, a drunk staggered into the office saying he had to pick up somebody or other at noon, and it had to be explained to him that he had come to the wrong place at the wrong time. "Thank God for Lil," Chris often thought. Chris wondered if the school could function without her.

Chris would head out to the parking lot, her pocketbook and her bulging blue book-bag bouncing. She usually appeared to be in a hurry even when she wasn't. She'd stride toward her small yellow station wagon. It had a baby seat in the back. As a girl, Chris had imagined herself driving such a car, a station wagon equipped for children. She had foreseen a bigger one with wood on its sides, like the cars that mothers drove on the wholesome TV shows of her youth.

To the west, the top of a crane in the Sullivan Scrapyard poked up above the chain link fence along Bowers Street. To the south were flat-roofed factory buildings. In the small park to the north beside the parking lot, the trunks of saplings were still wrapped in cloth, like race-horses' legs. There weren't many other trees in sight. Beyond the park stretched a weedy patch of vacant lots, and then old red brick apartment buildings with wooden porches, laundry hanging on clotheslines on those porches.

Kelly School is in an old industrial and residential part of Holyoke, a neighborhood long known as the Flats. Yankee investors, mostly from Boston, invented Holyoke in the 1840s out of the whole cloth of a small farm town. Immigrant Irish laborers built the city, damming the Connecticut River at its falls and making it flow through what would become the Flats, along an ingenious network of canals that fed falling water to the turbines of long blocks of tall brick mills. Holyoke was something new in America, one of the nation's first planned industrial communities, and the Flats was an essential part of the city's engine. For a time, around the turn of the century, Holyoke produced more paper than any other city in the world, staining the wide Connecticut a variety of colors all the way down to the city of Springfield.

Chris Zajac – née Christine Padden – spent the first two years of her life in this neighborhood. Her apartment building had stood just a couple of now half-demolished blocks to the north of the school. Her father worked about a half mile away, in the mill of a giant paper company called National Blank Book. He was a section leader, a subforeman, in the shipping and receiving department. He had walked to work among shoulder-to-shoulder crowds of men with lunch boxes, down streets that old-timers remember as having been clean. Perhaps they were cleaner in memory than they ever were in fact, but back then, in the late 1950s, the Flats still looked like a thriving part of a thriving city. But even by then Holyoke's industries had fallen into a decline, which by the 1970s became altogether visible.

As the city's population fell, from nearly seventy thousand at the peak to about forty thousand in the 1980s, the buildings of the Flats deteriorated. Some mills were abandoned. In the name of urban renewal – and partly in order to limit the size of the growing Puerto Rican population – City Hall presided over the demolition of many old apartment blocks. Most dramatically, the Flats burned. For years, flames lit the nighttime sky over Holyoke. Fires started in old wiring. Pyromaniacs and people bent on personal vendettas and professionals interested in insurance money set fires, and several were fatal. The fires changed the landscape utterly. Although they had abated now, the phrase "burned out" was still occasionally used in the hallways of Kelly School to explain why a child had vanished from the rolls.

Lately, the state and federal governments had put up money to rebuild part of the Flats, and landlords had actually renovated some apartment buildings. The far northern section of the neighborhood made local optimists declare, "It's coming back." The place was clearly in transition, but its next direction wasn't really clear. The train station in the Flats, which H. H. Richardson himself designed, now housed an auto parts store. On many streets, vacant lots accumulating trash and weeds surrounded lone, sooty red brick apartment buildings, which had the outlines of vanished neighbors etched on their side walls. They didn't look it, but even the most decrepit of those buildings had become valuable. Because so many buildings had disappeared and inexpensive housing was scarce in the region, and because the state and federal governments guaranteed a lot of rents, real estate speculators had lately moved in on the Flats and other run-down parts of Holyoke. They'd buy a tenement in the Flats or South Holyoke or Churchill, jack up the mostly subsidized rents, refinance the building, and, sometimes, sell it for a handsome profit. So far they had not greatly improved the majority of buildings.

Kelly School is in the Flats, but not exactly of the Flats. The people involved in its creation, back in the 1970s, had imagined Kelly School the cornerstone of the revival of the neighborhood, the phoenix rising out of the ashes of the Flats. They had built it into the side of a hill, on the high ground of those riverine lowlands: an imposing, complex structure of right angles, made of yellow brick with black asphalt trim along the eaves of its flat roofs. Its plexiglass dome stuck up like a tank turret. The designers gave it not just one but two fine, expensive gyms, in the hopeful thought that these would draw the community to its school. But the custodians locked up the school after hours now, because vandals had worked over the locker rooms.

Al Laudato liked to show visitors the front side of his school. He'd point to the saplings in the park and say, "When those grow up, hey, it's going to be beautiful here." He'd mark off with gestures of the hands a stretch of clean yellow brick wall that extended a mere twenty feet on either side of the front door. "From there to there we don't have any." Al meant there was no graffiti on that wall. "We're lucky here," Al said. He meant here at Kelly School, and he wasn't joking.

The school was still the newest and fanciest in the city. But walk around to its taller side and graffiti was everywhere: boasts and threats such as BORN TO ROCK THE FEMALES and WANDA THE PATA YOUR ASS IS GRASS, and many nicknames such as VAMP, PITO, COSMIC, DAZE, but only one reference to the staff inside, a reference to Al, which read, LAUDATOS DICK. In the evening, the school grounds became essentially unregulated territory. Then it belonged partly to thieves and vandals. Someone had busted all the exterior lights that were set high up on the walls, and someone had managed to pitch old bicycle tires over the lofty light stanchions. Rocks had dented and fractured sections of the wooden walls of the elevated walkways connecting the building's two wings. Those scars and the whitened patches on ground-floor windows, left by burglars who had tried to burn their way in, and the graffiti, which flowed across every surface reachable from the ground, across the brick walls and vandalism ordinance signs and ground-floor classroom windows and doorways (one of which always stank of urine in the morning), all gave the building a very melancholy aspect. Here and there on nearby side streets, old pairs of sneakers hung by their laces from telephone wires. In Holyoke, as in larger cities, hanging sneakers are small-time drug dealers' inexpensive advertising. After hours especially, the school looked like a fortress, lonely and despised.

A humble setting has one advantage. When grace descends, it is hard to miss. Heading for her car one fall day, Chris was greeted by the sight of a little battered automobile festooned with flowers in the school parking lot. Red, pink, orange, yellow, purple flowers were stuck in every crevice of that car, into keyholes and cracks around the doors, the windows, the hood, the gas cap. One flower was inserted into the broken shaft of the radio antenna. The car belonged to one of the Puerto Rican teachers. Many of her fourth-grade students had recently come from the island. They had sneaked out at lunchtime to decorate the car of their *maestra*.

Beauty always lurked somewhere in the school, but when Chris looked at its assaulted exterior, she felt depressed. This was her school and the Flats was part of her city and fully half of her class came from the neighborhood. She would say to herself, "I don't know why people want to destroy things." She felt sincerely puzzled, as well as sad and angry.

The apartment building where she had lived her first two years had been torn down. She didn't miss it, because she didn't remember it.

She'd never really known the Flats. She knew it now only through car windows and, vicariously, through her students.

Most routes out of the Flats lead across the canals and then uphill. Chris always took the shortest way, down Bowers to Appleton, under the railroad trestle, past an ivy-covered brick factory that looked like a castle, and across the first two canals, the western boundary of the Flats. From there it wasn't far up to High Street, the center of the old commercial downtown.

A lot of High Street, both the sidewalks and many buildings, had been repaired, but the storefront businesses still included a military recruiting station, a dance studio, a pornographic bookstore, and, near the corner of Appleton and High, a Salvation Army depot, where in the morning lines of people would stand waiting for breakfast. "I don't know if it'll come back or not," Chris often said when driving across High Street. Like many natives, she felt nostalgic for old Holyoke. She had also found that she preferred – infinitely preferred – living in Holyoke to leaving it.

Homesickness ran in Chris's family. Her mother had felt it keenly during those two years when Chris was a baby and the family had lived in the apartment in the Flats. Chris's mother had grown up in a small frame house in another part of town, in what Chris called "the lower-class Highlands." Her parents didn't have a car back then. Mrs. Padden would put the infant Chris in the baby carriage and walk back to the Highlands, out of the Flats, across the covered footbridge that still spans the railroad tracks, and up the hill, through the center of the city, through Old Ward Four, leaving behind smokestacks and tall Victorian brick factories and apartment blocks with their many-storied wooden porches, and walking into the narrow, tree-lined streets of her real home. Nearly every day, Chris's mother would make that journey, to spend a few hours where she'd been raised.

Most people think they will never come to resemble their parents, until the process is complete and they don't mind anymore. "I'm being like my mother now." Chris was saying that to herself more and more often these days, when, for instance, she found she just had to clean up her family room before she could sit down in it. Her mother would visit Chris and Billy's house and would reposition items in Chris's refrigerator. When her mother left, Chris would put the items back where she liked them, and laugh. "I'm being like my mother now."

Mrs. Padden said that she could hear her

voice in Chris's sometimes, but that Chris got her quick tongue from her father, and that Chris resembled both of them in her cautiousness. "I was a very, very timid person," said Mrs. Padden. "My mother told me that. I was afraid of Santa Claus." She went on, naming one of Chris's sisters: "Now my Mary was different. She was more adventuresome than Chris." As a young woman, Chris's sister had quit her job and gone off with a girlfriend on a bus, to see the country. "Chrissy said to me, 'I don't know how Mary could do that.' I don't know where Mary got her adventuresomeness. It must be someone in our past. But Chrissy *was* forward to a certain extent. It could've been third or fourth grade. It might have been second. She came home and said they were having a play at school, and the teacher asked if anyone could sing, and Chris said yes, she could sing. She sang the song, and I think it was something like, if you didn't have rain, you couldn't have flowers. To get up and sing on the stage in front of all the people, she had to have some kind of courage."

In fact, Chris was quite adventurous in a local sense. A colleague of Chris's, who knew only the Chris who taught school, once said, "If I had to sum Chris up in one sentence, it would be: Chris is not afraid to try new things." What did make Chris afraid was the idea of leaving home. She had tried leaving Holyoke once, and once had been enough.

Shortly after she got married, Chris went with Billy to live in Florida. Billy had a job down there on a newspaper. They moved into rooms in a suburban-style complex of furnished apartments, along with many transient military families — there was an Air Force base nearby. Chris had no friends and nothing much to do during the day while Billy worked. The women Chris met in the apartment complex actually talked about brands of laundry detergent, just like housewives on TV. She watched a lot of talk shows, doing her own talking to the screen. At Communion at a local church, the priest looked at her and said softly, "You're Irish, aren't you?" Afterward, outside, the priest took her hand and told her he could tell from her looks she was Irish. It made Chris think of home, and of the elderly men who would peer at her and say, "You don't look Polish. You must be Irish. Oh, you're one of the Padden girls, eh? I knew your father. He was Mayo. Your mother's people are Kerry." She did not belong in Florida. The air smelled wrong. The palmetto bugs that got into their apartment horrified her. She went to the bathroom armed with a slipper to ward them off. Easygoing Billy said they could make soup out of them. "Poor Billy. He was trying to make everything so nice for me, and all I did was complain." Chris couldn't joke wholeheartedly about the bugs until she got safely back to Holyoke. Then she told everyone, "They weren't bugs. They were birds!"

Back in Holyoke, the *Transcript-Telegram* had a job for Billy. Chris's exile in Florida lasted just one long month. "Hell on earth." Returning, she saw the city through the fog of tears, as she had last seen it, when she'd thought she was leaving it for good. It contained all she really wanted. It was a place where she could live according to the obligations of affection, among people who had known her as a girl, among family, old friends, and such comfortingly familiar sights as that boy from the old neighborhood, the one who used to be described as "a little simple," now physically a man, sweeping the sidewalk on Dwight Street every morning as she drove to school. Except for her wedding trip to Bermuda, the sojourn in Florida, and a few other brief visits away, she'd never had a reason to go more than several hours' drive from home.

Six hundred and twenty students had enrolled at Kelly School this year. Thirty were black, 11 Asian, 265 "white" ("Anglo" won't do in Holyoke, which annually stages the nation's second largest St. Patrick's Day parade), and

314 Hispanic, which mainly meant Puerto Rican. As always, the numbers would fluctuate throughout the year, but in a sense would remain the same; about a fifth of the students would leave, to be replaced by a roughly equal number of newcomers. About 60 percent of the children came from families receiving some form of public assistance. By design – the system was desegregated in the early 1980s – Kelly School's student body conformed statistically to the citywide population, and so did the student body in Chris's class.

Holyoke's borders enclose some working farms, some forest, and a gigantic mall beside the interstate, one site around which the new, suburban Holyoke is growing. Kelly School took in a fair cross-section of the city. Its territory included a suburban area, which looked like Anywhere, U.S.A. – one-story ranch houses, some modest and some grand. But only one bus from Kelly climbed into that region, and it didn't carry anyone from Chris's class.

Most of Kelly School's children came from neighborhoods in the old city. Seen from above, from the interstate, this old part of Holyoke is all smokestacks and church steeples. It has always been a city of labor and religion. Boosters advertise Holyoke as the birthplace of volleyball and as the place where the kitchen product

Lestoil was invented. In the old days, an ethnographer could have mapped it by its churches: Mater Dolorosa and St. Jerome's in Irish and Polish Old Ward Four; Precious Blood and Perpetual Help in South Holyoke, where Masses were French Canadian in liturgy and music; Immaculate Conception and Holy Rosary in the French and Irish Flats. Holyoke's small black population always had a Baptist church, now situated near the projects on Jackson Parkway. Uptown Protestants still have an Episcopal and a Congregational church, and uptown Catholics have Blessed Sacrament and Holy Cross, Chris's mother's church. Sacred Heart — Chris's church — in formerly Irish Churchill, now holds Masses in Spanish as well as English. The ten thousand parishioners who used to go to French Precious Blood, in the lower ward of South Holyoke, have dwindled now to about forty, while clustered around that old Catholic church are many little storefront Pentecostal ones with Spanish names above their doors. Holyoke remains a balkanized city. The divisions used to be more numerous. Only one sharp ethnic division exists anymore — between Puerto Ricans, the latest newcomers, and practically everyone else.

Several children in Chris's class this year came from Old Ward Four, just uphill from the Flats, a mixed neighborhood now of whites and

Puerto Ricans, generally poor. It is a greener neighborhood than the Flats, with more wood frame houses and far fewer vacant lots, but it too has apartment buildings and run-down sections. Chris's father grew up in Old Ward Four when it was simply called "the Ward." He lived with his parents in an apartment block near Dwight and Pine, now one of several notorious distribution points for narcotics. Chris had fond memories of visiting relatives in the Ward, but both she and her mother made a point of not driving through there anymore. The boarded-up storefronts and graffiti made them imagine Chris's father saddened. "If your father could see this now," Chris's mother had said to Chris the last time they had driven through that neighborhood together. And Chris had said, "He'd turn over in his grave."

In Holyoke, geographical elevations and incomes have always roughly coincided. In general, the higher up you go, the whiter the population, the fewer the vacant lots, the taller and more numerous the trees, and the larger the houses. The fewer the children, too. Hispanic Holyoke is very young, while white Holyoke has aged. Uphill from Old Ward Four the Highlands begins. In the middle of the Highlands stands a patch of woods – the Dingle, the so-called Highlands Dingle. This deep hollow, dense with trees, has long been the haunt of children eager to experiment with the adult side of life. Generations have worn footpaths among the trees on their way to growing up. The Dingle was another place of significance in Chris's life, one in which she had never set foot.

Twenty years ago, in the halls of junior high, Chris hugged her books to her chest and tried to look as though she didn't care while two girls — best friends of hers just days ago — sang, "Chris is a bay-bee." Chris had refused to go with them to the Highlands Dingle. Her friends were going to meet some boys there after school. Chris wasn't ready for necking in the bushes. She was always a very good girl. She rarely missed CCD, the weekly catechism classes, even in her high school years, when she'd grown to dread them. Her two erstwhile friends set several other girls on her. For a while, until she found a new circle to join, Chris walked the halls of junior high alone while those more daring, would-be bad girls taunted her with "Bay-bee," "Jerk," "Bay-bee." Chris went home from school in tears. As a teacher, Chris had always worried about children being mean to each other. Maybe the job itself keeps a teacher's childhood in view. Occasionally, Chris ran into one of that faction of former tormentors. Chris still couldn't muster more than mere civility toward her.

The Dingle is also a boundary. North of it, the world changes utterly. The upper-class Highlands begins. This used to be mill owners' country. "Don't you wish you'd lived in Holyoke in its heyday?" Chris once asked her best teacher friend, Mary Ann, who had grown up in Holyoke, too. Mary Ann said, "No. Because we'd have been cleaning other people's houses then." In fact, both of Chris's grandmothers had worked as maids in the upper-class Highlands. Chris remembered visiting a grade school classmate who lived in this fancy part of town. When she came home, Chris asked her mother why they didn't have a black maid, too. "Because you already have an Irish one," her mother replied. But Chris had just been curious. She didn't remember pining for a maid, or for a house in the upper-class Highlands.

Chris had three students this year who came from that part of town. Many of the houses there are large and still look grand enough to require maids. They have become less expensive than in the city's heyday.

Chris herself had come from the neighborhood south of the Dingle, her mother's old neighborhood. It was mostly to tease her mother that Chris liked to call it "the lower-class Highlands." In this mostly white section of one- and two-family houses, trees stand along the side streets. On the busier streets are some gas stations and body shops and stores and an occasional apartment building. Workers and not owners have lived in this neighborhood, but for many immigrants to the city, moving here has meant a figurative as well as a literal ascent from the Flats and the other lower wards. Chris had spent the rest of her childhood in this part of the Highlands, in a single-family house that her parents bought when they left the Flats. Her mother still lived in the house. Chris always stopped there on her drive home from school.

The street of Chris's childhood is only two blocks long and barely wide enough to allow for parking. Her mother's house has a front porch, like most of the others on the block. Mothers used to stand on their front porches in the evening, calling the children in, their voices caroling up and down the street. A dozen children lived in the house next door, and their mother's nightly call – "Jim-eee, Mare-eee, Billeee . . ." – sounded like a song. On the first days of school each year, Chris's father would assemble the children of the neighborhood for snapshots, out in front of the Paddens' patch of privet hedge, and there were so many children on the street back then that not all could fit in one picture. Now hardly any children lived nearby. "How times have changed!" Chris's mother sometimes said. For Chris, ever since her father had died, seven years ago, the whole neighborhood had felt incomplete, but it looked much the same, and she was glad to have the house in the family still, to connect her to her father and to her childhood. She had known Holyokers who could not wait to get through high school and clear out of town. But she thought she was lucky to have a street like this to go back to every day, and to have a stubborn mother who refused to move.

Chris remembered walking with the neighborhood kids to school, and, in later years, walking home along this street arm in arm with a couple of girlfriends, kicking out their legs in unison, as in a chorus line, and feeling risque while they sang:

"We are the Highlands girls.
We wear our hair in curls.
We smoke our sisters' butts.
We drive our mothers nuts."

Her mother's house is white and small and very tidy inside. Everything looked much the same: the landing at the top of the stairs, where Chris used to play teacher with her smaller siblings, and her bedroom off that landing, the small, darkstained desk still placed by the window. Chris could not recall a time when she hadn't wanted to be a teacher. In this house she conceived her ambition and also realized it, planning her first real lessons at that old desk when she was still unmarried, staring out the window and wondering what to do about her troubled pupils. From that window, she could see a part of the old brick firehouse, now closed up, where years ago indulgent firemen – Holyoke's firemen were less busy then than now – had let Chris and her friends play hide-and-go-seek. They would step into the firemen's big boots, which came up to Chris's hips, and hide behind the firemen's coats, which hung like drapery from the wall.

Chris's infant daughter spent school days with Chris's mother. It was a cozy arrangement, and Chris felt lucky for that, too. Coming by to pick up her baby, Chris usually stopped awhile to have coffee with her mother. Chris and Billy lived in another neighborhood nearby, newer than the Highlands but quiet and shaded by big trees.

The last part of her route home took Chris near the high school and one of the junior highs. Through her windshield she sometimes saw former students among the youthful, homeward-bound crowds on the sidewalks, and she would glance at them to see if they were carrying books – a good sign – or clinging to paramours — a bad one. Some days that fall as she drove home, her mind was full to bursting with thoughts about her class, the most worried, heated ones about Clarence. On those days she'd go inside and head right for Billy or for the phone to call her best Holyoke friend, Winnie. Most days a good talk was all Chris needed to clear her mind for home. She tried to guard against continuing at home the mannerisms of her school life. Sometimes, though, she'd enter the house and start giving Billy step-by-step instructions about some household chore, or she'd start wagging an index finger at him — her "teacher finger," as she said — and she wouldn't realize what she was doing until Billy said, "Chris? I'm not one of your students, Chris."

But if she could not always get completely untangled from her teacher self, she always felt relieved to get back to the kind of visible order in which she had been raised. Her neighborhood was just a few minutes from the Flats but a world away. People here pruned their shrubbery, mowed small front lawns and larger back yards, and kept up modest houses like her own. Her brick house, built in the 1950s, had previously belonged to a pediatrician. Not long ago a Puerto Rican family had moved in a few blocks away, and they had told Chris that an anonymous caller had welcomed them to the neighborhood by asking, "Can I get you to burn down some buildings for me?" But in general, serenity reigned on her street, and inside her house. Chris often said that her house was a mess. Her standards were high. She and her once-a-week cleaning woman kept it very neat. Last year cockroaches had invaded classrooms at Kelly School, and Billy had made her leave her bookbag outside the front door of their house, just in case she had brought home more than a few worries and mannerisms.

2

The year was in full swing now, days going by like a blurred landscape out the windows of a train. It was dark outside when she started her homework around seven o'clock, after washing the dishes and helping Billy put their children to bed. The beige carpeting in the dining room was soft under her stockinged feet. The wallpaper was of a calm pattern and cool colors, dark blue flowers against a white background. She sat at a round table made of blond oak, her grandmother's table. She remembered sliding around on her bottom under it, playing cowboys and Indians as a child.

Chris would spread her texts, planning and

grading books, and yellow legal pad on the table. First she would plan for about an hour. Then she would begin to correct papers, and, one by one, her class would file into this quiet, orderly room. Here many problems seemed manageable, or at least she could imagine that she had time to work on every child's problems. As the evening wore on and she felt the first wave of sleepiness, she would lift her eyes from a student's paper and the child's face would rise, too. She could see the face of the child whose paper she corrected, the child's face framed against the blackened panes of the small, many-mullioned windows of the dining room.

A stack of social studies tests lay before her on the table, slippery sheets of ditto paper, the questions in purple ink — fill-in-the-blanks questions that asked for definitions of terms such as "Tory." The test closed, as always, with an essay question; the children had to describe briefly a Famous Patriot. She stared at the stack of tests for a moment. "Do I want to?" she murmured to herself, and took the first test, Arabella's, off the pile. Chris's pen made a one-part scratching sound, inscribing red C's down most of the page, and she began to smile. "84 = B," Chris wrote across the top of Arabella's test. Sturdy, big-boned Arabella. Happy Arabella. Arabella's mother had told Chris that the girl was born smiling and hadn't stopped since. Arabella lived in the Flats. At Kingdom Hall, Arabella had acquired the habit of thanking God – for her parents, who always knew what was best for her; for her family's duplex and its two kitchens; for making her pretty; for the boy she saw at church, who, Arabella felt sure, liked her. As soon as she learned something, she was disposed to feel thankful for it. Arabella had made a lot of progress this fall. She had begun to learn to write coherently, and Chris had been able to promote her to the fourth-grade-level reading group. Arabella had now become its star. She was blossoming under Chris. Then again, Chris reasoned, a teacher who couldn't teach Arabella belonged in a different line of work.

One of Chris's secret pastimes was to pick out a boy and a girl from her class who, if she adopted them, would improve the Zajac household. She imagined bringing Arabella, sweetness and light, home. Chris would snap at the girl, "Your room's a mess. Go make your bed."

Arabella would smile. Arabella would chirp, "Oh-kay."

The boy Chris chose for imaginary adoption was Dick, who came from the upper-class Highlands. Dick was very quiet. All the other children liked him. At the first parent-teacher conference, Chris had told Dick's mother what a nice boy he was, and Dick's mother had said, "He *loves* you."

Chris's neck had turned bright red.

An incident summed up Dick for her: the day when he came up to her desk and said softly, "Mrs. Zajac, I'll help Pedro with his spelling." Two heads, Dick's white-skinned and sandy-haired and Pedro's dark and eager, hovered side by side over the spelling book. Back on the first day of school, Dick had guessed North America when Chris had asked the class for the name of their country. But Dick always got A's in social studies now. He had come some distance, too. "He better do well," she murmured to herself as she began correcting Dick's paper. Her pen scratched C's all the way down the page and on to the other side. She paused to read his essay. He had written about John Hancock. He had closed, "And on the Declaration you'll see a large . . ." Below, Dick had inscribed a neat facsimile of the patriot's famous signature. Chris laughed aloud, and with a quick flick of the wrist, scratched a big red C across the essay. Turning back to the first page of the test, she wrote, "100 = A + Super."

Next came Mariposa's test. For her nurse when she grew old, Chris would choose Mariposa, who lived in a part of the Flats, a stretch of Center Street, that some of her classmates avoided when walking home. Mariposa's father lived in Puerto Rico, Mariposa had said, and he didn't know where she and her mother and little brother were. Her mother had run away from her father. "My father was making trouble with her."

Mariposa was tiny, with corkscrew curly hair and an incongruously grown-up manner. One pair of her earrings nearly reached her shoulders. They looked like miniature chandeliers. Her experience with teachers had included being hugged fairly often and being entrusted with such chores as washing the boards. She would sigh happily and get to work. Mariposa liked to help out her teachers. Most of them, she believed, weren't very well organized. She was always helping Chris find things. She got only a 65 on the test. Chris let out a long breath. "She should do better than that." Mariposa loved to read, though. Just a little slump, Chris figured.

Cheered up by Dick and Arabella and Mariposa, Chris was ready for Felipe's test. Felipe came from the Flats, but dressed in clothes that he could have worn to a country club. Dapper, with jet-black hair – Indian hair, perhaps a mark of Taino blood. Felipe was too young, in the psychological sense, to be as consistently kind as some of the others. His face came to her in two versions. In one, Felipe's skin had changed color from light to dark brown, under lowered brows, and his mouth had tightened and would spit invective at her if he dared. In the other, Felipe grinned, crying out an answer to her question, wanting to be the first to respond whether he knew the answer or not. Often, after Chris reprimanded him, Felipe started limping. But he was a wonderful artist, even considering that Kelly, like all elementary schools, was full of wonderful artists. And Felipe was easily the most imaginative story writer in the class. On the other hand, he hated to rewrite.

Chris had to watch herself with Felipe. When he went into one of his sulks, she felt tempted either to shout at him or else to let his tantrums slide by in order to avoid another tiff. Most of the time she waited until the next morning, then took Felipe into the hall for a private lecture. Maybe the lectures had done some good. Recently, Felipe's teacher from last year had told Chris that his behavior seemed to have improved. It might just be puberty, Chris thought. If so, she wished Felipe's hormones would hurry up and grow him a mustache. Felipe owed her the second draft of a story. Chris turned to her legal pad and wrote on her list of things to do, "Felipe — story." She'd ask him for it first thing tomorrow. Her heart sank a little. Tomorrow would probably begin stormily.

Felipe got a 78 on the social studies test. Not bad. But he could have done better.

She put Felipe's paper aside and stared at Jimmy's. Jimmy could have done a *lot* better. Jimmy got a 28. She could see him, the Jimmy of Monday morning math class, cheek on his desk, glazed eyes staring at nothing. Jimmy came from the Flats. He had luxurious, long, curly brown hair. He was, in official terminology, a "white" boy. Imagining his ashen skin, Chris wondered what color it would be if she scrubbed him.

Jimmy had said that math was his favorite subject. "When it's math time, forget it. I'm always payin' attention." However, Jimmy had continued: "But sometimes I don't. Even though my eyes are open, I'm sleepin' inside. Because I'm tired. I don't know why I go to sleep late. I guess I'm just used to it."

Chris stared at Jimmy's test. He had not tried to answer more than half of the questions, and had not written an essay. Jimmy was the sleepiest boy Chris had encountered in years, also one of the stubbornest when it came to evading work that required thought. Jimmy had been absent a lot already, and when he came to class, he didn't do much work. Chris had badgered him about his homework. So Jimmy started bringing in homework in someone else's handwriting. Chris pointed this out to him. He confessed that his mother had written it. A few days later, Jimmy brought in homework that his mother had written but that Jimmy had laboriously traced over, not altering the looks of the writing but merely darkening the letters. Evidently, he thought that if he did that much, he could honestly tell Mrs. Zajac that he'd done the work himself. Chris explained to Jimmy that *tracing* over homework wasn't the same as doing it himself. A few days after that, she caught him trying to copy over on a separate sheet of paper, under cover of his desk, yet another page of homework written by his mother.

Chris would explain an assignment. Jimmy would say, "I don't understand." Chris would explain again. Jimmy would say, "I don't understand." Of course, he was waiting for her to do it for him. Like Felipe, Jimmy made it tempting for Chris to do the wrong thing. Jimmy's resistance was impressive, though — both passive and stubborn. Jimmy was to schoolwork as Gandhi was to violence. Jimmy wasn't stupid in the least. He was hibernating. Chris was going to wake him up. She hadn't yet. But, by God, she would!

Chris stared at the window. Maybe tomorrow, she thought, she'd make Jimmy take this test again. She went back to the pile.

Courtney got a 78, which wasn't bad, considering that she started the year by flunking everything. A white girl from the Flats. No father at home. A mother who got home late. Courtney wore a door key on a chain around her neck, like many other children at Kelly School. But this was one child whose name had been written less and less frequently on the lists of homework delinquents on the board. At first Courtney had looked shabby and dejected, but more often now she looked neat and pert. The other day Chris had staged a small graduation ceremony. She had moved Courtney's desk from its middle-person spot to a place on the perimeter.

Claude had been out that day. Chris had shoved Claude's desk into Courtney's middle-person spot, saying, as she did so, "I've got to have Claude up here where I can keep an eye on him, Judith." To Chris, it had not seemed odd by then that she should feel the need to explain herself to Judith.

Claude got a 70 on the social studies test. That was very good, for Claude.

Chris remembered Claude coming up to her desk, one day back in early fall, wagging his right hand rapidly, as if shaking down a thermometer, and saying, "Mrs. Zajac! Mrs. Zajac!" The mean sixth-grade boys on Claude's bus had dumped out the contents of his bookbag and had trampled on the second draft of his story, Claude said. So he'd had to throw that draft away, which was why he didn't have it, but he had done it. Claude made solemn nods, wide-eyed, and picked at his lip. There was something unfinished about Claude's face, something of the egg still about him.

Sixth-grade boys were picking on him? Chris said she'd see about that, and marched off, her hands in fists.

Chris returned to the room with her eyes narrowed. "Claude, no one was picking on you on the bus."

"I know," Claude said. He looked up earnestly at Chris. "I must've lost it."

Claude's pen ran out of ink one time. So, he told Chris, he couldn't do his homework. He left his bookbag at home another time. Claude said he would bring it in tomorrow. He did, but the homework wasn't in the bag. His hand shook, his eyes grew wide, he nodded his earnest nod. He said he'd taken yesterday's homework out of the bag last night, to finish it. But Claude, Chris said, you told Mrs. Zajac that you had finished it already. "I did," Claude said. "I just had a few things to do." For a while, she had tried cutting off Claude's homework excuses before they went too far. She was afraid they might inspire his classmates. Chris would thunder, "I don't want to hear it, Claude! I want to hear that you're going to do your work!"

But then Chris would come to a halt, standing over Claude. She often couldn't help herself. She asked, "How did it get lost?"

"I don't know. It wasn't on the kind of paper I'm used to," Claude said that time, looking up at her wide-eyed.

Claude told the class one Monday that over the weekend he had caught a thousand-pound marlin and had been bitten by a copperhead.

In her dining room, Chris smiled, and she shook her head over Claude's test. Why did his paper look as if it had been through a washing machine? "Get to Claude!!!" she wrote on her yellow pad. Then she gazed across the room, a hand covering her mouth. "I don't know if I'll ever get to Claude."

Margaret got an 80. Good for her. Margaret still followed Alice everywhere, one hand limp-wristed, laughing at what made Alice laugh. But Margaret had shown a flair all her own for creative writing. At the parent conferences, Margaret's mother had said to Chris that this was the first year ever Margaret said that she liked school.

"Margaret's another I have to get into," Chris thought. "There are a lot of those." Blanca, for instance, who could read sentences aloud without seeming to have any idea of what they meant, and who almost always came to school an hour late. Chris had badgered Blanca about her lateness, and this note had come from Blanca's mother:

Please excuse my daughter Blanca for being late. Right now we don't have no heat or power and we having a hard time getting the kids to school.

Chris had asked the office to get more information on Blanca. Chris had gotten her friend Mary Ann to test her informally, to see if maybe Spanish was Blanca's better language. It was not. Blanca worried Chris. The girl had frightened eyes.

On evenings like this, the children's faces came unbidden to Chris. But she always had to make an effort to summon Ashley's ghostly white and painfully chubby face, like the face of a fairy princess imprisoned in a tree. Ashley was one of the children who was much better at her self-defeating strategies than at any schoolwork. In her first essay, Ashley had written, "When I got to the 5th grade. I was kind of scared. I thought my teacher wouldn't like me. I sat quietly in my seat." Ashley hid less often now. "Mrs. Zajac, my dog had a puppy." "Mrs. Zajac, there was a robber in my house." "Oh, that's nice, Ashley," Chris would say, or, "Oh, Ashley, that must've been scary! That's something you could write about in your journal." But Chris never had time to draw the girl out, because Ashley always chose the busiest moments of the day to waddle up to Chris's desk and tell cryptic stories.

The house was very quiet. From upstairs came the sound of Kate, Chris's infant daughter, whimpering. Chris looked up from the shrunken pile of social studies tests. She glanced toward the kitchen. The clock on the wall there read eight-thirty. "She's a little late." Kate usually cried at eight-fifteen. Chris left her class in the dining room, took a glass of water upstairs, and helped Kate take a sip. Now Kate would sleep through the rest of the night.

Chris sat down again at the table. Pedro's test lay on the top of the pile. She read,

Tory. Like a grup of sogrs.

Chris placed her hand like a visor on her forehead. She stared at the blackened window across the room and slowly shook her head. "Poor kid."

Pedro had a happy-looking walk. He was short and darkskinned. His head and torso swayed from side to side in a sailor's rolling gait, and he smiled with his bulging mouth half open, so cheerful and perky it made her marvel. He didn't seem to know how sad he ought to be. She recalled the end of a day when the walkers stood at the door, and Felipe was again holding forth about how he yearned to become an astronaut, and little Pedro had touched Felipe's arm and said, "Someday, Felipe, your dream will come true."

Pedro's voice was deep out of all proportion to his size, and his voice had a garbled sound, as if his mouth were full of water, but sometimes perfect lines like that came out and made Chris wonder if Pedro really was, as she'd begun to think, mildly retarded. But maybe it was just the sound of Pedro's voice, the fact that he could speak at all, that was surprising. He didn't often talk. He never misbehaved. He almost always tried to do his homework. It was as another teacher had said: "Poor Pedro. He works so hard to get an F." His situation had seemed intolerable to Chris the very first day when, after assigning some simple classwork, she stopped to look over Pedro's shoulder, and he looked up at her and asked, "Did I do good, Mrs. Zajac?"

"You did *very* well, Pedro!" It wasn't entirely untrue; here in fifth grade, he could do some of the work expected of a second grader.

Then Pedro smiled up at her. His gums were very red and his teeth were covered with braces that resembled little checkerboards. Almost every morning, he offered her that red-gummed, metallic smile, but some days, before the lessons started, she looked up and saw Pedro weeping at his desk. No sound came out. Tears dripped off his chin. She would lead him by the hand to the office, the little-mannish boy gasping for breath, his wet eyes wide in terror. "I can't breathe, Mrs. Zajac. I can't breathe." She'd turn him over to Lil, and one of the outreach workers would drive him home, and then days, sometimes a whole week or two, would pass, and his desk would sit empty, before she'd see him again, walking up Bowers Street toward school. Pedro would wave to her and grin when she waved back.

Chris might have gone all year without knowing much about Pedro's life away from school, but that first question he'd asked her — "Did I do good, Mrs. Zajac?" — had sent her bustling to the office the second day of school to get the forms to start a "core evaluation" of Pedro.

A "core," as it was usually called — the student was the apple — involved a lot of paperwork and protocol, which always made the process lengthy, and an investigation of a child's background and a battery of psychological and intelligence tests. Eventually, a meeting would occur, and various administrators and teachers and experts would lay out a program for addressing a child's problems. In Chris's experience, the diagnoses were usually better than the cures. Most cores ended with an optimistic, carefully thought out "individualized ed. plan," which in practice meant that the child left his regular classroom for an hour or so each day for the Resource Room, where a specialist in learning disabilities would begin to put that plan into operation. But at Kelly, more than forty children with more than forty ed. plans went to the Resource Room teacher and her aide every day, and the poor woman who ran that room simply couldn't do it all. Chris didn't know much about what went on in there, but it wasn't miracles, clearly. Three boys from her class went, and she couldn't see any effect.

Chris thought that the wrong children often got, as the saying went, "cored" and sent to the Resource Room, children whose main problem with school seemed to be behavior, not ability. The Resource Room teacher remarked, "Its something of a dumping ground. I hate to say it, but it is." Nevertheless, a core was the only remedy available for Pedro. At least the testing might reveal whether or not Pedro really was retarded, and maybe it would give Chris some ideas about what she could do for him. But why hadn't there been a core evaluation of Pedro already? That question really bothered her. Was it because teachers had lost faith in cores, or was it because Pedro didn't cause trouble? Teachers had their hands full. Every class had disruptive children. It was easy enough to forget about a child like Pedro. In her time, she had forgotten some. From here in her dining room, Chris pictured this little boy sitting quietly at his desk, day after day, year after year, learning almost nothing, not even understanding half of what was said, and never complaining. She didn't like to criticize the schools, but that just wasn't right.

An administrator in the office had said that if Chris could get Pedro's mother – Pedro talked about a mother at home – to sign papers for a core, the process would be speeded up. So when the first parent conferences had come around, Chris had leaned on Pedro. Twice she gave him conference slips to take home. He brought back the first unsigned. The second slip came back with a note in Spanish on the bottom.

Chris took the note to Victor Guevara, the Puerto Rican teacher next door.

Looking at Chris gravely, Victor said, "I *think* it says, 'I am sick with high blood pressure. I can't walk much. I want to die.'"

"Oh, God!" said Chris.

Chris quick-marched to the office. She gave the note to Al. It was a story she would repeat at home to Billy and on evening walks with her

123

friend Winnie and maybe would tell for years to come.

Al wasn't pleased about the note. Was his school turning into a total social service agency? But Al called the police, who told him to call the suicide prevention center, who told him they couldn't act unless the potential victim asked explicitly for help. After saying to Chris, "Now, you gotta remember who we are here," Al dispatched the guidance counselor – Kelly School had only one for about six hundred students then – to Pedro's apartment house in the Flats.

Pedro lived on a littered, half-demolished street, behind an entry door with busted locks, up four flights of graffiti-covered stairwell that smelled of urine, in an apartment that was as clean as anyone could have made it, but that had unreliable heat and hot water, windowpanes that rattled in the wind, and lots of old woodwork painted dark brown, the favorite color of landlords. (One local house painter got so much call for that color that he kept large batches of it ready-mixed, in cans he labeled "Holyoke Brown.")

The scene in the apartment, as it was described to Chris on the counselor's return, was odd. Inside were a transvestite uncle of Pedro's and Pedro's tiny sixty-nine-year-old grandmother, the person Pedro called his mother. "I got four stepmothers," Pedro later explained. "My father never gets married with women. He don't like it. I got a whole lot of brothers. Like six. But they all from different mothers. Only three of us are Pedro — my little brother, my father, and me." It was hard sometimes to get the gist of Pedro's talk; he didn't have full command of any language; he knew less Spanish than English. Pedro said, "I was born and raised with my grandmother, because I was cryin' too much. And they took me to my grandmother, and my grandmother was takin' care of me, and my father gave my mother money, and my mother went to the circus. And sometime my mother used to come there without no shoes."

Pedro's grandmother had meant what she'd written in the note. Her husband had died at her age, so she believed her time to die had come. She said her favorite son had died some years ago of a heroin overdose and visited her bedside in the nighttime now. She spent her days cleaning, trying to scrub away years of grime from the apartment, and had left those rooms so infrequently the last four years that she could name every occasion. She had only one friend in the building, a woman so depressed herself that she seemed bound to die soon, too.

Hearing all that, Chris permitted herself a

useless thought: she'd take Pedro home with her.

But the worst didn't happen. Kelly School's counselor got a caseworker to visit the grandmother, and two days later, Pedro's uncle and grandmother got dressed up and walked over to the school to talk to Mrs. Zajac. Chris sat down with them and an interpreter in the vice principal's office, the tiny grandmother with her long gray hair tied back, wearing a simple dress with faded flowers on it, and Pedro's uncle in a leather vest, a tight white miniskirt, and black mesh stockings. Chris felt as if she were at a strange tea party, sitting on the edge of her chair and smiling brightly, and they all agreed that Pedro should bring his respiratory medicines to school, and a note requesting the core was drafted, which the old grandmother signed. She chuckled as she penned her name. The old woman seemed greatly cheered up.

But still there was no news about Pedro's core. Chris saw the boy walking in his perky way, in the mornings, up Bowers Street, ambling happily along toward another day of academic failure, and she thought that the strength of some children was amazing. Pedro just didn't know how hard his life was, but he'd be a teenager soon, and then he would, and the comfort dispensed by drug dealers would be waiting for him, Chris was afraid, if she didn't get him some help now. Chris told herself, "Okay, it's sad. Now what am I going to do about it?" But she was giving Pedro all the time she had to spare in class, and he still wasn't even spelling the spelling words right.

In her dining room, Chris wrote on her yellow notepad, adding to her list of things to do for tomorrow: "Check on Pedro's core!!!"

"36 = F," Chris wrote on Pedro's social studies test. If she was not honest, she would never have tangible evidence of progress or decline. Judith's test came up next in the pile.

Tory. A person that didn't think we should breakaway from England. John Adams. A fellow patriot that was one of the Sons of Liberty. He was the second president of the United States. He was one of the Signers of the Declaration of Independence. He was one of the Representatives of the United States with France. He helped fight the Revolutionary War.

"100 = A + Super!" Chris wrote across the top of the paper.

Sometimes in the classroom, when Chris was smiling surreptitiously − at one of Claude's homework excuses, say − she would look up and notice Judith, turned around in her chair and smiling, too, at Chris's efforts not to smile. Judith, usually the first to finish any assignment in class, would read while the others worked, and if while she was reading Judith's neighbor Alice touched her arm or whispered her name, Judith would make a little jump in her seat and clap a hand to her chest. "You scared me!" Judith had great powers of concentration, but she also seemed to be aware of everybody in the room and of what everyone was feeling, including Chris.

"Oh, Clarence, I'm so tired!" Chris remembered saying one afternoon, and there was Judith, turned around in her seat, looking at Chris.

"You *look* tired," Judith said.

"Oh, Judith, now I have to study fractions over the weekend. It's all your math group's fault."

"Students have to do homework," said Judith. "Why shouldn't teachers?"

"Oh, Judith, I'm so tired!"

"I don't blame you," said Judith. "I'd rather go in the Army than be a teacher."

"I don't know about *that*." Chris sat up, somewhat invigorated.

"Well," said Judith, "you got a battle here every day." And Judith hunched her shoulders like Miss Hunt and gave Chris a lovely grin.

That story Judith wrote about having to move to the Flats from her family's last, nice little house, and the part of the essay about her mother sitting on the porch steps and Judith sitting down beside her, and neither of them speaking but each one knowing just how sad the other felt — that was an essay by an adult. "This girl is about as mature as I am," Chris thought. "And smarter."

Judith's eyes fascinated Chris. It was possible to imagine that they were centuries old, the eyes of an ancient soul in a girl's body. In fact, Judith's eyes were slightly myopic, a secret that Judith, who didn't want glasses, had kept from all of her other teachers and, for a while, from Chris.

Judith had moonlit skin, a thin figure, and brown curly hair, which she kept very long, because her father was an old-fashioned Puerto Rican of the countryside, a *jíbaro*, and he insisted that his daughters wear their hair long until they got married. Judith tied it up artfully with lacy ribbons. She was physically a year older than most of her classmates — twelve instead of ten and a half or eleven. Judith hadn't started school until she was seven. But the main reason she seemed much older than the rest probably lay elsewhere. Judith could not remember a time when she hadn't been fluent in both English and Spanish. She had served, from the age of about eight, as her parents' main interpreter to the English-speaking world, at stores and clinics and welfare and housing offices. So she knew first hand about the ailments, financial worries, and humiliations of immigrant adults stuck in poverty.

Chris had noticed that praise made Judith shy. It had taken Chris a while to realize that was because Judith was even smart about being smart. When she got an A on a paper, which was usually, Judith put it away in her desk before her classmates could see it. Judith felt that her teachers had always praised her too openly. "I like the way I do good in school, but I don't like overpraising. It makes me feel like, like the other kids look at me like someone else. So I try to do good in school, yeah, and I do try to be like a kid, you know?"

But Chris knew Judith's life was more confined than any child's ought to be. Judith lived down in the Flats, in a housing project of gray three-story units. Her father didn't feel free, Chris realized, to let her walk the few blocks to school, as most children did without incident. Her father drove her to and fro, carrying Judith from one safe place, as safe as he could make it, to another.

Judith read a great deal, and she knew a fair amount about politics and geography. Judith said that she did well in school because she chose to do so, and that was because she wanted to get a good job when she grew up. But it sometimes seemed that her world was even smaller than the Flats itself. She said, for instance, thinking about her future, "I'm not gonna be livin' off welfare." She added, "Like most people."

Kelly School was right next door to what is called the Five College Area, but Judith had not yet heard of Smith, Mount Holyoke, or Amherst College.

From her classroom window in the crisp, dying days of fall, Chris would watch her students at recess on the playground below. She looked out to see if Clarence was in a hitting mood, and to see which children were making friends. Through the window, about a month ago, Chris had begun to see Judith hanging around in a group that included a very tough thirteen-year-old fifth grader from another homeroom, a pretty girl with a dirty neck, who leered at handsome boys and was often seen sitting on the bad-boy chairs outside Al's office. Then one day Chris saw that girl stuff some clothes under her coat at recess and promenade around, pantomiming pregnancy, while a small group of girls, which included Judith, watched. It looked as though Judith was laughing.

A while back Chris had bragged about Judith to a teacher friend. The friend had asked,

"Have you considered moving her up to sixth grade?" Chris decided she should do that right away. Losing Judith from this class would be like losing an adult friend. The thought of the room without her made Chris feel bereft, and that made Chris feel it was her duty to promote Judith. She'd get Judith away from that tough girl and shorten the number of dangerous years between Judith and college.

The vice principal, Paul, talked Chris out of the idea. Wasn't Judith doing well? Didn't she seem happy? Paul asked. Chris was willing to be persuaded to keep Judith.

Every other day in Holyoke, a teenage girl was giving birth. Someone on the staff had carelessly remarked that Judith would probably get pregnant in a few years. But Chris refused to believe that.

"Judith, come here," Chris had said when class was winding up one day early in the fall. Judith came with her cheek laid against her right shoulder. "What do you want to be?"

Judith laughed.

"Do you want to go to college?"

Judith looked around her. The other children were getting their coats and weren't noticing. "Yes."

"Good," said Chris. "You should. You're a smart girl. If you keep working hard, you'll get a nice scholarship. So keep it up. Okay?"

Chris had been feeling very optimistic about Judith since the parent conferences. Judith's father had attended. He looked much older and less prepossessing than Chris had imagined him. He wasn't much taller than Judith. He wore rough work clothes. He spoke softly in Spanish.

Judith stood beside her father at the front table and translated into Spanish Chris's words of praise for her.

"Tell your father that you're an excellent student, Judith."

Judith obeyed. She seemed to be trying not to smile at the absurdity of it all.

Chris brought up college. Judith's father spoke. Judith said, "He says that maybe I can get a scholarship."

"Yes!" shouted Chris.

It was during that conference that Chris decided she hadn't understood the full extent of Judith's gifts. The girl had a huge English vocabulary and her parents didn't even speak the language. For Chris, there was no question now. This was the brightest child she had ever tried to teach.

When Debbie, the librarian and director of the reading program, came asking for children who could be spared to help out in the library, Chris volunteered Judith, during spelling. Judith didn't need spelling lessons. Then Chris decided to send Alice, who would certainly be going to college, along with Judith to the library, to keep her company. Pretty soon – Chris could have predicted it – Debbie was leaving Judith and Alice to run the library by themselves for half an hour in the mornings. Chris was afraid that Judith might get bored with school. Chris made sure to spend some time with her every day. But it didn't feel like enough. Chris kept looking at Judith and thinking, "If only I had more time."

When was it exactly that Chris noticed something wrong with Judith's eyes? Probably that time when Chris wrote a sentence on the board and, while turning to watch Clarence, asked Judith to read it aloud. Judith made just a quick squint when she must have thought Mrs. Zajac wasn't looking. But Chris saw the squint from the corner of her eye. Chris pounced. For weeks now, she had been cornering Judith near the door at the end of the day, cutting her out from the herd of other walkers and saying, "Judith, you'd look so pretty in glasses!"

Judith would lift her eyes to heaven, put her hands on her hips, shake her head, and smile at Mrs. Zajac. The girl was still resisting, but the struggle was fun, and it seemed worth the effort, if only for its symbolism. It was something Chris could do for Judith, who was always doing something for Chris. Just recently, for example, at the end of a very bad day with Clarence, Judith had said, "Mrs. Zajac? Do you mind if I take home a dictionary?"

In the dining room, Chris turned to Alice's test. Alice had pink cheeks and silky brown hair. She wore shirts with the designer's name on the front. The sight of an injured or weeping classmate clearly troubled her. Her hands, the nails brightly painted, would flutter nervously. If a crying child was within reach, Alice would rub the child's back. Chris could not remember a fifth grader with a more fully developed sympathetic imagination. Alice was spunky, too. One time Chris left the room and returned to find Alice standing up at her desk, glaring at Clarence. Evidently, Clarence had snatched something from Judith and Alice had snatched it back. When Chris entered, Clarence was saying to Alice, "You do that one more time, I'm gonna make you cry." But he was backing away from Alice, who stood resolutely, her little jaw firmly set, facing him down.

Chris imagined pretty Alice returning home to the upperclass Highlands. That daily event was life as it has been dreamed of in popular American culture: Alice in her snug house, working on her homework in a sunny family room. Alice was one of only several in the class who lived with all the trappings that every child has on TV sitcoms designed for the whole family: safety, fine expectations, no rats or roaches, only birds chirping in the yard outside, a mother who sat down and listened to everything Alice wanted to say, and a father always willing and able to help Alice with her homework. Her parents could have sent her to a private school, but they believed in the idea of public education. They thought she was getting a good one. Some girls at school picked on Alice out of envy of her clothes; her father thought that at public school Alice would learn resiliency.

Alice lived just a few minutes' drive but a socioeconomic gulf away from Judith's project. Chris figured that what the two girls had in common was probably more important: each had two parents who took pains with her. In school, adeptness with language usually matters most, and preschool training often has a lot to do with aptitude for language. Alice's parents had read to her from infancy; Judith's father had always told her stories. In grades and standardized test scores, the two girls resembled each other more than they did anyone else in the class. Alice ranked number two, a little behind Judith in most subjects.

Chris often corrected Judith's and Alice's papers after the others. They helped her get to sleep. "96 = A Very Good!" Chris wrote across the top of Alice's test.

"Oh, Alice," she said, "why don't I have more of you?"

Chris's pen made a regular, two-part sound, like windshield wipers, when it hit wrong answers and drew an X beside a question on the test. It was as if the pen were saying, "That's wrong." Her pen scratch-scratched down the page, then over onto the other side, saying, faster and faster and more and more angrily, "That's wrong, that's wrong, that's wrong, that's wrong." Chris made a face. She said aloud, to Robert's paper, "Robert, you got a thirty. Isn't that wonderful?"

Sarcasm is wrong; it tears down a child. Chris hated it, especially in herself, even when she directed it at Robert's paper and not Robert. Clarence wasn't the only very taxing child in this class. Robert was a genius at bringing out the worst in her.

Robert had crew-cut black hair. His wide face looked as if it had been cut from a square block. He was big all over, with the ample belly of a middle-aged softball player. He had an improbably squeaky voice. On one of the first days of school, Chris asked him, "Robert, please, could you put this package of markers over on my desk?" And Robert did a shimmy at his desk, rolling his shoulders, a patch of jiggling white belly showing. "Who? Me?" he said. Then he looked up at Chris with that smartass grin on his face. "Robert, I'm not asking you to move a refrigerator," she said, but wouldn't she have liked to slap that coy grin away.

There was always an accidental quality to the life around her in her room. On the one hand, there was Judith, who wrote the following cinquain:

Space
is a dark void. Cold
stars and planets live up
there. Big Dipper and Mars. We
explore.

And on the other hand, Robert, who Chris knew had the equipment to do well in school, and who wrote this:

Garbage is disgusting
garbage is wet and smells
garbage drips all over the ground.
It smells

Robert's paragraph about his ideal birthday party described a cake fight at his house, during which his mother's boyfriend got the cake "right in the face." Reading that here in her dining room one night a while back, Chris had thought, "They probably haven't cleaned up the mess yet. Maybe that's where the roaches in the room came from." Robert was getting to her more than he could possibly know.

He lived in an old, rundown apartment building in the lower-class Highlands, not many blocks from where Chris grew up. Maybe that was part of the problem. Maybe Robert made the kind of life Chris dreaded seem all too near at hand.

Where had Robert learned that the best way to deal with failure is to embrace it? One time, after Chris handed back a test, Robert said loudly, "F. F's my specialty!"

Another time, Chris told Felipe he had to stop leaning back in his chair. She tacked on a cautionary tale of a former student of hers who had fallen backward and cracked open his head.

"Did blood spurt all over?" said Robert, grinning.

Chris tried to add some fun to Friday's spelling tests by putting the children's names into sentences: *"Firefly.* Mariposa caught a *firefly* in her hand."

"And squished it," piped up Robert in his squeaky voice. He gurgled.

"Smother," Chris said during one test. "You

shouldn't put a pillow in a baby's crib, or it might *smother* itself."

"That'd be a riot," declared Robert.

That time Alice spoke for Mrs. Zajac. "Robert! You could kill the baby!"

Robert made his gurgly laugh and looked around the room, as if searching for more of that kind of approbation.

Robert was capable. Chris had asked Robert's reading group what sort of teacher she would be if, like the girl in the story they were reading, she didn't care for her job.

"You'd let the kids do whatever they wanted," said Robert without hesitation.

His misspent intelligence angered her. "He could be at grade level. Easy. He could be getting A's," she thought.

Once in a while, Robert did get A's. One day that fall, he even came in with all of his homework done, and did all his work in class. Chris wrote a note to his mother, saying that Robert had a very good day in school. Maybe his mother said the wrong thing when she saw the note, or maybe the note frightened Robert. He was acute enough to sense that the surest way of hanging on to his teacher's attention was not to do the work. He didn't do his homework again for weeks.

The second day of school, Chris wrote Robert's mother a note.

Robert's mother wrote back, in part: "I want to know everything he does. So I can stop it."

Which seemed both discouraging and encouraging. By immediate return note, Chris tried to institute the old homework-signing deal: Chris would make sure that Robert wrote down his assignments correctly and would initial the paper; Robert's mother should make sure that he did the work and she should sign it. A few times after Chris sent a note to his mother, Robert did his homework. But his mother could not have checked Robert's work very often because he rarely did any, and the little that he did always came back unsigned.

Finally, Robert's mother called Chris on the phone at school. The woman sounded angry. She demanded to know why Robert was being kept after school. Chris said it was because Robert hadn't done his homework for a long time. His mother said that surprised her. Robert did his homework. Chris said she never saw it. Then Robert's mother said that if her son wasn't doing his homework, maybe it was because the work was too boring for him. Chris held her tongue. Then the woman said she wanted Chris to keep Robert after school *every* day. Chris said she couldn't do that, and the mother soon hung up. "She just wants free babysitting," Chris thought. Here at her table at night, Chris had imaginary conversations with that woman. They usually turned into shouting matches.

She didn't always find it impossible to like Robert. He once said, "School would be better if they didn't have teachers. Just robots. Yeah. And we'd rewire 'em." Chris felt a little wave of admiration for him when he blurted out statements like that, or when he told her she was said to be the meanest teacher in the school. She'd think, "Boy, I'd never have had the guts to say that to a teacher." And Chris felt a little ashamed of herself, for her thoughts about Robert, when she read his scrawled writings about his father, whom Robert had never met. Without being able to say so, Robert seemed to feel that in the great mystery of who his father was lay the secret of himself. But Robert's mother evidently felt that a meeting with his father might lead Robert astray. A couple of times in class, Robert wrote letters to his father, letters that would never be mailed.

Dear Dad
were do you live I want to come and see you I love you but the only thing is do you love me. Why did you leave my mother in the first place because you had another lady on your mind or something.

By
Dad

142

Teachers' manuals say it is best to ignore a showoff, but Robert wasn't just a showoff. His penmanship itself was distressing to look at — sometimes round, sometimes angular, sometimes utterly indecipherable. He'd sit at his desk, dismantling a notebook or a pen, covering his hands and pants with ink, then grinning at the mess. He'd sit there and start crying out, "Oi, oi," then turn to tuneless song, then utter cries that sounded like imitations of sexual passion: "Oh, harder!" Chris would turn to him and see him tearing a hole in his jeans with his ruler. Or he'd have wedged a very sharp pencil between the edge of his desk and his groin, the tip facing groinward, and she'd see him pressing harder and harder against the pencil point with a distressingly placid look on his face. Without warning, he would start attacking himself, first patting his thighs, then slapping them, then pounding them with his fists, all the while wearing that bemused look. He would slap himself in the face, harder and harder. She'd grab his hand. "Robert, stop it!" He would enter one of those maniac, masochistic periods, and then, just as quickly, he'd go silent and sit drooped over his desk, staring at nothing, radiating gloom.

Chris sat in her classroom one afternoon and

read this essay of Robert's:

I don't now what to write because I have
noten in my mind so I just want to say
hello and good by to every body because I
am moving to A New town A New house a
New world like I'm out of my mind like
Nobody cares if I Leave. Because parent's
are so stuPid that if I were going to light a
building on fire there just get out of the
apartment and watch it burn down I have a
poem to go withe it do you want to here
the poem too bad you listen to it anyway it
goes fill the halls with gasalin fa la la fa la
la light a match and watch it gleam fa la la
la la la la la watch your school burn
down to ash's fa la la la la fa la la la arent
you glad you played with match's fa la la la
fa la la la la la ha ha ha ha ha ah

One morning, taking a slightly different route
to school, Chris passed the public mental
health clinic on Maple Street. She thought
about Robert on the instant. It was not a large
leap of imagination; it was the kind of perception that seems to account for everything and
explains nothing.

Chris could manage Robert. He would back
down, unlike Clarence. If Robert started talking
back to her, she'd just get her face close to his

144

and he would shut up at once and drop his eyes to his lap, blushing. But what could she do for Robert? Maybe, somehow, she could talk his mother into taking Robert to a psychiatrist. In the meantime, she'd just keep trying to get him to do his work. She'd lecture him, and tell him he was smart, and keep him in from recess now and then, and for after-school detention when she could bear it. Sometimes Robert did his work in class, and did it well, and more often he didn't. Whether he worked or not seemed to have little to do with measures she undertook, except occasionally for one strategy. She'd tell him she was finished with him and wouldn't pay any more attention to him until he made an effort, and then sometimes he would stop singing or slapping himself or gazing moodily at nothing, and get to work, quite happily, it seemed.

The clock on the kitchen wall read nearly nine when Chris's son appeared in the dining room, wiping tears away with the sleeve of his pajamas. In school today, he had said to a classmate that he hated his best friend, and now he was afraid his classmate would tell his best friend, and his best friend would tell his parents, who would yell at him for saying that.

Chris smiled. "Come here," she said.

"There's nothing to be upset about. I think you're just overtired."

"I'm not," he sniffled.

"Come here. You want a little ice cream? You want to sit here a couple minutes?"

"Okay." The boy's nose was stuffed.

She corrected a few more papers while the child watched.

"Guess whose test I just corrected."

"Whose?"

"Clarence's."

Her son smiled. "What'd he get?"

"He did good. Did well. He got a seventy-nine!"

Clarence must have studied for once. Could he have cheated? No, Chris had made sure his desk was shoved far away from Mariposa's. She had moved Clarence's desk several times already, most recently next to Mariposa's. She'd hoped that maybe busy, efficient Mariposa would have a calming influence on Clarence. Arabella, Clarence's previous neighbor, had complained. Clarence had been singing at Arabella, "There's a fat girl sittin' next to me."

If Clarence had studied for this social studies test, it was the first time this year. He did do all of his homework and classwork one time earlier in the fall, and back then she'd thought that perhaps a change was beginning. Chris didn't let herself believe that now.

Her son frowned at the news about Clarence's doing well on the test. He went behind the doorjamb in the kitchen doorway and peeked around the corner at Chris, imitating Clarence, banished to the hall and peeking back inside the classroom. He had heard enough stories to think that Clarence would be fun to play with. Her son had asked Chris if she would bring Clarence home someday.

Chris kissed her son and sent him back upstairs to bed. She returned to Clarence. Even here at her dining room table, she would look up from other students' papers, only to find Clarence's face there instead, blocking all the rest.

Chris tried to bury memories of troublesome students from years past. She wasn't sure, but she thought she'd never had a more difficult child than Clarence. By the end of the second week of school, his pattern had become unmistakable. She remembered one day out of many like it: Clarence wouldn't work. Chris told him gently that if he didn't, he couldn't go to gym. That didn't make Clarence comply. Instead, he beat up Felipe, his best friend and usual victim, in the hallway. A scolding followed. Afterward, Clarence ripped down part of Chris's bulletin board display. Chris planned to keep Clarence after school, to try to talk to him, but he managed to get away — she let him go fetch his little brother from kindergarten, telling him to be sure to come back, but Clarence didn't come back. She went home that afternoon and told Billy the whole story. Billy started to say that maybe Chris shouldn't take gym away from Clarence, and Chris started scolding her husband. "Don't tell me I shouldn't take gym away! I don't want to hear I shouldn't have done what I did!" It wasn't a serious argument, but Chris couldn't believe she'd let this boy disrupt her home that way.

When she felt calmer, Chris devised a new plan. It did not seem naive back then. Clarence would win a star for each day he behaved well and did his work. He would get a special reward for three stars in a row. The next morning, Chris called Clarence up to her desk to tell him about this new deal, and he seemed to like the idea. But when she got to the part about behaving well and asked Clarence gently if he knew how, as if to say that of course he did, Clarence started crying, and said he didn't.

"Did you see that? That's emotional disturbance," said Chris to Pam Hunt, the student teacher, afterward. Chris's voice sounded a little desperate.

Then there was the day when Clarence got angry at Alice over a classroom game; kicked Alice in the back of the legs on the way to reading; was rude to Pam, who scolded him; got even by punching Arabella during indoor recess; hit Arabella again, right in front of Chris, which was unusual; and when Chris got him out in the hall, called her a bitch. Chris decided not to send Clarence to Al that time. She sent him to a guidance counselor. This was early in the fall, when Kelly School still had two counselors. One was a woman who didn't seem to understand English fully, or boys like Clarence. Clarence sneaked away from the woman and went home. (Al soon had that counselor transferred.) Chris had decided that what Clarence needed most and yearned for was stability – consistent rules and consequences – and, she felt, the boy had defeated her again.

Clarence got only one star in three weeks before Chris let that frail attempt at behavior modification drift into oblivion. During the third week of school, she had started the paperwork for a core evaluation of Clarence. Actually, it was Al, not Chris, who insisted that Clarence be "cored." Then if Clarence did something truly bad, Al could prove that the school had already taken some action. Once in a great while, a core ended up with a child's being sent to one of the special so-called Alpha classes, which were notorious. Al said, "Clarence isn't an Alpha kid. He isn't a killer." Chris didn't think a core was what Clarence needed, but it couldn't hurt. Anyway, nothing would come of it for months.

From here at her dining room table, the year so far with Clarence looked like a one-boy crime wave. Chris could remember a long series of incidents: the disappearance of the special pens for story writing, of the playing cards from the cabinet, of Arabella's candy at one of the class parties. Again and again, after Chris asked the class if anyone had seen those things, Clarence would say "Nope" and shake his head much too earnestly. From the moment she heard Pedro's labored breathing and saw his heavy braces and protruding teeth, she worried about other children mocking him, and sure enough – it was around the third week of school – there was Clarence in the doorway, saying to his friend Pedro, "Get out of my way, buck teeth." There was the angry teacher telling Chris about that little fourth-grade girl who was shaking, literally shaking, and crying with fright at the end of a school day. The girl was afraid to leave the building and walk home across the Flats because Clarence had told her that morning, "You're dead meat. I'm gonna get you after school." Confronted by Chris, Clarence said of the tiny girl, "She starts trouble with me!" Chris warned Clarence. He turned his face away. Clarence threatened the little girl a few more times. Then, evidently, he lost interest in that, and it stopped.

Another day, Clarence beat up a boy in the bathroom. Clarence didn't act sorry. He gave Al a blow-by-blow demonstration in the principal's office. It might have been funny, except that the other boy was sobbing in the corner.

Sometimes Clarence seemed intent on destroying the community of her classroom, or on reshaping it to his own liking. Clarence's vigilance over all nonacademic matters in the room had now become a routine of the class. Now he would hiss at other children to get back in their proper seats, and tell them to be quiet right before and sometimes after he had gotten up in the midst of one of Miss Hunt's lessons and wandered around, refusing to sit down. Scold or punish Clarence, and he would get even with Chris through the other children, always ones who were weaker and almost always out of Chris's sight.

Chris, returning from coffee break, found Felipe sobbing because Clarence had kicked him and hurled him against the wall.

Chris, returning to the room, found Arabella – cheerful, enthusiastic Arabella, who was always kind to everyone – with her head buried in her arms on her desk, her shoulders heaving. Mariposa whispered to Chris that Arabella didn't want to tattle, but Clarence punched her very hard and made her cry for no reason that Mariposa could fathom.

Clarence, furious and feeling persecuted about being kept after school for not doing his homework, waited until Chris left the room and then took over, moving his chair into one of the aisles, playing the troll. Chris came back that time and found Clarence shoving away and threatening all children who tried to pass and get to their desks.

Clarence had taken a fancy to Judith. One day he passed this note down the rows to her:

Dear Judith,
You are so pretty that I would like to ask you something I love you But if you say no I will love you OK!!

"At least he has good taste," thought Chris when she found it a few days later. But the note was both actually poignant and an attempt to be poignant. Clarence had tried out many winning smiles on Chris when she asked him for homework he hadn't done. When smiles didn't work, Clarence sometimes tried tears. Most often he went stony. At the gentlest remonstrance, at the slightest insinuation that he could not do just as he pleased, Clarence would begin to turn away, as if on a motorized wheel, and refuse to look at Chris and refuse to answer. She felt tempted to plead for his attention then. If a less experienced teacher did plead, as Miss Hunt did early on, the suggestion of a smile on Clarence's face would give him away.

Chris felt she couldn't let him win the little contests that he staged, and give in to his cuteness or his stoniness. However, if she spent half her time and energy on Clarence, she would cheat the other children. He was like a physical affliction. Keeping down her anger at his attempted manipulations exhausted her, and so did the guilt that followed from letting some of that anger out. He was holding her hostage in her own classroom. Sometimes she felt that way. But lately, Chris thought, she was controlling Clarence, and herself with Clarence, better.

After school a while ago, Pam had told Chris about how Clarence had mocked Pam to her face in front of the class. Pam was searching for a general explanation of Clarence. "With a kid like him," she said, "maybe it's the structure of the school."

"You think he should be in another environment," said Chris, her chin on her hand, gazing at Pam.

"I guess," said Pam. "He's not really *bad*. He just wants to move around."

"I know what you mean, Pam," Chris replied.

"But this is what there is. There is no other place for Clarence."

And because that was, or seemed, true, and Chris and Pam weren't going anywhere else either, Chris settled uneasily for an equilibrium dictated by Clarence as much as by herself. Sometimes Chris got some work out of him. She was very pleased with the couplets he wrote. One of them read:

The wind is cool as cool could be
But it is not as cool as cool as me

"These couplets are wonderful, Clarence!" Looking at his other set of couplets, Chris added, "But no 'Beans, beans, musical fruit,' okay?"

One of Clarence's cinquains read:

Christine
The best teacher
Sometimes she is so good
That she is so soft and cuddle
Christine.

Clarence, as Judith observed, could be "very sweet." In spite of everything, he was growing on Chris. She found a folded piece of paper on her desk one afternoon not long after she scolded Clarence gently —

she was certainly trying to be gentle — for not doing his work. I LOVE MRS ZAJAK, the anonymous note said. The handwriting was unmistakable. Alice whispered to Judith that Clarence was just trying to butter up Mrs. Zajac, but Chris felt moved. "Thank you, whoever wrote this," Chris said.

She could remember peaceful afternoons with Clarence, such as the one Chris didn't want to wreck by making a fuss because Clarence had forgotten both grammar book and homework again. "Why is it," Chris said to him, leaning her elbows on her desk (Clarence now sat at the desk closest to hers), "that I have to remember fifty thousand million things, and I'm an old lady, and you can't remember one book?"

Clarence turned around in his chair and looked at Chris. "Old?" he said.

"Yes! I'm an old lady," said Chris.

"You don't look like it," said Clarence, solemnly shaking his head.

One Friday afternoon, she peered into Clarence's desk, putting on her stupefied look, her mouth agape and tongue lolling out, at the chaos inside. "I'd hate to put my hand in there," Chris said to Clarence. "It might get bitten off by the animal that's back in there."

Clarence looked up at her and shook his head. He grinned, revealing the slots where his eyeteeth would be. "Nah," said

Clarence, "it don't bite."

Chris gazed down at him. "Clarence," she said. "You are an original."

But Chris didn't imagine she'd begun changing Clarence's life. Not long ago he jettisoned one of his spelling books on the playground, to get even with Miss Hunt — there were no small children around for him to hurt that time. The soggy book was discovered, and Chris sent him to the office for destroying school property. Afterward, Clarence, suddenly the most prolific of writers, had composed this rough draft of a story:

Hunten house

There once lived a witch her name was Mrs. Zazac and she was a very bad witch and never like no body there was a boy name Clarence she didn't like and she lived in a hunten house an it was bad no one will go in there then one day Clarence went in there was bats all over the place and Alice Judith Felipe Dick and they say watch out look beside you and the witch saw their eyes lid up and the children ran and Clarence look behind him there was Mrs Zazc the witch I didnt believe it and she came right after me than the goust starad to come after me i was right in the corner they haged me up and i was about to di into Judith came she had an big ax to cut down the rope it was to late then we all got trap in a cage where ghousts lives and pretty soon we got batter to them they helped us out then we were called goustbusters and put on our lazer guns we killed our teacher and alice judith felipe and i started to cry and we sad we did what we had to do and that was the end of the wicked witch. the End.

Chris had talked to the class about setting a scene. To his story, Clarence had appended:

part two
   About the wicked witch she died outside it look it was and a nice gradering big color tree big brown rocks and

Perhaps the school psychologist would want to see the story. Chris put it in one of her desk drawers and said to Clarence, "I'm sorry you think I'm a witch, but I wasn't the one who threw away your spelling book." And that was the end of it.

Their truce was of the sort then raging in Lebanon. Chris preferred not to send children to the principal's office, except for violent, dangerous behavior. But she had taken Clarence there many times already. If on one day

Chris decided that Clarence's behavior really had improved at last, and it was time for her to find new ways to get him to do more schoolwork, on the next or the day after the next, she would be marching down the hall toward the office, her arms swinging high and hands in little fists – her taking-a-kid-to-the-office walk, as one colleague called it.

Clarence would be trailing some distance behind, his face sullen, his hand running down the grooves in the cement block wall. Chris would turn back to wave Clarence onward. "Do you remember yesterday, when we talked about consequences? This is the consequence, Clarence, when you don't control your temper."

Clarence would answer angrily, saying of the usually more innocent Felipe, *"He* starts the trouble!"

For Chris, Clarence's life outside school seemed too distant even to imagine. She knew only that Clarence lived in the Flats with his mother. She'd have taken action if she'd seen any physical signs to support the schoolhouse rumors about Clarence being beaten, but she had been keeping a lookout and hadn't seen any. She couldn't do anything about his life away from school, whatever it was like. She told herself, "Let's face it. I as a teacher have to deal with things as they are in the classroom, whatever the situation is at home."

When Al suspended Clarence, Al would send along a message that Clarence's mother had to come to school the next day to get her boy reinstated. This inverted form of kidnapping always worked. The first time Al used that strategy, during the first weeks of school, Chris excused herself from her class in order to confer with Clarence's mother in the vice principal's office. His mother was a big woman, much taller than Chris, and was dressed in slacks and sandals. "Okay," she said, looking out the window, when Chris had finished describing Clarence's latest offense.

Chris set up the old homework-signing deal. And maybe, said Chris, Clarence's mother could come to school every two weeks or so to talk to her about Clarence?

"Okay," said his mother. She had a deep, musical voice. "I'll give it a shot. I did it last year."

"It's only September," said Chris. "But he's sliding, and we've got to stop it now. He's not a happy kid. I think he comes to school with a chip on his shoulder some days. How is he at home?"

"He's good," said his mother. "He plays good outside." She sighed. "Well, can't give up."

"Oh, no!" said Chris. "He's much too young for that! If we work together, we can help him have a good year."

"Yeah, well, give it a shot," said his mother, looking again toward the window.

But she could not have checked Clarence's homework any more often than Robert's mother checked his, because Clarence, too, almost never did any. Clarence's mother did not come to see Chris again that fall. She did come to Kelly periodically, to get Clarence reinstated. Once, Chris saw her in the hall, and for a moment could not remember which infraction Clarence had committed this time. Lately, Chris had all but stopped sending Clarence to the office, although he still gave her cause. Sending him there, or home, hadn't done any good.

Thinking about Clarence tonight didn't lead to any new strategies. She'd just go on trying to ignore small offenses and to get him to do his work. She'd keep on trying to talk to him. Maybe she had made some progress. She still heard bad stories from other teachers who dealt with him. But he was behaving fairly well now for her, or at least better than in September. That was a start maybe. He'd done well on this social studies test. There was always reason for hope.

Chris put the social studies tests in piles. There were four A's, four B's, four C's, two D's, four F's, two absent. "I don't want that to happen. I want the majority to be in the A's and B's. But Clarence. I've really got to praise him. And Ashley, who I didn't think was paying *any* attention, she got a C. So did Claude." Propping up her chin with her hand, Chris gazed into her kitchen at the clock on the wall. "Oh, what am I going to do about those four who flunked? Jimmy. Well, maybe if I move his seat . . ."

It was past bedtime.

Chris's parents had always recited the rosary at night. Sometimes Chris did, too, while trying to get to sleep. Her reasons were less pious, she guessed. Chris thought of prayer as a better way of counting sheep, and of keeping her students' faces out of her bedroom. If she failed, she wouldn't sleep well, and all the next day her voice would sound to her like branches snapping.

Discipline

Passing by the door to Room 205, Chris's best teacher friend, Mary Ann, heard screams and a thudding like soldiers tramping. Chris and Pam were sitting at a table down in the library, working on lesson plans. Mary Ann called down from the balcony, "Chris, you can't believe what your class sounds like. Are they supposed to be doing that?"

"They're having music," Chris called back. "And, Mary Ann, I don't want to hear about it."

A little later, Mary Ann called down again. "Chris, it's getting worse."

"It's not my problem, Mary Ann."

Late on Wednesdays, as a gesture toward integrating Spanish- and English-speaking children, half of Chris's class went to the bilingual room next door and half of the bilingual class came into hers, and while Chris went outside with her texts and planning book, the children had art, which often entailed the teacher's screeching for quiet and often ended, a half hour later, with the children sunk into a sullen, grumbling obedience. Then the children in Chris's room had music, which was different from art.

The music teacher was cheerful and buxom. She had a lovely soprano voice. Lifted in song, it commanded attention. Lifted to declare, "I'm in a mean mood today, children," it lacked credibility. The music teacher said those words once at the start of her lesson, and Clarence jumped up, flexed his biceps, and yelled, "Me, too!" The music teacher would arrive out of breath, with a bongo drum under one arm and, in her other hand, a satchel stuffed with cowbells and maracas, the ends of flutes and recorders and xylophones sticking out of the bag. It sometimes seemed as if she were bringing equipment for a riot. When they were reminded that they had music today, the children would emit soft purrs. They'd cheer when she appeared in the doorway to supplant the art teacher.

When the music teacher walked in that afternoon in October, to deliver the lesson that alarmed Mary Ann, Clarence jumped up from his chair and ran furiously in place for a few seconds. Then he put the eraser of his pencil to his lips, as if it were a rap singer's microphone, and cried, "Everybody clap your hands!"

The music teacher didn't seem to notice. She explained to the class — she had to raise her voice to be heard the minute they spied all the instruments and the big tape recorder — that she wanted to celebrate Halloween by making a recording of spooky sounds. Today, she would hold auditions to see who could do the best imitations of ghostly moans, rattling chains, loud footsteps, door creakings, and window slammings. "And I need one person who can do a really fantastic scream," the music teacher said, her high voice raised still higher because they caught on right away.

In a moment, the children were standing on their chairs and their desk tops, stomping their feet, while Clarence went bounding in one mighty leap over a desk and then sprinted twice around the room. Felipe rolled around on the carpet, wrestling with a chubby boy from the bilingual class and crying out, "Get off me, you starving pig!" Some children tried to outdo each other's moans, and others tried to outdo each other's screams, and even good Arabella was using the maracas both to imitate chains and to bonk her friend Kimberly on the head.

"Time out! Time out!" cried the music teacher, but she didn't sound angry.

Judith and Alice were the only two sitting down, in their usual seats. They clutched their stomachs and alerted each other to various sights. "Look at Clarence!"

He had mounted the cart of encyclopedias and sat on top, a grinning emperor on an elephant, while another boy wheeled the cart around. Clarence was pounding the encyclopedias against the metal shelves to imitate heavy footsteps.

"I guess we can't do this, boys and girls!" cried the music teacher, but she still didn't sound angry at all.

"Hey, teacher! Hey, teacher! I got a door slammin'!" yelled a boy who was vigorously kicking the metal cabinets near the window. Another boy executed somersaults. Clarence dismounted, and did a somersault, too. Children strutted to and fro, stiff-legged, imitating Frankenstein. Clarence disappeared under desks. His head popped up, grinning at Judith and Alice. Someone was beating the bongo drum, and the music teacher's voice was growing hoarse.

"Children! Children! Sit down in your seats. Or else we can't do this."

They crowded around her and the tape recorder instead, and finally, though it was impossible to say how it happened, they all quieted down for a while. They had just finished the recording when Mrs. Zajac opened the door. Before her lay the aftermath of music: the slightly sweet odor of children's perspiration, the flushed faces, and the form of Clarence still crouched beneath a table, Clarence's huge eyes and white grin lurking in the shadows. The children were ignoring the music teacher's cries of "Sit down in your seats!" when Mrs. Zajac entered and said, "I don't think some of you heard. Get in your seats."

"It's wonderful when you're quiet like this," said the music teacher to the class then.

Over at her desk, Chris murmured, looking around, "I can't believe this. Now I have to clean up this room." But she smiled and applauded, too, as the class applauded itself, when the tape recording was played and the last Halloween sound, the really fantastic scream, was dying away. It was the sort of event that becomes a part of the oral history most teachers keep of their classes to distinguish one from the others over the years. No other event that fall quite rivaled it, not even the rhythm bee, which the music teacher staged several weeks later.

2

Ancient Greek and Roman schoolmasters adopted various instruments for classroom management, such as ferrules, switches, and taws, which nineteenth-century English pedagogues found useful. In some of Germany's nineteenth-century Latin schools, children passed by whipping posts on their way to class, and when they got in trouble had to visit the Blue Man, the official in charge of punishments – the Blue Man always wore a blue coat, under which he concealed his tools. Although the practice has been greatly reduced, formal beatings of school-children still happen in America; most states still permit them, though not Massachusetts, at least in theory. Some medieval European and some colonial American schoolmasters probably thought they were doing their students a favor by literally beating the Devil out of them. Historical records make it plain that some teachers and school administrators enjoyed having licenses for their tempers, and perhaps some still do. But a central fact in most sorts of schools has always been the fear of the Lilliputian mob. In America, corporal punishment began to wane around the time when elementary education was becoming universal and compulsory – around the time, that is, when keeping order probably became more difficult. One sociologist of teaching describes the situation as "dual captivity": the children *have* to be there, and the teacher has to take the children sent to her.

The problem is fundamental. Put twenty or more children of roughly the same age in a little room, confine them to desks, make them wait in lines, make them behave. It is as if a secret committee, now lost to history, had made a study of children and, having figured out what the greatest number were least disposed to do, declared that all of them should do it.

Some people think it must be easy to manage a room full of children, but if that were the case, it wouldn't often be said that adults who have been behaving badly have been behaving like children. A man recently out of college came to Kelly School one day that fall to try his hand at substitute teaching. It wasn't even noon when Al, making his third visit to restore order in that substitute's room, told the man that he might as well give up and go home. The screams of his pupils had broadcast his failure throughout the classroom wing. He left with his collar loosened, his necktie askew. He had to go down the main hallway to get out of there, and he walked as fast as a man can without running, and kept his eyes lowered, avoiding the looks from the teachers, mostly women, whom he passed.

Classroom management, as Mrs. Zajac practiced it, required an enlargement of senses. By now Chris could tell, without seeing, not only that a child was running on the stairs but also that the footfalls belonged to Clarence, and she could turn her attention to curing one child's confusion and still know that Clarence was

171

whispering threats to Arabella. She was always scanning the room with her eyes without moving her head, seeing without being seen. Peripheral vision gave her that glimpse of Judith squinting at the board. And there had developed in Chris a sense not easily accounted for — like a hunter's knack for spotting a piece of furry ear and inferring a deer standing in a thicket — so that, for example, she could sit at the slide projector, pausing in a film strip to lecture the class on the Iroquois, and know that, behind her, Robert wasn't paying attention. In fact, Robert was playing baton with his pencil, noiselessly flipping it in the air. Chris didn't stop talking to the class or even turn around. Extending her left hand back toward Robert, she snapped her fingers once. Robert stopped flipping his pencil and, as usual, blushed.

Once when Chris was busy on the other side of the room, Dick, the quiet boy from the Highlands who loved social studies, leaned over to a classmate and, inclining his head toward Mrs. Zajac, said, "She knows every trick in the book."

At the end of a day in October, Pam said to Chris, "I don't know how you do it." Pam looked sad. "You just come in and they're quiet."

Actually, they posted sentries when Pam's

lessons were nearly over. Clarence or Robert or Felipe would look out the doorway and hiss, "Mrs. Zajac! She's comin'!" Clarence would dash back to his seat, vaulting into it like a stunt man into a car. So when Mrs. Zajac walked in, she would find Pam standing there with her jaw looking hardened and the class sitting with its collective hands folded, the last whispers fading, all eyes on the door.

"What am I doing to this poor, sweet girl?" Chris asked herself at those moments.

Now when Chris drove down to the Flats, the canals steamed in frigid air. She started wearing her green cloth winter coat, which would answer for all the seasons and all the fashion she needed from now until after St. Patrick's Day. For her week of recess duty in November, she brought wool socks to slip over her stockings before going outside. The first snowstorm struck just before Thanksgiving. At home that evening Chris kept peering out windows; Billy told their son, "Mom's on blizzard alert," the way he always did; and Chris spent the next day at home, rejoicing about snow days until nightfall, when she got out her homework and reminded herself that this day would still be served, tacked on to June. A few small epidemics passed through the class, and children with puffy eyes and reddened noses, walking Petri dishes, were driven home by the outreach workers, leaving temporary holes in the room.

In October, fire had gutted the tenement where Lisette lived with her mother and her mother's boyfriend. The girl moved away in November. Chris had set out, as her first goal for Lisette, to get the girl to smile, and though Chris had succeeded only a few times, she had begun to see flickers of aptitude, if not of great interest, in the girl. Lisette had written compositions about several boyfriends, and of "rapping" with them, sometimes with two on the same day. Unfortunately, Chris, who always had to play catch-up with the latest student lingo, did not know until long after Lisette had left that "rapping" had acquired new meanings, which ranged from kissing to intercourse. Chris mourned Lisette's departure: "I thought I was making some progress with her. And now where is she?" As for the children, only Clarence, as usual noting any change in the room, mentioned the fact of Lisette's empty desk.

The potted plant on the corner of Chris's desk died from lack of water. A teacher friend had sent it to Chris on the first day of school. It was the only plant in the room. Chris hummed the funeral dirge – "Dum dum dum, dum da-dum da-dum da-dum" – and dumped the withered remnant in the wastebasket, saying, "I don't have time to water plants."

Massachusetts law didn't require that school-children say the Pledge of Allegiance. The Jehovah's Witnesses, of whom Chris had several, weren't allowed to say it. She led the class through the Pledge only once that fall. The exercise turned up the fact that Clarence wasn't quite sure which hand was his right, which suggested that there might be better things, arguably more patriotic, for Chris to do with those few hurried minutes before math.

That fall, Chris ran the class and Pam practiced on them for a while every day. For the first several weeks Chris sat in on Pam's lessons, and afterward gave her advice. Pam tried to cover too much ground; Chris showed her how to plan against the clock. Pam spoke too softly. "We need to give you a mean, horrid voice like mine," Chris told her. All in all, Chris felt pleased about Pam's teaching. She liked the way Pam enfolded her lessons in games for the children. She could tell that Pam labored over her lesson plans. Pam came from Westfield State, which was Chris's alma mater. Chris imagined her planning at night in her dormitory room, just as Chris had done in her own practice-teaching days. One time Chris told Pam, "Jimmy loves you," and Pam replied, "I think I'd rather have him hate me and do his work." Chris felt pleased. Pam had the right instincts, Chris thought.

Above all, Chris approved of the emotion that Pam brought to the job. In Chris's philosophy, a brand new teacher needed to feel strong affection for her first students in order to sustain her. The first days of school, when Pam merely sat as an observer in the back of the room, Chris spied on her, including Pam in the searchlight sweeps she made of the room. She saw Pam gazing fondly at the children. Some, especially Clarence and Felipe, kept turning around at their desks to smile at Pam. Pam hunched her shoulders and smiled back, a smile she might have used to entertain a baby in a crib. Pam was falling in love with these children, Chris thought, and the gentle spectacle took her back to her own first class, to a time when she had felt that there never were more fetching children than the ones placed in her care, and she had indulged herself by crying a little at night, in her room at her parents' house, over her first deeply troubled student – the boy who had stolen the class's goldfish. That boy had possessed so little sense of right and wrong that when the fish had been extracted, gasping, from his pockets, he had declared indignantly, "I didn't hurt 'em. They're still breathin'."

Chris felt confident that Pam had all the equipment to become a good teacher. She needed only to learn how to control a classroom. "The discipline part," Chris thought.

"She's got all the rest of it."

At the end of her sixteen weeks of practice, Pam would have to teach the class for three entire days without Chris in the room. After the third week of school, to start breaking Pam in, Chris left her alone for a half hour to teach spelling. The first couple of times, Pam's spelling went well. On a Friday, however, Clarence struck.

Pam was trying to administer the weekly spelling test. Robert, Felipe, Arnie, and Clarence kept telling each other to shut up. As Mrs. Zajac had advised, Pam gave them all warnings, and then she wrote the next offender's name on the board: Robert. That meant he was in for recess. Robert shrugged. Then Pam wrote Clarence's name on the board, explaining that he was not to disturb the rest of the class anymore.

"So?" said Clarence, glaring.

"If you don't care, then go out and stand in the hall," said Pam. Mrs. Zajac had said to put him out there if he was disturbing the class and wouldn't stop.

"No," said Clarence.

"Yes," said Pam. But she didn't make him go. She wasn't sure how to do so. If she laid hands on the boy, he'd make a fuss, Pam thought. So, instead, she told him, "You're not impressing anyone by having that attitude. Clarence, get up and go sit at this front desk. Clarence, right now."

He obeyed, but he banged chairs as he went.

"I feel bad for the people who want to take the test and do a good job."

"So?" said Clarence angrily.

"Don't answer me back!"

She turned her back on him and read the next spelling word. Behind her, Clarence muttered, making faces at her. She wheeled around. "Clarence, get up and go stand in the hall!"

She lowered her voice. "Please."

She stood over him and said softly, "Please move your body into the hallway."

Clarence jumped up. He made a small cry. In the doorway, he turned back and said to Pam, "I'll punch you out! I'll punch you in the face!"

"All right!" Her voice hit her upper register. "You can say that to Mr. Laudato!"

Mrs. Zajac had said that you need to know your ultimate threat, which at Kelly was usually Mr. Laudato, but that you should never go to it right away. And as Pam explained later, "The reason I get wishy-washy, part of me wants to yell at him, and another part wants to wait until he's cooled down a little and I can talk to him." Now she obeyed the second impulse. She didn't take Clarence to Mr. Laudato.

Behind her, Robert was chortling. "He said he'd punch her!" Robert squirmed in his seat.

Julio and Jimmy grinned at each other.

Pam returned to stand in front of the class. Behind her, Clarence edged himself around the doorjamb. He peeked in. Several children giggled. Pam turned. Clarence vanished. "Clarence, I don't want to see your face!" Pam turned back to the class to read the next spelling word. Clarence's face came back around the doorjamb, mouthing silently at her back, "Fuckin' bitch. Gonna get you." The class giggled. Clarence began to grin.

Pam went to the door. Clarence's face disappeared. She closed the door and said to the class, "I hope you'll just ignore him." But in that contest of personalities, hers as a teacher still unformed and divided, she was bound to lose.

The door was closed, but Clarence's face now appeared in the small, rectangular, gun-slit window in the door, his nose and lips distended as he pressed them against the glass. Even Judith ducked her head and shook with the giggles. Others laughed openly. "I'd appreciate it if you'd ignore him and not laugh. You're making things worse," said Pam. But how could they help it? School days were long and this was something new.

Clarence was making faces in the window, bobbing up and down in it. The sound of his drumming on the door — *bang, bang, bang* —

accompanied Miss Hunt's reading of the words for the remainder of the test.

The dénouement was predictable by then. Pam tried to talk to Clarence in the hall, and he wouldn't look at her. So she held his chin in her hand, to make him, and a few minutes later he got even with her by sneaking up behind Felipe – in the hallway, on the way to reading. Quickly thrusting both arms between Felipe's legs, Clarence lifted his friend up and dumped him, face down, on the hallway carpet. Felipe arose weeping. Clarence got suspended. Pam spent the afternoon worrying about his mother punishing him.

Chris stayed after school with Pam that day. They sat at the front table. Pam told Chris the whole story. Chris said, "You've got to remember there are twenty other kids, and you *are* getting to them. Clarence may be beyond us. We'll do our best, but don't let him ruin your time here. It's not your fault. He walked in like this. You've got to take your little advances and try to forget things like this."

Pam nodded and smiled. She had a confession to make. "The thing is, I almost cried, and then he'd know he'd gotten to me, and I'm thinking, 'He's only ten years old. I can't let him make me cry.' "

Chris went home worried. She told Billy the story. When she got to the end, she said, "Oh,

God. If she had cried . . ."

Chris didn't want to preside over the destruction of a promising career. She worried that Pam would lose her enthusiasm if being alone with this class turned into torture. Chris wanted Pam to taste success, so from time to time Chris continued to sit in on some of her lessons. The children always behaved on those occasions. It was obvious why. They kept glancing at Mrs. Zajac. "If I stay in the room, she won't learn how to discipline," Chris thought. Within months Pam would become a certified teacher. Next year, probably, she would have her own class. Then there'd be no Mrs. Zajac to intervene and help out. Pam had to learn how to control a class now. So for the most part, when it was Pam's turn to teach, Chris gathered up her books and went out to the hall, and told herself as she left, "You have to sink a few times before you learn."

Chris did her own practice teaching in the old West Street School, where, war stories had it, the staff wore mittens indoors in the winter and often got bruised when breaking up fights on the playground. Chris's supervising teacher eventually left Chris alone, to teach her lessons in a dank, decrepit basement room − one day the blackboard fell off the wall. Chris found herself with a class of thirty-four children, many of whom didn't speak much English. Chris remembered coming into that room one day and finding the class bully perched on a chair with one chair leg planted on the stomach of a writhing classmate. She didn't do much real teaching, she thought, but in truth she always could manage, almost from the start, to get a class under control. Chris's skills had grown. Now she could make discipline into a game, as on the day this fall when, apparently looking elsewhere, she noticed some girls passing a piece of paper down the back row during reading. "I'm not even going to ask you for that note," Chris said ten minutes later. The girls' mouths fell open in astonishment. Chris smiled at them. "Teachers have eyes *all around* their heads," she said. She leaned down to get her face close to the girls' faces and drew her fingers all the way around her head, as if encircling it with a scarf. "That's why I don't cut my hair shorter. I *hide* them."

Chris knew that confidence is the first prerequisite for discipline. Children obeyed her, she knew, because she expected that they would. But that kind of confidence can't be invented. Pam would have to find it herself. Chris tried to help. For an hour on Wednesday afternoons, during art and music, Chris and Pam would sit down on the brown vinyl sofa in the balcony corridor between Room 205 and the boys' lavatory. Then, and also after school, the two women would sit facing each other, both dressed in clothes fit for church, the elder looking old only in comparison to the neophyte, the rookie teacher eyeing the veteran respectfully. Pam compressed her lips and nodded as Chris gave her tips:

– No college course prepares you for the Clarences and Roberts, so don't think that you should have known how to handle them when you got here. You are doing a good job, at least as good a one as the other practice teachers in the building.

– Don't let yourself imagine that you are a cause of a troubled student's misbehavior. If you do, you become entangled in the child's problems. You must cultivate some detachment. You have to feel for troubled children, but you can't feel too much, or else you may end up hating children who don't improve.

– When teaching a lesson, don't only call on the ones with their hands up.

– While you teach, scan the room with your eyes for signs of incipient trouble.

– Don't put a child in a situation where he, for the sake of his pride, has to defy you.

– If a child starts getting "hoopy," call on him at once. Stand beside his desk while you teach the class.

– If he acts up anyway, send him to the hall.

You must not allow one child to deprive the others of their lessons.

– Before you even start a lesson, wait until all the children have taken their seats. Don't try to teach until all of them have stopped talking.

That was easy for Mrs. Zajac to say. Before starting a lesson, she would simply fold her arms and, leaning a shoulder against the front chalkboard, stare at the class. The children would scurry to their desks. They'd stop talking at once. But what if Pam did that and some of them just went on talking and wandering around the room? What should she do then?

Pam wanted the class to do some work at their desks, quietly. She was trying to get Clarence to sit down first. He was walking around the room backwards. She touched his arm. He threw her hand aside and proceeded, walking backwards. She turned to Robert, who was making choking, chuffing sounds. "Robert!"

"My motor ran out of gas," Robert explained.

She turned again, and there were Felipe and Arnie wrestling on the carpet. She ordered them to stop, but while she was doing that, Courtney had gotten up from her desk and had gone over to Kimberly's to gossip.

"Courtney, go back to your desk."

"Wait a minute," said Courtney, who had

never talked back before.

"No, I'm not waiting!"

Robert was babbling. "That cold. Cheat. Cheat. Cheat. Five-dollar food stamps." He stood up as Pam approached, and did a shimmy in front of her, his big belly jiggling. He was protesting that he couldn't get to work. "I don't have no book," he said.

Mrs. Zajac walked in. The sentries had failed.

"Then you go over there and get one!" thundered Mrs. Zajac.

Robert froze. His face turned pink.

Pam was trying to show a film strip about colonial days, but Clarence kept putting his hand in the beam. Then Robert put his hand in the beam. Then the usually well-behaved Julio tried it, too. Then Clarence put his hand on the rump of the colonial maid on the screen. Felipe leaned way back in his chair, laughing and laughing.

Pam stopped the film strip. She put the names Clarence, Robert, and Felipe on the board, which meant they couldn't go outside after lunch. As the class arose for lunch, Clarence said, right in front of Pam but as though she weren't there, "Lunch! I'm goin' outside."

"*I'm* goin' outside," said Robert.

As for Felipe, he refused to get up and go to

185

lunch at all. He had his arms folded. He pouted.

"Felipe, you are going to lunch," said Pam.

"No, I ain't!"

"Yes, you are!"

"Read my lips!" said Felipe. "I'm stayin' here!"

"Tsk, tsk, tsk," said Robert.

"Because we were laughin', then she had to put my name down. I hate her! I'm sick of her!" yelled Felipe as Pam, twisting her mouth, decided to leave him there and get help.

One day, when sent to the hall, Clarence stood in the doorway, pointed a finger at Pam, and declared, "I ain't stayin' after school either." Then he watched Pam wrangle with Robert. He cheered Robert on, saying, "Crunch her, crunch her."

Pam said, "Okay, Robert, would you get up and go down the hall to the office?"

"No, please. I wanta stay," said Robert, smirking up at her.

"Robert, get up," she said. "Robert, get up."

"I wanta stay here."

"If you're going to stay here, you have to be good."

"See dat?" said Clarence from the doorway. "She doesn't make Robert go. She prejudice, too. See, she didn't get Robert."

"Shut up, Clarence," said Robert.

"Robert, go to the office," said Pam.

"No," said Robert, smirking.

Another time, Pam said to Clarence, "Shut your mouth!"

Clarence replied, "No. It's *my* mouth."

Pam said to Robert, "You can work on your story now."

"No, I can't," said Robert. "I don't know what to write."

"Use your brain," said Pam.

"My brain gooshed out," said Robert. Then he looked up at her and began beating on his cheeks, a popping sound. Then he gnawed on his hand. Then he slapped his own wrist.

"I don't want any more foolish comments!" she thundered. "Do you under-*stand?*"

Clarence watched. "She not human," he said.

Pam turned to Clarence. "You don't disturb twenty other people."

"There aren't twenty people," said Clarence. "There's . . ." He started counting.

"He knows how to count," said Robert.

Chris returned to find Pam sitting at the teacher's desk, staring out the window, with her jaw misaligned.

It wasn't as if Pam did no teaching. The children would sidle up to her table throughout the day, bringing her pictures they'd drawn and asking for help. She tutored many individually. Some of the lessons she taught without Chris in the room went smoothly. Once in a while when Miss Hunt was teaching, Judith or Alice or Arabella spoke up and told Clarence and Robert to be quiet and stop making trouble. But usually that just egged the boys on, especially Clarence. Some of those boys' responses to Pam's efforts to tame them seemed surprisingly sophisticated, as if they themselves had read handbooks on classroom management. Once, for instance Pam turned her back on Robert, and Robert called to her, "That's right. Just ignore me."

As for Clarence, he often wrote his name and Judith's on the board, as if to claim her, but that didn't give Judith any special power over him. He told her once that she needed someone "to pop her cherry." One time, after he had been especially nasty to Pam, Judith told him, "You have the brain of a caterpillar."

Without hesitation – the lines seemed to have been already planted – Clarence replied, "I'll take yours out and put it in your hand and make you eat it." Clarence made his slow, threatening nod at Judith.

Judith looked skyward. She said to Alice, "How did God make such a mistake? He had no choice but to put Clarence on earth. He didn't want him up *there*."

On one of those bad days that fall, on the way to lunch, Judith said softly to Pam, "Are you

188

reconsidering your decision to become a teacher?"

"No, Judith," said Pam, and she smiled. *"You* make it all worthwhile."

Judith herself had begun reconsidering her embryonic plans for becoming a teacher. She wondered why Pam kept coming back, and didn't even take a sick day. Judith believed that Pam had to be a very strong and admirable person, but even as the days of Pam's travails wore on and Clarence's antics lost their novelty, Judith still couldn't help laughing when Clarence, banished to the hall, did a soft-shoe routine for the class in the doorway. As Robert indignantly pointed out – "Hey, the teacher's laughin', you're not sposed to laugh" – even Pam couldn't always hide her amusement. For example, the day when she told the class that primates have tails, and Clarence stood up, poked out his rear end, patted it, and said, "Check out mines."

Chris didn't witness those scenes. Leaving Pam alone in the room for a period, Chris would go out to the sofa in the hall and try to work on her plans for next week's lessons. She had a hard time concentrating. She'd hear distant, muffled sounds of commotion, then Pam's voice, high and angry, then more commotion. Chris would flinch. She'd get up and peer down the corridor, to see if Pam had put Clarence out in the hall. One time, when Pam had put him out there, Chris waylaid a passing teacher and said, "Give Clarence a dirty look when you go by, okay?" When boys came by on the way to the bathroom, she waylaid them. "Felipe, come here, please. What's going on in the room?"

"Miss Hunt is in a bad mood," said Felipe. "Clarence was talking back to her, and everybody laughed. He wrote on the board, 'Miss Hunt is a jerk.' She kicked him out, and he wanted to come back, and she yelled at him, and he's mad."

"Okay. Thank you."

Felipe moved on. Chris sat on the couch, fuming. "Children can be so cruel when they sense a weakness. I'd like to go in there and . . ." She bared her teeth.

On the bulletin boards in the hallways, Halloween displays lingered almost until Thanksgiving. Most of the displays were store bought or inspired by books of ideas for bulletin boards, on sale at all stores that cater to teachers. No child would have recognized his fears in the black cats, toothy pumpkins, and witches on broomsticks. They all looked much too benign. But some of the witches' faces that hung in the classroom, over the closets and under the clock, had malevolence, especially high-strung Felipe's. His witch's face was long and distended, like an El Greco, and her mouth suggested an appetite for little children. And Clarence had acquired a pair of plastic fangs, painted red, which he wore for the class during one of Pam's lessons.

As November wore on, Pam taught more and more. Chris grew increasingly restive out on the couch in the hall. Now and then Chris felt a little consternation at Pam. One afternoon, she stood on a chair just outside the door, taking down an old bulletin board display. While she pulled staples, Chris eavesdropped. A fair amount of noise came out of the room. "Does it always sound like this?" Chris muttered under her breath.

From the room came Pam's voice. "Felipe! Why are you out of your chair?"

"That's a good question, Miss Hunt," muttered Chris. "Why is he?"

Sometimes rivalry develops between a practice teacher and the one whose class she borrows. Neither Pam nor Chris committed any rivalrous deeds, though. Chris really liked Pam. She ached for Pam while she sat on the sofa imagining trouble back in the room. But Chris had more on her mind than Pam's travail. In December, the real test began, both for Pam and Chris. Pam took over the class for three whole days in a row. Chris couldn't sit still. She roamed the olive-carpeted halls like an expectant father. Two days went by. Finally, Chris sat down on the sofa. "Oh!" she exclaimed. "I want my class back!"

3

A dusting of snow covered the playground. Heavy coats filled the closets. Out in the hall, just before Pam's last grammar lesson, one of the last lessons she would teach the class, Chris said, "Well, Pam, are you ready to slam down the book, and close the door, and let 'em have it?"

Pam looked at Chris, and then Pam hunched her shoulders and smiled.

Chris went to the sofa. In a moment, she arose and sneaked up to the door of Room 205. She peeked through the gun-slit window. "Oh, good. Pam just threw down the book. I wish I could hear what she's saying. I told her to get right up to Robert's face with her teacher finger."

Chris went back to the sofa. From there, she could hear Pam's voice, not the words, but the form of it, loud and angry but confident. In a moment, all was still. This time, quiet endured.

Afterward, Pam told Chris that the class behaved well after she slammed down the book and let Clarence have it. Pam said she felt better. She said she believed that the class had been waiting for her to do that, and that they felt better, too.

"She's learning," said Chris after school that day.

They gave Pam her farewell party on a day in mid-December. Chris, Judith, Alice, and Mariposa organized it. Chris sent Pam on an errand so they could hang up crepe streamers. Felipe got so excited during the preparations that Chris had to send him out to the hall. "So you can calm down."

When Felipe came back in, Clarence, now on his best behavior, looked at him and said, "You still ain't calmed down."

On the front table was apple juice and a cake inscribed "Good Luck." Pam had brought each child a candy cane and now laid them on the desks. Robert refused even to touch his. He refused to get into the class picture that Pam took. He sat at his desk, and while the other children scurried around and chattered, Robert pulled his sweatshirt up over his mouth, to his nose. Then he clawed at his eyelids. Then he began slapping himself, harder and harder, in the face.

Chris stared at Robert from her desk. "Look

at him! I gotta get him out of here."

She took Robert down to the office to see the counselor, but the counselor was busy, as usual. So she sat Robert down on one of the bad-boy chairs outside Al's office. "Why didn't you want to make a card for Miss Hunt?"

Robert shrugged. "I didn't have no paper," he said in a squeaky voice.

"Don't give me that!" said Chris. She lowered her voice. "What's wrong, Robert?"

"Nuttin'!"

She left him there. Maybe the counselor could get something out of him. Probably not. Later, she'd wish that she had asked Robert, "You're sad Miss Hunt is leaving, aren't you?" At the moment, though, Chris had to get back to the party.

Pam gave Chris a new, larger bookbag and a note that concluded, "You are a very special person and a dear teacher."

Chris had decided that she missed Pam already. So had the children, including most of her tormentors. They were putting on their coats.

"Bye, Miss Hunt," said Jimmy.

"We'll remember you," said Felipe.

Pam smiled and gulped.

The time arrived for the walkers to leave. Judith pulled Arabella back by the collar and delivered her to Pam. Arabella hugged Pam. So

Felipe had to hug her, too. Judith, who had said she'd like to give Pam a present but couldn't think of anything except maybe earplugs, gave Pam a casual, one-armed hug. Last was Clarence. He hugged Pam hard for a long time, burying his face in her dress.

"Bye, Miss Hunt."

"Goodbye, Clarence. Be good and do all your work."

"I *will!*"

Then it was Chris's turn. Walking Pam to the door of the room, she said, "I think you'll do well. I really do. I hope you have an easier class. And remember, the first day it's gotta be *grrrr.*"

All of the children except Robert had made cards for Pam. Clarence's was the longest and most elaborate. He had decorated the outside with hearts, inside which he had written, "Spelling BEST" and "Teaching is the BEST." Inside, in very neat lettering, he had written:

Dear Miss Hunt

I am sorry you are leaving Today and I now how i been bad to you but i Want to say something before you leave That here it is I Love you And thank you for all the help i needed Thank you Miss Hunt?

Merry Christmas
Your Friend
Clarence by!

Once again, Chris felt moved by Clarence's note. But when, several weeks later in the Teachers' Room, someone said that Westfield State should pay part of Pam's tuition to Chris, Chris remarked, "Actually, they should pay Clarence." She added, "Pam took Clarence 202."

4

The Mrs. Zajac of Mondays was strict, and you obeyed her quickly. The first homework was on Monday night, so on Tuesday morning, if you hadn't done yours, she would probably put your name on the board and give you a lecture, and if you missed a few times, she might keep you in for recess or talk about the late bus, and her voice might sound angry, especially if you didn't do the work you were supposed to do in class. But at least you knew what to expect.

Down on the handball court in the Flats, one of last year's fifth graders told Julio, the tall, quiet boy who was being held back a grade, "Yo, Julie. You got Mrs. Ajax, bro? She is *mean*, bro. If you do your work, she tears it up. She used to scream at me for *nothin'!*" But Julio said, "Now I believe for my own self she ain't as mean as they say. She's fair, because if you do your homework and forget it, she says that's all right but bring it in the next day. But if you keep on skipping, she'll get mad and try to get even."

You were supposed to raise your hand before you asked or answered a question during one of Mrs. Zajac's lessons. If you didn't raise your hand, she would probably call on you. You could count on that. But she gave you a lot of time to answer and she wouldn't get angry if you couldn't, unless you hadn't been paying attention, and she wouldn't let your classmates make fun of you. She said she always made mistakes herself, and that was true. She was always losing the key to her closet and asking Mariposa to find it. If you tried to tell on someone, she'd say, "I don't want to hear it," unless someone had hit someone else or was being mean, usually Clarence, and then if you told, Mrs. Zajac wouldn't let Clarence know it was you.

She was always correcting kids' grammar. If someone said something like, "Mines is good," she'd make herself look like a crazy person and pretend that she was going to run her nails down the chalkboard. She'd say, *"Mine!* Not *mines!* Mine!"* It was funny. Maybe some kids sometimes said "mines" or "ain't" just so she would go into her crazy act. You had to be careful not to say swears, or "It sucks." She'd say, "That's street talk," and she was sure that your mother and the other kids' mothers wouldn't want their kids to hear that kind of language, and she wouldn't either, if her son was in the class. She said please and thank you and excuse me, and if you didn't, she'd say the words for you. She'd say to you, "Thank you, Mrs. Zajac, for finding my book." Some kids would say "Huh?" But after a while they'd catch on.

She didn't know some things. For instance, she thought you still thought Michael Jackson was a fresh, bugged-out homeboy. But she knew some of the new words. She liked to say "chill out." And you could joke with her, especially at the end of the day, when a lot of kids hung around near her desk and told stories and talked about movies and TV shows. You could play the game called "arshhht" on Mrs. Zajac then. It was just a silly game that a lot of kids played on each other around Kelly. You'd ask the other person a question, like "Guess what?" If the other person was off guard and said "What?" back to you, then you'd say "Arshhht," which meant you'd fooled the other person. Clarence would come up to Mrs. Zajac's desk at the end of the day and ask her, "Guess what, Mrs. Zajac?" Mrs. Zajac always fell for it. Then Clarence would yell "Arshhht!" and Mrs.

Zajac would laugh. "Mrs. Zajac loves to laugh," Clarence told Pedro one day, after arshhhting her.

Sometimes she'd make up games – the boys against the girls, or one side of the room against the other side – to review for a test, or she'd make up a mystery. One time she picked up the stapler and the pot of glue and the pot that the plant used to be in and a piece of crepe paper and several other things, and she started putting them on kids' desks. She almost put the glue pot on Robert's, but then you could see she changed her mind, and, of course, you knew why. Felipe kept saying, "What's this for?" and Mrs. Zajac just smiled. Then when she was all done, she said, "Now why have I put these things on your desks?" And Felipe yelled, "I don't have the slightest idea!" and Mrs. Zajac said, "I've just given each of you something," and Clarence said, "We get to keep these?" and she said no, it was just pretending, and then she started telling you about the words, such as "yours" and "hers" and "mine, not mines," that meant something belonged to someone.

If she caught you passing a note, because you wanted to tell Kimberly that the new boy liked Arabella, and it was Monday, Mrs. Zajac would probably take the note and put it in her skirt pocket, but you could get away with notes and a lot more on Friday, and especially on a Friday before a vacation. Fridays were the best times, not as funny and crazy as some of Miss Hunt's lessons when Clarence was talking back, but peaceful and happy, like reading aloud, which was another good time, when, after recess, Mrs. Zajac would sit on the front table and read stories or books, and you could listen and write letters or draw pictures or organize your desk, as long as you didn't bother anyone else.

Judith was the smartest in the class, Claude announced one time, and Mrs. Zajac said, "Thank you, Claude, for deciding that for me." She asked Claude, if he did his work and studied for tests, wouldn't he be as smart as Judith? Claude said he guessed so. Of course, everyone knew Judith was the smartest, but Judith appreciated what Mrs. Zajac said. Mrs. Zajac praised her a little too much for comfort, but not the way some other teachers had, not by saying to other kids, "Why can't you do as well as Judith?"

Mrs. Zajac had a high temper, and she yelled at Clarence and Robert. "It makes things not so nice," Judith thought. But, all in all, Judith approved of Mrs. Zajac. "I think she's one of the best teachers I ever had," Judith had decided. "She's really nice, and she's up front. I like blunt people. They take after me. You don't have to wait for her to be blunt with you.

She just tells you. Sometimes kids might get mad, but that's the way it goes. She's kind, but she's strict. And she's fair." Judith did some Sunday school teaching herself. "That's one thing I admire in a teacher, being able to control a class like ours and still be fair," said Judith.

5

Al came by the room and said, "It's ho-ho time, Chris." He meant that he wanted her to change the bulletin board outside her door, and that Christmas vacation was near. For Chris, the period just before vacation was the happiest so far this year. Pam's practicum was over. The interregnum had ended. Chris missed Pam, but she had missed her class more. She thought she could count some real gains, in all subjects, by most of her students. She had vowed in the fall that this year she would get the parents more involved, and she'd had a good turnout at the first parent conferences, which is to say that a little more than half of the parents had come. The many notes she'd sent home doubtless encouraged some parents. Others came at the urging of their children. Felipe had told his father that Mrs. Zajac was strict, but that it was for his own good – of course, Felipe knew his father would like to hear that. Mariposa had talked her mother into coming; she'd told her that Mrs. Zajac was nice. And Julio's stepfather had come. Here was a man who worked two jobs and still could make time to visit his stepson's teacher. So much, Chris had thought, for one favorite theory of certain white Holyokers: that all Puerto Ricans came to town to get welfare.

The deficiency lists on the upper right hand corner of the board did not vanish, but Clarence behaved remarkably well, for Clarence, in that period just before Christmas. At lunch in the cafetorium, among his buddies, Clarence would talk knowingly about girls who liked to "rap." Once he pointed to a sixth-grade girl and said, "She smoke reefer, bro." But no one is sophisticated about everything. Chris overheard Clarence talking about Santa Claus. Clarence said he wanted a new dirt bike. She figured he didn't want her to tell on him to Santa Claus.

The windows were closed now, and the heater under the window ran all the time. Its hum replaced the sounds of the factories outside. Clarence had discovered that a piece of paper would levitate if he put it down on the heating vent in the counter under the window. Snow had come, gone, and come again to the landscape outside. In early afternoon light, the snow on the playground made the colors of the small factories look bleaker, especially that one hospital-green wall of Laminated Papers, which opened periodically to let in trailer trucks. But in the morning, sun streamed through the half-lowered blinds on that east-facing window, which stayed clean because it was too high up for graffiti. The children's coats in the morning and after recess were sachets full of the thrilling smell of winter air. Over the window hung the class's pictures of Famous Patriots. Felipe's portrait of John Hancock looked down on the room with a small, smug smile, as if that gentleman were still pleased with himself for having signed the Declaration in the boldest hand.

Chris had her class back and under control. She often grew weary of the role of disciplinarian. She'd say at the end of a bad day with Clarence and Robert, "It's exhausting being a bitch." But she never wearied of what discipline brought her. It allowed her to teach.

Of all the subjects, Chris liked teaching social studies most. She had loved social studies ever since her college course in American history, when she had discovered that it was a story, and didn't even resemble the boring lists of dates, the names of good guys and bad guys, she'd had to memorize at Holyoke High. She had not read deeply in history, but she had read some, and had concocted most of her own lessons. She used the social studies text mainly as an outline. Chris thought the book both too hard and too boring for most fifth graders to read.

In Room 205, the Revolution began just before Christmas. Chris had begun reading them a novel about the Revolution, from a boy's point of view. The first day she warmed them up. "We are *not* – and some of you will be disappointed – going to get into the blood and guts of the war. We're going to get into why there are wars and, in particular, why this one. She talked about taxes, about the distance between England and its American colonies, not lecturing exactly, but, as was her custom, asking such questions as, "What are taxes? Felipe?" with a note in her voice that seemed to say she wondered, too. (One of the best teaching manuals says you should ask a question first, then name the child you want to have answer it. That so the other children won't lose interest. Chris always questioned that way, but for a different reason: so that the child she was going to call on wouldn't have time to get scared and forget every thought.) She mentioned such figures as King George III, saying, "He's going to be an important character in our story." She wondered out loud, "What was the

Boston Tea Party?" and answered, "That's one of the things we'll find out." These were all by now familiar ploys, but applied with such vigor that Clarence actually blurted out, "It sounds like a movie!" That was high praise.

The next morning, just before lunch, Chris went to the board and wrote, CAUSES. She turned around so swiftly that her skirt swirled, and she sashayed toward their desks. "What name did they call the war between the English and the Americans? Clarence?"

He had been gazing toward the window. Now he turned and grinned at Chris. He seemed to be in high spirits today. She was going to make use of Clarence.

"If you don't know, Clarence," she said, "you'd better pay special attention." She began to pace before the class, her hands in her skirt pockets. "All a war is, is a gigantic argument, and how many of you have ever been in an argument with someone?" She stopped and folded her arms. There were lots of responses: "I have!" "Me, too!"

"And as with all arguments, there are two sides," she went on. She made both arms flow out to her right, her hands cocked with the palms toward her, until her arms were fully extended, whereupon she rolled her hands out flat, like the tongues of party favors. "You think one way, and your friend thinks the other." Her arms flowed out to the left. Then she repeated the movements in abbreviated form: hands to the right, palms on edge, set like facing walls, then hands like walls to the left. "And if the fight goes on, sometimes you hit each other." Her hands chased each other in a circle, divided, and then came back, one over each shoulder, the thumbs up, like an umpire's declaring an out. "When you were younger. I hope you're not doing that now."

Clarence was watching her intently, mouth slightly ajar. "Yup," he said, and he grinned.

"Is there one person that's always right in that situation?"

"Yeah!" said Felipe. The hand-raising rule was tacitly suspended. Many of the girls were shaking their heads.

Chris let her tongue loll out briefly and lifted her eyebrows. "Felipe, if you have an argument with your sister, you're always right?"

"No! She is! Because I always get in trouble all the time!"

But with the assent of Dick and the girls, Chris insisted that in a war no side was completely right. "Also, you don't just go up and punch your friend for no reason," she said, suddenly advancing, with a fist readied, toward Julio, who looked up from the pens he had been fiddling with, shied away, and grinned.

Clarence threw a punch at the air. "Pow!" he said.

"You have reasons," Chris went on, glancing at Clarence. "And we're going to talk about them.

They had reached the issue of the colonists' desire to become independent. Chris told them that her baby daughter had recently decided she wanted to feed herself. Chris described her baby in the high chair, pushing away her mother's hand. "She wanted to be . . . what's the word? I, n . . ."

"Impossible!" yelled Felipe.

"Well, she *is* that," said Chris.

"Independent!" yelled Felipe.

"Yes, she wanted to be independent."

"You let her?" asked Clarence.

"Yes," said Chris. "Maybe the colonists started like babies. When you were a baby, your parents did everything for you. But as you got older, you wanted to do more things for yourself. Jimmy, pay attention. I'm going to be asking you questions about this."

When they came to the issue of the trade laws, and discussed the ones that favored the colonists and the ones that didn't, Chris called Arabella to the front of the room.

(Arabella usually wore glasses in class. She didn't have them on. As she passed Clarence's desk, he hissed fiercely at her, "Wear your glasses.")

Chris whispered in Arabella's ear. Then she turned Arabella around to face the class, standing behind the girl, her hands on the girl's shoulders. "Arabella is French. I'm English. Now, all of you colonists out there, I'm offering you a hundred and fifty dollars for your tobacco. We got a deal?"

"Nope," said Clarence.

"I'll give you two hundred dollars," said Arabella to the class, and, having delivered her lines according to Mrs. Zajac's whispered instructions, she covered her mouth and giggled, and sat down.

"I'll give you a hundred and fifty dollars, and Arabella just offered you two hundred. Who you gonna sell it to?" Chris asked the class.

"Her," said Clarence, pointing at Arabella.

"Yeah, her," said many other voices.

"You can't," said Chris. "I just made a law that says you can't."

"Awww!" said Clarence. He was pouting.

Many others groaned, as if she had just announced, "Homework."

She let the groans die down and asked, "How do you feel?"

"Mad," said Clarence. "Sad," he added.

"Sad and mad," said Chris pensively. "Well, too bad. You have to sell it to me."

Judith was smiling, watching Clarence, then watching Mrs. Zajac. Smiling as if at herself,

Judith added her voice to the many that were saying, "No way!"

Julio piped up, at England, "You wish!"

"Too bad!" sang Chris, arms folded on her chest now, a stance rather like Al's imitation of the Colossus. Her eyes were partly closed. She shook her head. "You have to sell it to me. Because I *own* you!"

"But that's not fair!" cried Felipe. "That's like prejudice!"

"I'm *paying* you," said Chris. She made a face and shook her head at them. "You like the trade law I made that said I can't sell anybody else's tobacco in England, I can only sell yours." She made such a face as mothers of teenagers often receive. "Oh, you people in the colonies want it all your own way."

"So?" said Clarence angrily.

Ashley was vigorously shaking her head at Mrs. Zajac. Felipe had taken up the cry of "You wish!" Jimmy, cheek still resting heavily on his hand, looked annoyed, but at the noise, not the unfairness of England. But most of the rest were denouncing King George, in the person of Mrs. Zajac, and the Revolution was launched with perhaps greater fervor than some patriots had felt. Chris had to raise her voice to be heard over the hubbub. "All right. I'm just trying to make you see how England felt." She added, "The colonists, on the other hand, felt, 'Hey, it's our tobacco. We should be able to sell it to whoever we like.' "

She brought them down gradually and told them to transcribe the list of causes she would write on the board. Later on, she'd administer a quiz, which for once nearly everyone would pass, even Clarence, Julio, and Pedro. Retiring to her desk right after that lesson, Chris glowed. Her face was flushed. She called that method of instruction "Rambo social studies." She was very glad to have seen Ashley, Pedro, and Julio engaged in the lesson, and wished that Jimmy, Kimberly, and Blanca had been, too. Felipe was marvelous, and as for Clarence, she wondered for that short, sweet moment how she could ever have thought of him as difficult.

Clarence *was* difficult during the Christmas party, the last afternoon before vacation. He turned up his nose at the McDonald's gift certificates that Chris gave each of them. "What's this? I don't want this." Chris felt a little sad, but that was not the time for a lecture on manners.

Then Clarence and Felipe nearly wrecked the party by getting into a fight during the game of Seven-Up. But Chris didn't scold them.

She pretended not to hear when Robert, after

giving her a box of candy, said to anyone who wanted to listen, "I got her the two ninety-nine. I coulda got her the three ninety-nine, but she ain't worth that much."

Chris sent them away for vacation with smiles all around and many cries of "Have a nice vacation."

She grinned at the empty room. It had turned into just a room. It had lost its power over her. "This is freedom!" she cried. She foresaw Christmas carols, gingerbread, Christmas parties, leisurely mornings with her own children, who had only normal problems. She'd start to feel that life was too serene a few days before she had to come back, and when she returned, the children would look new to her again, and all of them really would be a little different. She knew that at least one morning she'd wake up in the dark, look at the clock, cry out, "Oh, God, I'm late!" and then, feeling doubly relieved of her duties, fall back to sleep.

Sent Away

Chris had been one of the model pupils whom teachers use as surrogates; the principal put her in charge of the school office for a day in sixth grade. She could still remember every time when a teacher had reprimanded her. Chris thought of her childhood as very happy, but also as constrained. She felt that she'd lacked confidence as a girl. She grew up obeying the many voices telling her what not to do, such as those of the nuns at CCD.

One of Chris's grandmothers was the sort of person whom people describe as saintly, a woman too kind and even-tempered to fit the usual profile of a real saint. Chris remembered hearing someone ask that grandmother why she went to confession. What could *she* possibly have to confess? "Angry thoughts," her grandmother had said. Recalling that line, Chris exclaimed, "Angry thoughts? I'd be in confession for a week!"

It seemed as though there was a part of Chris

that felt pent up, and that her classroom was one place where she could let it free. In the classroom, she could be aggressively good.

Among other adults, Chris had a shy, reflexive way of turning aside compliments. She'd try not to smile and would utter a self-deprecating remark, as if to say she appreciated the compliment but didn't think she deserved it. Some people who'd served on committees with her thought she could be a little blunt, but when she spoke bluntly to adults whom she didn't know well, Chris often added a patter of laughter to her voice, as if hastening to say, "I don't think my ideas are better than yours, and I could always take them back if they offend."

She was different in her room. There, she had great physicality. Her friend Mary Ann, tall and blond and slightly dreamy-looking, would stand behind a girl in the hall and chat with Chris while braiding the child's hair. When Chris touched children, which was often, she would put them in bear hugs and head locks. Whether scolding or comforting or merely making sure that a piece of work was understood, Chris got very close to the children. Sometimes, leaning over them, she'd almost touch her wide, changeable eyes to theirs. They could smell her perfume, hear her breathing, and some, such as Felipe and Jimmy, would go all squirmy, like kittens rubbing their flanks against their master's ankle, while Clarence might even relax his vigilance and fail to see a stranger at the door. Chris could be squeamish. The day back in the fall when she spotted a cockroach skittering across the carpet, she cried, "Somebody kill it. *Please!*" and for the next half hour scratched at her arms. A few children carried in strong odors, which bothered her, but she denied none of them her close presence.

In the room, her confidence seemed unlimited. One day she stood beside her desk, holding aloft and shaking a sheaf of social studies quizzes on which none of the class had done well. She told the children they had to study harder. Then she declared, "Mrs. Zajac wasn't a very good teacher to you yesterday." So saying, and with a wild-looking smile, she tore the quizzes in half and dropped them in the wastebasket, throwing her fingers open to let the papers fall. She left her fingers splayed wide above the basket for a long, dramatic moment.

And when laughter came over her in her room, at something a student said or did, it wasn't at all nervous-sounding, but deep and raspy, erupting under glowing cheeks and widely opened eyes from a place in the throat where laughter can't be manufactured. In the room, all shyness left her, and her voice had the booming ease of carnival barkers and other practiced, shameless exhibitionists who love to work a crowd. Chris felt very comfortable in the classroom. For all her tricks, she felt almost completely honest with children.

As a teacher and as a woman, she liked the sorts of males whom she'd been taught to stay away from as a girl. Billy was a high school classmate, a member of several crowds including the fast one. He cut some classes and put peroxide in his hair. Chris would never let Billy forget that, any more than he'd let her forget that she was the only girl in their class who had worn her blue jeans pressed. Billy always liked Chris. He showed it in high school by joining the adolescent pack that lingered in the halls, making suggestive comments about the prim, proper girls of Chris's set. Chris would hug her books as she passed by, hating him. She had thought he liked her.

She remembered, from a time several years later when she and Billy were courting, talking Billy into coaching her girls' softball team. He was very patient but got quite annoyed at the female outfielders who, when bored, started weaving dandelions into their mitts. These days, Chris thought, Billy was an even more serious person than she, more devout and stricter with their children. She had married one of the bad boys, and reformed him. Of course, it wasn't that simple. Billy had only dabbled at being bad, and mostly he had just grown up. But reforming bad boys was a pattern of intent with Chris.

Chris liked a lot of the supposedly bad boys at school — catching them at their tricks especially. She worried sometimes that she played too rough. She'd had a cautionary dream about that in the fall: Al walks down a hallway toward her with one of the gang from her last year's math class. The boy has reformed. It's the talk of the school. This is amazing. But Chris sees that his shoelaces are untied and flopping around. Aha! she thinks. She sneers. "Haven't you learned to tie your shoes yet?" barks Chris at the boy. On the instant the boy regresses. He stands there flicking boogers at her and making armpit farts. Al snarls at her, "Time out, Chris! You just ruined everything we did with this kid!" She woke up, and for a moment that dream felt like something interfering with her breathing.

Chris tried not to go too far. She attacked the behavior of children such as Robert and Clarence, but never the boys themselves. In her rough-and-tumble way, as Judith noticed, Chris was kind.

On a winter morning, a new member of the class was brought into the room, a girl named

Juanita. She was slender, with light brown skin and very curly brown hair pulled back in a fluffy ponytail and big, shapely mollusk ears. The vice principal led Juanita in. She looked as if she were being delivered to an executioner – on tiptoes, her head bowed before Mrs. Zajac.

Later, Chris would unearth an explanation for this child's shyness. Juanita's parents had gotten divorced. Juanita's mother didn't want the child living with her. Juanita's father had remarried. His new wife didn't want the girl around either. So Juanita had come to live in Holyoke with an aunt and cousins. In the evenings, Juanita cried in the bathroom at her aunt's apartment. She missed her father and her sisters and brothers. She had been placed mistakenly in a bilingual class at Kelly. Actually, she knew English far better than Spanish. Perhaps Juanita had tried to disguise that fact, and had aided in her own misplacement at the school. She had wanted to be in a bilingual class, she'd said, so that she could improve her Spanish, which was her father's principal language. She wanted to learn how to talk to her father better, she had told her bilingual teacher. Apparently, Juanita thought that if she improved herself in that way, her father might let her come back and live with him.

Chris didn't know the details then, but she

felt she knew this girl at once. She brought Juanita up to her desk. She looked at the girl's address. It was in the area of Dwight and Pine, that newly tough part of town that Chris and her mother didn't like to visit anymore. The number of Juanita's apartment building was familiar. It had great significance for Chris. Chris smiled at Juanita, who kept her head lowered and peeked at Chris. She said to Juanita, "Did you know that's near where my father lived a long, long time ago?"

Juanita shook her head earnestly and looked at the floor.

This was the saddest, shiest, most frightened-looking girl Chris thought she'd ever seen. Juanita walked stiffly back to her desk, like an acolyte carrying something sacred who is afraid of making any noise at all.

But this was not going to be a difficult case. Chris started right in on Juanita during math. "*Very* good, Juanita! I'm impressed!"

Juanita could not read aloud very well, but she understood everything she read. "Very good, Juanita!" Chris said during reading. Chris leaned toward her, so that she was looking right in Juanita's eyes, and declared, "You're going to fit right in here!"

Toward the end of that day, Chris stopped in front of her desk. "I like having you here, Juanita." Chris leaned down, looking again at the shy girl's eyes. "Do you like being here?"

Juanita nodded.

"Good!"

For about her first half hour in the room, Juanita would not look at Mrs. Zajac. But after Chris began to tell Juanita, in that emphatic, no-nonsense voice, that this was a place where she was entirely welcome, the girl's eyes followed Chris everywhere around the room. It seemed as if Juanita were afraid Mrs. Zajac would disappear. Two days later, Juanita wrote this in the rough draft of an essay:

remember if you have a new teacher just give her a chance she might be the nices teacher you ever had. And if you have a teacher and you're a girl you could try to wear some of the clothes she wears.

When Chris took her class to lunch or gym, she took them in a line. She did not insist that it be perfect. It was always slightly ragged, children trailing out behind her as she led them along the balcony corridors that overlooked the library, through carpeted hallways, and down uncarpeted stairways. Al sometimes played the local mood-music radio station over the hallway speakers to encourage serenity. Mrs. Zajac's class made a peaceful picture, in procession through the halls, to the sounds of homogenized soft-rock songs — "Da-doo-run-run-run. Da-doo-run-run."

When Chris watched her boys walk, and especially when she saw them running on the playground, stiff-ankled, to keep their unlaced sneakers from falling off, she thought they looked very young, running as though they had loads in their pants. Many of the girls wore outfits that made them look in a hurry to be grown up: one lacy black glove, big black belts slung low and outlining their incipient hips, the fronts of those belts sloping down in front in suggestive V's. One girl in her reading classes wore a pair of plastic handcuffs on one of those belts. A few girls and boys occasionally wore salacious T-shirts — "Liquor Up Front Poker In The Rear." T-shirts like that made Chris wonder who was running things at home, but she knew that for the most part fashion dictated their costumes. Leading them in their line, Chris thought she was like the mother duck in the children's book *Make Way for Ducklings*, leading her chicks safely through the world.

The world outside seemed perilous. Taking her class to lunch one day, she saw, on the balcony corridor opposite, a former Kelly student carrying a baby. The girl was all of fourteen now, and had come back to show her old teachers her first child. Chris hurried on with her class.

The tough fifth-grade girl who had worried Chris by hanging around with Judith had run away from school early that winter. Chris heard rumors that she had an evil stepfather. No agency would agree to look for the girl yet, for the ridiculous reason that her parents would not report her as missing. A pretty young girl on the winter streets - the thought made Chris shudder.

In January, a sixth-grade girl started crying when one of her classmates tried to take a snapshot of her, and a week later she spilled out a story of years of sexual torture at home. An agent from the Department of Social Services took that child away.

And the boy who had figured in Chris's cautionary nightmare of the fall, who had not in fact reformed, fell out of his teacher's line and was sent to Church Square, an alternative junior high for children expelled from the regular ones. That boy was too old for Alpha, the special classes for troubled elementary students.

Even in appearance, Church Square was desperate and depressing. Chris knew it only as a big red brick former church, which looked like an armory or a nineteenth-century mental hospital. The director of Church Square once described part of his student body this way: "Some of these kids are very smart. We have

224

smart fifteen-year-olds functioning academically on a first- or second-grade level who are living the lives of twenty-five- or thirty-year-olds, with heavy sex, crime, drugs, and violence. Lots of these kids have seen people hurt violently, even murdered. We have one boy who saw his brother get doused with gasoline and set on fire in New York last year."

Chris couldn't imagine a child she cared about being sent to Church Square. And, in her imagination, Alpha wasn't much better. Alpha classes were situated in a few of the elementary schools, though not at Kelly. An Alpha class was merely house arrest compared to Church Square, which was Siberia, but Alpha usually meant omega. Children rarely came back from Alpha to regular classes; some were bound to end up at Church Square. Even the name Alpha, now officially abandoned but still in use, had a scary, ironic connotation, like the word "asylum." Chris had never seen an Alpha class. She imagined rooms full of children as difficult as Clarence, and no Judiths, Alices, or Arabellas to compensate. She couldn't imagine trying to teach a class like that. She couldn't remember ever having a child leave her class for Alpha.

Chris had a recurring dream from years past. In it, she is leading a class down the second-story corridors toward gym. As sometimes actually happened, she abandons her place at the head of the line to talk to another teacher, and the children get ahead of her. She looks up and sees her class filing out the door to the stairs, which lead to the playground and its many exits to the city. She runs but can't get to the door in time. She yells at the class to stop, but the children don't seem to hear her.

2

January went well for most of the class. Chris had come back from Christmas vacation full of energy, with plans for improving her reading and science lessons, which she knew to be her weakest, and with a two-page list of things to do. In January, Judith finally got glasses. "Well, Judith, you've got them on your desk. That's a start. Your desk can see fine." That ploy worked. "Oh, Judith, you look so pretty in them! Can I try them on?" At long last, Felipe seemed to be getting the beginnings of long division. "Felipe, you did all these problems by yourself! A light went on up there in the old attic, huh? You should be proud of yourself. Are you proud of yourself?" Felipe shrugged coyly. He did look proud, but Chris was prouder than he, faintly smiling from her desk at the volatile, black-haired, gleaming child.

She printed out on index cards the steps to long division, and taped the one that read COMPARE to Manny's handsome forehead. That made Manny grin and, for the time being anyway, remember. Her introduction to astronomy was, she felt, far and away the best of her science lessons so far: a tour of the solar system with charts and glossy photographs, the children arguing loudly with each other when Arabella, playing Galileo before the Inquisition, suggested that the sun might be larger than the earth, and Chris chuckling to herself and lifting her eyebrows and saying, "We'll find out." Now, after scolding Robert, she would add, "You're a smart boy, Robert." She homed in on Jimmy. She'd creep up on him from behind, in morning math class, and say in his ear, "Wake up and smell the coffee, Jimmy," adding to a Jimmy who looked both annoyed at being awakened from his nap and pleased at the attention, "You think everyone is smarter than you, but you can do the work. When you do the work, Jimmy, it's beautiful. You're a smart boy, Jimmy." She thought she might be getting to him. One day, after she caught him with a book report copied from the description on the book's back cover, Jimmy wrote this:

I did do my book Report What dose she

want from my blood. If she doesn't like it
go to Hell then. all teacher are Dickhead
like stinky on floor cleaner Mrs Azaic the
sheat lady.

Chris laughed when she read that. The essay
seemed like progress. Jimmy generally wrote no
more than, "Today is a boreing day theres
nothing to do today." Compiling the grades for
the second set of report cards, Chris thought
she saw evidence of an upward trend in Jimmy's work.

She made her usual midwinter, post-report
card, "clean chalkboard" speech to the class,
likening the empty board at the front of the
room to her grading book, and asking once
again, at the end of the exhortation for "quality
work": "If you bring in a paper that looks like
it's been through the mill, what's Mrs. Zajac
going to do?"

Alice got the answer out quickest. "Make us
do it over."

"Make you do it over," Chris chanted.

Driving down to school in the mornings,
steaming plumes from smokestacks at the horizon, she passed by snow piles growing dingy
and, on the corners awaiting their buses, many
Puerto Rican children with sun-kissed skins,
huddling in winter coats and wearing bur-
gundy earmuffs (this year's most popular

color). Chris had met a teacher from a little rural town up north who had told of watching with her students as a Great Snowy Owl flew by her classroom window. Glancing out her own narrow window, Chris remarked, "Wouldn't I love to look out and see a Great Snowy Owl instead of a great snowy trailer truck." The world outside the window lay frozen. Footprints had solidified, like dinosaur tracks, in the snow. Snow covered the factory roofs outside. On many days now, the playground was empty during recess. The intercom said, "It's indoors." Annoyed-looking teachers on recess duty prowled the halls, quelling disturbances inside the rooms, out of which came the raucous sounds of children confined for too long. In Chris's room, a few small pink wads of gum had become embedded in the blue carpet, which was coming up again at one of its seams. There was no morning light some days, just an ominous grayness outside, the wind whistling at the window, Henrietta saying in math class, "Mrs. Zajac, I hear something sounds like a ghost." News of coming snowstorms made the children fidgety and for moments too distracted to teach.

Chris could manage weather and the "hoopy" days the weather sometimes brought. A couple of early-winter events distressed her, though. Looking back, she would feel that they came and went much too quickly for their importance. They were like gunshots.

Without warning or any real explanation, Blanca's mother came to the school one morning and took that puzzling girl with the frightened eyes away for good. Chris had no time to do anything except to give Blanca a hug and tell the class, "Blanca's moving to a new town. Let's all say goodbye to Blanca."

That morning, the police had called the school to say that Blanca's mother had called them last night: the girl hadn't come home. She had spent the night at Courtney's house. Blanca's mother didn't know that. She couldn't have known her daughter was safe, and yet she hadn't shown up at the school first thing in the morning. Al had sent the counselor to Blanca's address. The counselor had found not Blanca's mother but two men there, neither of them related to Blanca. About an hour later, Blanca's mother had finally appeared at the school and, saying she was moving, taken the girl away. Why, Chris wondered in the aftermath, hadn't Blanca gone home last night? Was she afraid of those men in the apartment? Why had the mother taken her away so suddenly? Was the family involved in a welfare scam? Or was something worse going on?

Judith had watched Blanca leave. "Blanca was scared!" Judith said. She added, "Adults

230

never do think about children."

Then Lil, the beloved secretary, got sick, and only one week later the news came that she had died. It was around the time of those events that Chris started having trouble sleeping through the night. Not every night, but about once a-week. She lay awake worrying about Blanca and thinking of Lil. One night she woke up – bolt upright, she later said, at three A.M. – with this hardly startling revelation: 'Jimmy hasn't been doing his homework lately." Other nights, it was Clarence on her mind.

In late January, Chris was sitting on her table reading to the class when from afar she heard Clarence's mother coming down the hall. *"Where's Clarence! I want Clarence now!"* Clarence had stolen twenty and maybe sixty dollars from his mother's purse. His mother took him away. Down the hall they went, Clarence in the lead and scurrying along, his mother not far behind, thundering, "You get on home, boy!" and Chris in the rear, trying to catch up, arms pumping like a drum major's on parade, saying to Clarence's mother's back, "I think we should wait for the counselor. He's very good at handling this sort of thing."

Clarence came back the next day, not bruised but very hungry. He said he hadn't eaten for a day. And Chris thought, "If that isn't an argument for free lunch and breakfast."

She and Clarence had yet another spat, caused in the usual ways, and she kept him for a few minutes after school, to try, as unsuccessfully as usual, to reason with him. After she let Clarence go, Chris stood at her desk, collecting her homework. She heard a splat behind her — a snowball. Another hit the window. Chris waited until she got her grin under control, then cranked open the casement and called down to the playground, "Clarence, if you throw one more snowball, you won't be here tomorrow."

They stood facing each other for a long moment, Clarence standing shin-deep in the snow and scowling up at her, dressed in his aviator-style jacket, and Mrs. Zajac high up in the window, meeting the boy's angry glare with dangerous looking eyebrows of her own — Romeo and Juliet in winter.

She kept on telling herself, "Clarence *has* to start doing his work," and she lectured him after school again and again, as gently as she knew how, saying, "It doesn't hurt *me*, Clarence. Do you understand? It's only hurting *you*." He'd avert his face. One time she said, "I'm not giving up on you, Clarence."

Daily games of cat and mouse with Clarence on the stairs began. Children had been spotted in the building after hours. Teachers had reported little items missing from their desks and rooms. Al had ordered the staff to make sure every child really left at the end of the day. Chris would take her walkers to the top of one of the staircases that led down to a rear door. She'd watch them leave. Again and again, Clarence would not be among them. She'd go down to the next landing and see him hiding inside, pressed against a wall, and make him leave.

In early February, Clarence and Robert, who had threatened each other for months, got into a fistfight outside the nurse's office. The yearly lice epidemic had hit the school. The nurse inspected the children's heads. Robert said, "Clarence got bugs," and Clarence started swinging and kicking. Robert got in only a couple of swings before Chris had both boys by suddenly limp arms, a tableau that might have replaced the eagle on the Kelly School pennant, under the legend "Woman Civilizing Boys."

Al suspended both Robert and Clarence. For the first time that year both boys were absent. Chris herself had just begun to notice how serene the room felt when one of the children said aloud, "It's *quiet* today."

"Well," said Judith, "Clarence and Robert aren't here."

Chris called a pause in creative writing for a class discussion. She didn't let them criticize Clarence and Robert, but she asked them how they felt about the room today. Many of the children said they liked the quiet. They said, in effect, that the battles between Mrs. Zajac and those boys made them feel that they were being punished when they hadn't done anything wrong.

Chris already knew as much. She had heard Judith and some others murmur "Good" on several occasions when she'd sent Robert or Clarence to the hall for disrupting the class.

When Robert and Clarence returned, she gave both of them lectures. Mainly, she told them what the class had said. Robert behaved quite well after his talking-to. She gave Clarence his after school. It was the same old scene. How many times had she skirmished with him in the emptied room, Clarence sitting alone, a little island of sullenness and fury among upturned chairs, while the hefty janitor passed through, collecting the trash can. Chris gazed at the boy, looking for words that might improve that empty feeling she had about him, that he was like a calendar with no numbers on it, a future without hope, already determined. She lectured him again, and softly, about consequences, about taking the better of two choices, about self-control. She told him he was smart. He could be the best boy in the class. But neither she nor the class would put up with his misbehavior anymore.

Face averted, Clarence yelled, "What about Robert! Robert started the trouble!"

"I gave Robert the same directions," she said. She felt weary. She could hear it in her own voice. She took him all the way down the stairs to the outer door.

Clarence shoved the door open and went out. As the door closed, Clarence turned back, showing her a face of rage and tears, and yelled, "Bitch!" Then he ran.

Chris held on to the bar handle of the door and stared out through the door's scratchy gray plexiglass window at the factory wall across from it. The wall was white and blank. The world was picking on Clarence. That was what Clarence thought. He would go on thinking that, and would say it to his next teacher, and then to his boss, and then – she just couldn't help thinking so – to the police. Then to his probation officer. "Well, you didn't catch *him* sellin' drugs. You're just pickin' on me." And yet, she thought, she liked him. She really *liked* him.

Chris used the word "love" cautiously with children. She reserved it for her own son and daughter. She would keep her feelings and responsibilities in proper order. It would be very dangerous to feel toward strangers' children who were merely passing through her life that particular attachment and all the hopes that "love" implied. If she let a student into that special circle of her affections, she would resent him if he called her a bitch. She knew that she was a better, more objective teacher since having her own children. Too much feeling for a boy like Clarence would only get in the way of what she wanted to do for him.

And yet Clarence seemed to have taken up residence in her mind, even to the point just lately sometimes of shoving her own children aside. And why was that? Not just because he was cute to look at. Felipe was as cute. And it wasn't just because Clarence demanded her attention. Felipe demanded it, too, and she didn't often go home worrying about him. Felipe didn't need her as much. Maybe that was the reason. None of the children could charm or infuriate her as thoroughly as Clarence. And Clarence, like Judith, seemed acutely alert to her inner moods, as if he'd known her a long time. Tomorrow, probably, he'd make a drawing for her, or write her an anonymous love note, and for a while tiptoe around her, saying his pleases and thank-yous. He was often like that on days after storms. He liked her, too, and he needed her.

"But what about the rest of the class?" she asked herself. She had let Clarence affect the atmosphere and tempo of events in her room far too much. The class had in effect told her so. The rest of the class needed attention from her, too. Even the ones who didn't seem to need her as much as Clarence had a right to her attention. The strain of trying to give it to them, while always having to keep an eye on Clarence, had accumulated. He was much more difficult than Robert, who only hurt himself and whom she could usually silence with a look. She felt angry now when she had to stop a lesson or some special tutoring for one of the other needy children, such as Julio or Pedro, in order to try to get Clarence to do some work or in order to deal with another of his eruptions. If she yelled at Clarence, the other children felt distressed; she could see it in their faces. But keeping in her anger left her feeling exhausted, sometimes too exhausted to get to sleep on time and too drained to work up the enthusiasm she needed in order to be as good a teacher as she wanted for her class. Clarence was wearing her down. Either that, or he was getting worse. Or both.

Clarence reappeared after February vacation with his brown jacket torn all the way up one side. White stuffing showed. When she saw the jacket, Chris felt newly worried. Children often changed slightly over vacations, and the torn jacket seemed to depict an alteration in Clarence. He had never defied her openly, except when he was angry. Now, not once but several times, he was casually, airily fresh to her, and seemed almost indifferent, surly without being angry, when she called him to her desk and said, "Give me one more smart answer like that, and you're not lasting in this room."

"I'm controlling him a lot and teaching him a little. Very little," Chris thought, watching Clarence saunter back to his desk. Would this more rebellious Clarence be impossible even to control?

3

The core evaluation of Clarence that Al had ordered in the fall was scheduled for a Wednesday in late February. Chris hadn't requested the core. She didn't have to get involved. But she feared that if she didn't, the usual pat plans would be put in place, and Clarence would end up going to the already ridiculously over-crowded Resource Room for an hour a day. That would do no good. She'd keep Clarence with her for the rest of this year, and do her best, but she wanted to ask that a realistic program be laid out, one that might really help him.

She had not wanted to hear about Clarence's past in September, but by November she had begun to ask for information. She got most of it from his teacher last year, who knew Clarence well and liked him. Chris knew her to be a gentle and trustworthy judge of children. Her Clarence stories troubled Chris, because they resembled the ones that she had been telling Billy after school all year long, except that Clarence now was even more unruly and less studious. More nearly violent, too, and now, it seemed, right on the verge of open defiance. She'd keep trying this year, but she didn't want to close her eyes and simply pass him on to another teacher. She didn't know the right program for him, but maybe the experts would.

She was tired when she got to school the day of the core. She hadn't slept well again – and events of that morning wore her out. She felt ready with her arguments for the core, but the meeting was postponed. The woman in charge of running cores came to the room no fewer than five times that morning: first to tell Chris that Clarence's mother hadn't arrived, then that the mother still hadn't arrived, then that the core couldn't be held today, then that it might be rescheduled for tomorrow, and finally that it would take place tomorrow, with or without the mother, as the law allowed. Chris felt testy all day. Once, she scolded Clarence when she really shouldn't have.

The room was full of eyes. That morning of

the aborted core, Clarence was especially watchful.

"Mrs. Zajac!" he whispered.

Mrs. Zajac looked at him. He pointed to the doorway, at the woman from the office.

Every time that woman from the office showed up, Clarence was the first to spot her in the doorway.

That woman kept coming back. Mrs. Zajac kept saying "Excuse me" and bustling out to the hall. From inside the room, the words the two women said were just murmurs, Mrs. Zajac and the woman standing outside the door, Mrs. Zajac's hands flying every which way, now and then Mrs. Zajac going silent and her jaw dropping, now and then her head turning to look back into the room at him. Clarence watched from his desk, eyes fastened on the doorway. His mouth hung open. The two women kept looking at him. Then Mrs. Zajac called his name.

"Clarence? Is your mother coming in today?"

"I-I don't know."

Clarence looked worried. Had someone told on him about the twenty dollars he had hidden, from the money he'd taken out of his mother's purse?

The woman stopped coming finally. But then Mrs. Zajac yelled at him for not raising his

240

hand when he wanted to tell her he didn't understand. That wasn't fair. She always said to tell her if you didn't understand. But Clarence didn't feel like pouting. In a minute, he figured out what Mrs. Zajac wanted. She wanted them to copy down something from the board. He wrote fast. Then he stopped. He'd made a mistake. He raised his hand, and this time he waited to be called on.

"Ca ca can we put Thomas Jefferson?" Clarence said very rapidly.

Mrs. Zajac blinked. Alice and Margaret giggled. But Clarence didn't look angry about that, the way he did when he thought someone was laughing at him. He didn't even seem to notice the giggles. He looked up expectantly at Mrs. Zajac. She looked puzzled for a moment. "Oh," she said. "Can you put *Thomas* Jefferson instead of *President* Jefferson? Sure."

And Clarence let out the breath that he'd been holding in.

Story writing commenced. Yesterday, Mrs. Zajac had told him she'd keep him after school if he didn't get to work on his story. So he'd written this:

I hate Someone in this class and it start with a Z and 1 time when she was reading my brother Sam. I rised my hand she didn't say anything and she saw me rising my hand and when 2 girls walking in the door she stop reading and stop for them that why i hate her today i don't know what to write. And she told me to turn around and i started to write about her.

Mrs. Zajac had seen this story yesterday and had told him it was fine, he should just keep writing. But now Clarence got it out of his desk and tore it up and dumped it in the wastebasket, fast, when Mrs. Zajac wasn't looking. He began to write a new story, bending over the paper, designing the words carefully, his tongue sticking out of a corner of his mouth. Mrs. Zajac was nearby. He made little glances to make sure.

Then suddenly, she wasn't there! Clarence looked up, and Mrs. Zajac was heading for the doorway again! In the doorway stood the school psychologist, the woman who had taken him to a room in the office a while back and given him a lot of tests. She was nice.

Clarence stopped writing. He gazed at the doorway with his mouth hanging open.

The school psychologist was about Chris's age and a little taller, with large, inquisitive eyes, which she kept trained on Chris's face. Chris did likewise to her. Chris felt suspicious of psychologists, especially of their lingo,

which she thought was designed to obfuscate
and not to explain. She hardly knew this psychologist at all, but Chris was a good reader of
eyes, and as the talk proceeded, she realized
that this woman was no fool. They talked in
lowered voices, and both talked fast, right in
each other's faces. Evidently, the psychologist
had thought that Chris wanted Clarence taken
from her room. When Chris said that she had
every intention of keeping Clarence for the rest
of this year, the conversation pivoted. The
psychologist smiled broadly, looking into
Chris's face as if she'd just discovered Chris.
She wondered if maybe she could help
Chris with Clarence. "If, on occasion, you
found him doing something well, he loves
praise."

"I do praise him," snapped Chris.

"Oh, I'm not saying you don't!"

"No, no," said Chris. "I'm just self-evaluat-
ing."

Chris was talking on, explaining herself,
when that sense of another presence, that feeling of something out of place on the periphery,
stopped her, and she turned, and there was
Clarence standing just inside the doorway, a
few feet from her.

"Mrs. Zajac," Clarence said. "Felipe's drawin'
pictures of me on the wastebasket."

Clarence tattling when he wasn't in trouble

himself — that really was unlike him.

The first thing Chris noticed, after lunch on the day of the aborted core, was how placid Clarence had become — a complete turnaround from the first two days of the week, when she'd thought that he was edging his way toward open defiance. She thought, "I think he knows something's up."

Judith had observed Clarence when she was feeling bored, and she had come to this conclusion a while back: "What I think about Clarence is that he hides behind his funny things. He's like, he's afraid to come out and say he doesn't understand something. So he hides behind the things he does. But he cares. I *know* that. Sometimes he doesn't understand the work. That's what *I* think. He doesn't understand the work, and he hides behind the things he does, to make himself funny, he hides behind it."

At the end of the day, Clarence sat quietly at his desk, trying to fill out the form Chris had given the boys, an application to become a Boy Scout.

"Mrs. Zajac?"

"Yes, Clarence?"

"What do a-d-d-r-e-s-s mean?"

"Address," said Chris. She thought he simply couldn't read the word.

But Clarence knew less than that. He said, "Yeah. What do 'address' mean?"

Chris looked at him. Had he ever openly confessed to such basic ignorance before? She was surprised. She said offhandedly, "Where you live." And Clarence went back to filling out the form to be a Boy Scout.

He didn't know what "address" meant? Well, children sometimes had surprising gaps in their basic knowledge. Chris didn't give the episode much thought just then. But, in Judith's terms, Clarence had begun to come out of hiding. It had been a long day for Chris, and a terrifying one for Clarence.

4

It is remarkable how much of the time of how many adults in a school one child can command simply by being difficult. The meeting happened Thursday. Past the long desk in the office and into the windowless, overheated conference room at a little before noon went a parade of five experts on troubled children. Chris went in, too. The only person missing was Clarence's mother, though she had been officially notified again.

When, about an hour and a half later, the

parade came out of the conference room, Clarence was no longer a member of Chris's class. The news traveled quickly through the office. Clarence would go to an Alpha class as soon as paperwork permitted. Chris was flushed, all the way from her forehead to the collar of her blouse. The fringes of her black hair were damp. Her face looked grim. She hurried toward her classroom.

As she thought of it later on — and it was a long time before she could stop thinking about it — the situation was impossible. Nobody had told her ahead of time that Clarence might be sent to an Alpha class *this* year. She hadn't had time to find a settled attitude. But even after the decision was made and she had all too much time to think, she still didn't know how to feel.

Chris worried about Clarence. She had reason. To send him away was to tell him the same old news: he was a problem; he had failed. And to help Clarence by placing him in a special class among a number of other notoriously unruly children — might as well say his behavior would improve if he was made to join a street gang. She couldn't argue for doing that to him.

And yet at the same time, removing Clarence from the class seemed like a just solution. He had not committed any acts of extreme violence;

he hadn't thrown chairs at other children or come to school with weapons. But he did beat up and intimidate other kids. More and more since Christmas, he had begun to seem like a wrecker in the room. Was it fair to let one child's problems interfere with the education of nineteen other children, many of them just as needy as Clarence? When she looked back and imagined herself saying, "No! I don't want him taken away," she imagined herself feeling just as guilty as she would have if she'd said, "Yes, by all means, Alpha." In retrospect, sending Clarence to Alpha seemed like a decision to accomplish something that was probably right by doing something that was probably wrong.

She had one awful, sinking fear. Had she wanted, deep down, to get rid of Clarence? She hadn't acted on that desire, but had she felt it? "I don't want to get rid of him. I don't!" she told Paul, the sympathetic vice principal, later. "I mean" – she looked up at Paul – "I do and I don't."

Would Clarence suffer? Many educators feel that separating children thoroughly from the mainstream of school is never a good idea. But as such programs go, Alpha looked reasonable on paper. Clarence would go to a class of only ten children, with three adults in charge: an aide, a trained, fulltime counselor, and a head teacher who was reputedly adept. Alpha classes did have an evil reputation, but everyone had taken pains to tell Chris that the class picked out for Clarence was different. The new teacher was first-rate. She'd really turned that program around.

Chris wanted to see the class for herself. She had asked Al, in the doorway to his office, "I don't suppose I could go and see that class sometime?" She had sounded at that moment like shy Juanita asking permission to go to the bathroom.

Al had said, "No. But don't worry about it." He reasoned: "I can't allow her to do that. I can't let a teacher go up there and say, 'Oh, no, I can't send him there.' It's not for her to make that decision."

The genius of committees is that they can make decisions that no one would want to make alone. Chris didn't have the authority to say what would be done with Clarence. She was simply the most knowledgeable witness about the boy and his effect on her class. The person who had final say, the director of Church Square and Alpha, didn't know Clarence. He had run into situations in which teachers simply wanted to use Alpha to get rid of troublesome children. But he figured that couldn't be the case here or he'd have heard about Clarence back in October, not now in March. He was impressed that Chris intended to keep her troublemaker for the rest of this year. Thinking back, the director would say, "We need more people like that, who don't want to give up on the kid."

So to him, Chris's descriptions of Clarence seemed completely credible. Chris's account convinced him that Clarence belonged at Alpha. "I heard her saying she'd done everything possible." In effect, it was decided that Clarence be sent away partly because Chris was willing to keep him.

5

Clarence might have been a model pupil if someone could have staged the commotion of a core around him every week or so. For most of the following week Clarence didn't know what was happening to him, but he sensed danger. Maybe Mrs. Zajac's special gentleness warned him, but then again, he did not, the whole week that followed, give her many reasons for not being gentle.

There was a deep intelligence in Clarence. But it had been directed mainly toward the arts of escape and evasion and sentry duty. It would have seemed misdirected almost anywhere, except in a school for infantry or on some city streets. He didn't become angelic overnight. Yet everything that Chris had hoped to bring out of Clarence – with rewards, detentions, praise, lectures, and scoldings – he now delivered without being asked. He didn't hit or threaten anyone. Just like that, he stopped talking back to Chris. And he did his work. For several days Chris did not know what to make of the metamorphosis. She did not let herself.

When on Friday morning, the day after the core, Mrs. Zajac announced the weekly spelling test, Clarence looked up at her and said, "I didn't study." She didn't answer. Halfway through the test, he blurted out again, "I didn't study!" He sounded angry, maybe a little frantic.

With plain curiosity on her face, Chris said softly, "Clarence, I appreciate your honesty. But if you didn't study, what do you expect me to do about it? You haven't done your work all year."

Clarence stared at his paper, full of misspellings, and his mouth hung ajar, as it had when he spotted his mother in the doorway that time after he'd raided her purse, or the other day when strangers kept arriving.

The following Monday, when Chris wrote down the homework assignments on the back board, Clarence, whose attention usually wandered at this time, turned around and watched her with his pencil poised. "I'm gonna need two books tonight," he said loudly. *"Three!"* he cried.

When she asked them to turn in their topics for their astronomy reports, Clarence cried out, "Report? On what? What's it about?"

She explained.

He wrote furiously.

Normally Clarence didn't like being sent to the board to do a problem in front of the class. During a grammar lesson the first week after the core, he volunteered to go up and punctuate a sentence. The one Chris gave him had the word "buildings" in it. Clarence stared at the sentence. He turned back to Chris. "Wha wha what's that word right there?" He pointed at it, his face all earnest expectation and his mouth hanging open.

On Tuesday morning, Clarence didn't do his pirouettes or linger over the menus on the closet door. He sat right down and did his penmanship, and then he asked her if he could take the attendance sheet to the office, a job that in their community was bestowed only on children who had done their homework.

When Chris went to the Teachers' Room that morning during spelling, she paused over the coffee machine and decided to take the pot of decaffeinated. She hadn't slept well for days. That problem was much worse. Maybe, she told herself, the reason was caffeine.

It would be "unprofessional" to get very upset about Clarence's leaving. Unprofessional. Sometimes that term seemed to apply best to teachers who used it most often. And yet it would apply to her in this case if she let her feelings show. Everyone involved had tried to do the best thing for the boy and for her class. Alpha was not a terminal illness. These things happened in school. This problem Chris was having with her sleep should not have to do with Clarence. She'd have to figure it out by herself. She couldn't talk it out the way she usually did. Professional colleagues didn't discuss such things. It just wasn't done.

She couldn't even really talk to Mary Ann about it, though Mary Ann gave her the chance. "It's so sad," Mary Ann said. "Just because this happened, yesterday I walked in your room, and he's being perfect. Today I walk in, and he's being perfect. Ohhhh."

But Chris looked away and, as if reciting, hurriedly said, "But I also have to consider the other kids in the room. And there are no real alternatives. I think that's not a great statement about Holyoke, but I don't know what other towns have to offer. There's always the danger he'll be influenced by the other kids there. But that's balanced by the fact that there's a fulltime counselor there, and everybody says the teacher's excellent."

She couldn't even talk to herself openly. Chris went home the day she gave up caffeine, had a pleasant evening with Billy and the kids, and thought, "Thank God. I'm over whatever it was," and then she woke up in the middle of the night, gritting her teeth.

She said to Billy, "I think this is the first kid who's ever left my room this way."

Billy said, "No, it isn't. You had one your first year at Sullivan."

"I did?"

"Yes," said Billy. "If you say the name, I'll remember."

"Oh!" she said. "But he came out of a program like Alpha, and I only had him two weeks." She laughed, remembering that boy. "Everything I said, he used to give me the finger." That was long ago, and she'd had nothing to do with that boy's being sent away.

6

Chris began to feel the way she had the year her father died. She had hated teaching most of that year. Ordinarily, she would have tried to understand her difficult students and have looked for remedies, but that year, seven years ago, a lot of her class became unconquerable antagonists who wouldn't behave, wouldn't work, and wouldn't learn. Chris called that "the year I thought I was burnt out" – the term is very popular among teachers; it carries an unfortunate note of finality; at the very moment when a teacher needs to search for ways around her unhappiness, "burnt out" suggests that there is nothing she can do.

In Chris's childhood household, her mother had been the organizer and chief disciplinarian, a cheerful one. Spankings were infrequent. Her parents sometimes raised their voices, mostly at Chris's brother, but real anger came over her father so rarely that everyone in the family remembered this incident: her brother had thrown a wooden block at Chris. He missed. The block crashed through a window. Up the stairs in a moment, really shouting, came her father. Her brother got beneath his bed. Her father stood over the bed, trying to lift it. He shook it. Her brother, on his back underneath, held on to the metal frame for dear life. Chris yelled in fright. Then her father let go of the bed, and he started to laugh.

Jim Padden is remembered as a thin, quiet man with a quick wit. "Pretty good on the repartee, eh?" he'd say to Chris's mother when he'd gotten off a good one. He and Chris's mother had a way with children. Chris and her siblings and their friends usually chose to play at the Paddens'. Chris's brother remembered a time when a friend of his hurt his leg badly playing in the street. His friend didn't want to be taken home; he wanted to be taken to Mr. Padden.

Even at his death, her father was still drawing a crowd. Hospital workers who had gotten to know him during his long illness drove all the way out from Boston to go to the funeral and wake. In Irish parlance, "wake" is also a verb, evocative of a heritage that is both pious and mystical, as in, "We waked Jim Padden last night." No one wakes the departed by recalling his faults, but the testimonials at her father's wake were impressive: from the young man who'd worked under him and whom Jim Padden had talked into going back to school; from several men who remembered how Jim Padden would forgo his own chances at earning overtime so that they, who had young families, could get the money instead; from men who'd had him as a boss and remembered being sick and Jim Padden, who almost never took a sick day himself, covering for them.

Her father didn't drink or boast. "He wasn't one of your − I hate to say it − bullshitting Irish," Chris would say. For her, his memory defined the term gentleman. He had not made it very hard for Chris to please him. He loved to read, and she decided she did, too. They often talked about books, describing ones they'd liked to each other. He would take her to the library and bookstores and book fairs as other fathers take children to baseball games. He didn't preach to her about college, but she knew he wanted her to go. In that household, youthful expressions of ambition were taken seriously. Both her parents felt that teaching was the right profession for Chris. When playing teacher with her siblings on the stairs, Chris was allowed to write on the wall opposite the landing, which cannot have been a small concession in a house as tidy as the one Mrs. Padden always kept. When Chris made the National Honor Society, her father put the newspaper clipping that mentioned her name inside his wallet, where it crumbled after many showings.

In Chris's family, one went to Mass every week. There was no discussion or argument. Even when Chris reached the age of choice, she attended church, but mostly out of habit and because she knew her parents wanted her to. She didn't know how much religion mattered to her until her father got sick. Then she didn't know what else to do except to pray. She prayed as doggedly as she did most things. She tried to cut any number of deals with God. When her father died anyway, she felt very angry. In church she might be on her knees and look devout, but in her mind she said, "You killed him. Why him? He was a good man, and we still need him."

In his eulogy, the priest, still one of Chris's favorites, offered an answer that would have resonance for anyone whose family history included the terrors of immigration. The priest probably drew inspiration from the Gospel of John. Chris's father had provided well for his family here on earth, and was still providing for them, the priest said. Her father had gone on ahead, to prepare a place for them in Heaven. He had died now so that they would not feel frightened when they followed him.

Occasionally, Chris asked herself, "Where *is* my father?" But with her heart she accepted the priest's explanation, and hung on to it through what remained of that worst year in her life. Her father had died in May, before school let out. In July, she lost her second child to a miscarriage. Then her mother's routine physical turned up something ominous. There had been too much death around her and inside her. She spent August living through the news ahead of time, that her mother was going to die, too. If she lived it out in advance, the worst would have happened already, and her mother wouldn't have to die. She made another deal with God, on her knees at Sacred Heart:

"Please make my mother healthy, and I'll stop blaming You and the world for my losing my father." Chris kept her end of the bargain. The doctor declared her mother fit the day before school started. "It was like everything just left me. I saw I had so many things to be thankful for. Billy looked at me and he said, 'Thank God. I never thought you'd be normal again.' The first day of school, I was exhausted, but I felt like a new person."

Chris didn't talk about religion, except in church or among people very close to her. That God made people for a purpose seemed plausible to her, however. She thought God had intended her to teach, and if He had not given her the power to alter the lives of every troubled child who came into her room, He expected her to try.

So would her father. In her classroom, she would look at Clarence refusing to work and would consider just ignoring him. But then she'd say to herself, "No, you give me a hard time every day. I'm going to give you one." And she'd also remember the time when she began her student teaching and her resolution faltered and she said to her father that maybe she should become a lawyer. Her father had told her, "Oh, come on, Christine. You can't give up *that* easily."

Over the years Chris had gotten in the habit of wondering when she would burn out. It was like waiting to catch the flu and, at the first intimations, like waiting to see if flu would turn into pneumonia this time. Now in the room, during the week after the core, she kept having a feeling of doubleness. She didn't want to be here. The real Chris wasn't here. Now and then she lost her temper at one or another of the children for offenses that would not have upset her before, and her voice sounded harsh and shrill to her, like the voice of someone else, someone she didn't like. The little leaps of the clock's minute hand, which had seemed to happen much too quickly once, now seemed to come after endless delay. On the surface, her lessons seemed adequate but plain. In her mind, as she taught some of them, she thought, "I'm boring myself. I'll just get through this one. I'm not really here. I don't know what's wrong." She told herself, "It's March. I do this every year. I say, 'Uh-oh, it's March. I'm supposed to feel terrible.' But in the middle of a social studies lesson on Tuesday, she felt as if she were listening to someone else drone on before the class, and she asked herself, "Oh, God, am I losing it? Am I burnt out?"

Little incidents distracted her. As if to remind her that Lil was gone from the office and not coming back, Al's mood music got piped into the classrooms by accident for a little while and made her interrupt her lesson until the place stopped sounding like a dentist's office.

Nothing visible had changed. The room was the same. The bright-colored children's chairs had the same old air of prearranged forced cheerfulness. The flecked blue carpet, designed for wear, hid the little messes that inevitably occur in a classroom over years. What went on here now was just one little play out of many already staged and to be staged. Through the thin walls came the sounds of other classes going on just as before. The room was filled, as always, with the prettiness of children, and the many stacks of books and papers lay, as always, on the cabinets, on the front table, on the corners of Chris's desk, in the carefully organized disarray of a craftsman's workshop.

School goes on, but Chris felt as if it went on without her all that long week. Robert's arriving without homework, as usual, sent her to the phone by the door, to call the office and say, "Al? Robert. I can't deal with him today." (Al, who was not a stone, as some teachers thought, showed up just moments later and took Robert away for several hours.) The class seemed different to her. As the week dragged on, more and more children ceased doing their homework. Chris looked up at the quadrant of green board where she recorded debts of effort, and the lists were full of children who had been making lots of progress just a while ago, and by midweek the only name that she would not have minded seeing there now had vanished. The pattern was all wrong. For the first time this year, Clarence did all of his homework two days in a row. She looked at Clarence playing the little scholar, working on his penmanship without being reminded, his tongue pinned in the corner of his mouth. He made his cursive especially neat – she'd always praised his handwriting back when she had to search for ways to praise him.

She would have to tell him soon.

For a while Chris thought Clarence's mother might do that job for her. On Wednesday, his mother showed up. She said she hadn't heard about the core.

She wore a colorful cloth bandanna wound around her temples. She was tall. Her voice was deep. She looked exotic and powerful, and maybe even dangerous if crossed. And yet, in this setting, she seemed meek. Many adults feel a little nervous going back to school. Standing in the hall, leaning on the balcony railing beside Chris, Clarence's mother seemed more like a wayward pupil than an adult.

"And we thought it would be the best thing

for Clarence to go to a special class," Chris said.

"A *special* class? Oh, no." But his mother's deep voice had no power behind it.

The counselor took the mother to his office. She was talked to by several others involved in the decision. The mother nodded. She looked a little sad sometimes. She made her musical laugh over jokey remarks from the counselor. She was extremely polite. She wanted to know how long Clarence would stay in the special class. Probably through sixth grade, said the counselor, who did not tell her any lies. "I think he'll like it, and you can always go up and take a look at it," said the counselor.

Clarence's mother didn't ask for a ride to see the special class, though. The counselor offered to explain anything she didn't understand about the class and about the forms she had to sign if she agreed. She said, "Well, give it a shot," and started signing.

Chris felt sorry for the woman, but while she'd talked to her briefly that day, Chris was thinking, "We're picking up your pieces. We have to try to figure out something to do for him. And *I* have to feel lousy about it."

That afternoon Chris told the class about an essay contest. She said it was optional, and Alice and Judith said, in that case, they didn't want to participate. Chris looked at them sternly and said, "I know I have a lot of good writers in here."

"Yeah, me!" declared Clarence.

He lingered after school. She didn't tell him to stay. She took the other walkers out and, returning, found Clarence sitting at his desk, copying down the homework assignments.

"Mrs. Zajac? What's that word? E-s-s-a-y?"

She stood over him, looking down at the busy boy.

Clarence looked up at her craftily. "Mrs. Zajac. I got a joke for you."

She lifted her eyebrows.

"There's a horse name Nobody. If that was the only horse on earth, who would you marry? No! If *you* and the horse was the only ones on earth, who would you marry?"

She smiled, half closing her eyes. "Nobody."

Clarence grinned. Then he asked her if he could wash the boards for her.

That night Chris woke up gritting her teeth again. She imagined Clarence's mother telling him about Alpha. That was his mother's job, but Chris wondered if she shouldn't have told him first.

Thursday morning, Chris felt as if she were holding her breath when Clarence came in and got to work on penmanship.

"Clarence? Come here, dear."

He leaned on the edge of her desk, his legs

spread and far out behind him, his about-to-be-frisked pose for pleasant talks with Mrs. Zajac.

"Did your mother mention anything to you last night? About school?"

"No." He shook his head. He looked at her, his mouth slightly ajar. "Why?"

"Just wondering," said Chris.

So she'd have to do that job herself. She needed time to think.

That afternoon, when the children had gone to gym, Chris sat at her desk and read over some papers of Clarence's. She looked off at nothing. The papers proved again how far he was behind most of the rest. Maybe, she thought, he would be a star at Alpha. That was the main reason she hadn't fought against it, she told herself.

She guessed she'd have to tell him tomorrow.

7

Friday morning Clarence sat right down and asked her if he could work on his essay instead of penmanship. So he really planned to enter the essay contest. He might be gone, she thought, before the contest was judged.

She felt tired. Her daughter had been up half the night with stomach flu. Her own stomach felt as if it were drifting from its moorings. She felt grateful for her morning chores. But when she got to the attendance sheet, she stopped. She dropped her pen, let her shoulders droop, and gazed off at nothing, one hand covering her mouth. "I don't know how to tell him," she thought. "Oh, God."

"Clarence, come here a minute."

Clarence took his usual stance, leaning on the edge of her desk. Pitching her voice low for this private talk, she said, "We had a meeting about you last week, and I was therrrre and some other people were therrrre . . ." She heard in her own voice the exaggerated cadence adults use to coax little children off to sleep, a voice that rarely works, of course. Perhaps the strangeness of her cadences put Clarence on his slowly turning wheel. He was standing sideways to her by the time she had managed to tell him that he was going to a new class.

She had her old voice back at least. "So anyways, I don't know when you're going there, but I want you to know that's where you're going. I *also* want you to know that you're not going there because of the way you've behaved or anything like that. Mrs. Zajac isn't sending you there for a punishment. She's sending you there because I think it's going to help you. I think you'll *like* it, as a matter of fact. You'll probably like it more than this school, because there's only twelve kids in the room and the teacher will be able to give you more attention. What do you think of that?" She waited. He didn't answer.

"Think you're going to want to go?"

He shook his head.

"Why not?"

He wouldn't speak. His eyelashes fluttered. No other part of him moved.

She tried for a while longer, and then she said, "Well, if you have any questions about it, you come up and ask me. Okay? Maybe you can think of some when you're sitting back down. As I said, it's not going to happen on Monday or anything like that. I don't know when, but I'll let you know. Okay?"

He walked slowly back to his desk. He sat staring at the board, mouth ajar. Then, in a flurry of movement, he pulled out pencil and paper and started working on his essay for the contest. A moment later, with the quickness of a woodland creature, Clarence turned his head toward the doorway just as Courtney, arriving late, appeared. Clarence looked at Mrs. Zajac. "Courtney!" he whispered.

By the end of math, Chris's ears were clicking. All day her illness expanded, and as it did, she grew markedly gentler, as she always did anyway on Friday. At the start of the day's last hour, she led the children down to the library to do research on their astronomy reports. She sat at a table a little distance away from them and didn't even try to work. Now and then children came up to her.

"Mrs. Zajac, there's lava on the moon!" said Felipe.

Ashley came up. "Mrs. Zajac, a comet is a fuzzy star."

Chris smiled. Her eyes were puffy. Her words were full of the sound of the letter *b*. She watched Clarence while holding tissues to her nose. He sat several tables away. He was pretending his chair was a horse. She smiled. She ached too much to try to do her duty by him. In sickness, she felt better than she had for days. All week the room had seemed to harbor the secret of Clarence's banishment. Now the feeling of intrigue had been swept away. The worst was almost over, and the revelation that had lain in front of her for the last six days, like a figure in the carpet, was not impossible to face. She had waited all week for the old Clarence to return. He had not. He had been trying to make up in a week for all the lessons he had missed in his six years of school. He looked happy now and mischievous, rocking in his chair and chewing gum openly, and she was glad. How frightened the boy must have been this past week and a half! she thought. And what amazing instincts he had.

Since the core, there had been important differences between what Chris knew and what she told herself and friends. She was relieved to feel so weak and aching that picking up a book was hard, and to blame microbes and not herself. Maybe she'd been coming down with flu all week, she told herself, and then she made a face. She gazed at Clarence. She wished she could think that others had made the decision to send him away. She had tried to believe that all week. Well, in fact, they had. She had not argued for Alpha. But she hadn't really argued against it. Only she had made the decision not to try to *prevent* the decision. "I let him down in a way," she thought. "That's why I can't sleep." There. She'd faced it all.

"Every hundred and fifty years Pluto moves into Neptune's orbit," Judith said to Alice in a loud voice a few tables away.

This week's scary gloom might not have come entirely from Clarence. In any case, Chris thought it was a warning. Maybe she was getting stale. She'd take her usual counter-measure and make a change. Al had asked her to teach sixth grade next year. That would mean new colleagues and a new cur-riculum. She'd have to spend a lot of summer vacation working on new lesson plans. But that would be fun. She liked that part of education, she thought. She was glad that she still did.

Chris was sick all weekend, and she slept and slept. She called in sick on Monday. The substitute, a college freshman on spring break, had it easier than Pam, because Clarence was still behaving fairly well.

When Chris walked in on Tuesday morning, her face was pale. At the start of math, Manny bickered with Horace.

"*Just* a minute!"

Chris stood before the low math group with her arms folded on her chest.

"Whether you realize it or not," she said to them, "Mrs. Zajac is *back!*"

They quieted down. In a moment, though, Manny started whispering to Jorge. Mrs. Zajac advanced on Manny. He stopped and lifted his eyes to her.

"Do I look like the sub who was in here yesterday?" she said to Manny.

Manny leered up at her. "No," he said. "She was younger."

Color moved up the nape of Mrs. Zajac's neck. She laid a hand flat on her breastbone and, tilting her head back, let loose her high-pitched, raspy laugh. The members of the top group stopped their work and turned around to see what they had missed.

269

On the Tuesday she returned, Chris got word
that Friday would be Clarence's last day. She
would tell him so at the end of school on
Wednesday. She'd wait until Friday to tell the
class and find a way to explain it to them.
Meanwhile, on Tuesday, the old Clarence rema-
terialized. He hadn't done his homework,
wouldn't do his penmanship or stop whispering during the spelling lesson, tried to bolt
before the other walkers at dismissal, and
wouldn't look at Chris when she tried to talk to
him after school. At the outer door, Clarence
yelled at her, "I hate this school," and ran. But
Wednesday morning, Clarence went right to
work on penmanship. He had done his
homework. He knew he was going to the Alpha
class now. She knew that he was trying to
prevent it. She would make it through this
week somehow.

The clock did not move quickly Friday.
When Clarence came in — the new Clarence,
the one who went right to work on penmanship
— she saw that he was dressed differently.
Yesterday she had reminded him that he would
visit his new class today, and today, instead of
the usual T-shirt, he wore a white oxford shirt

with a button-down collar, a little frayed in back. He had buttoned the top button but not the ones to the collar. She imagined Clarence choosing his own best clothes that morning and dressing himself.

And no sooner had he started his penmanship than he turned around to her again and said, "My mother said I was goin' to a special class. Why am I goin'?" She took him to the hall and put her hands on his shoulders, so he couldn't turn around. He did avert his face. "Clarence, as much as you're going to miss this class, we're going to miss you. It was a very hard decision. I had to think what's best for Clarence."

The counselor arrived around this time and made cheerful talk to Clarence about his new class, and Clarence just slowly shook his head. Chris sent Clarence back to the room.

"They're all like that," said the counselor to Chris. "Scared to leave, you know?"

"No," said Chris. "The problem is, I'm a witch, and he likes me. He's used to witches." She added, "He got dressed up today. My heart is breaking."

From her desk, she kept a Clarence watch. He batted his eyelashes. He left his mouth ajar. He knew she was watching him, she thought. But when he thought she wasn't, he tried to trip a classmate. His grin blossomed. Then he saw her and it vanished. The pattern was familiar to her after all these years among little boys. When he knew she was watching him today, he would extract every thrilling tickle of sympathy he could, and she would let him have what he wanted.

After the spelling test — he had studied for it this time — Clarence went away with the counselor, to visit the Alpha class. In the car, the counselor chattered away at Clarence, invoking visions of picnics and roller skating parties at the Alpha class. Clarence sat in the back seat, gazing out at the melting, muddy March landscape as the car ascended through Holyoke, Clarence answering by saying "Yup" over and over again.

At the outer door to his new school, Clarence fingered his collar button. He bent down and smoothed the cuffs of his pants.

The desks in the Alpha room had high partitions on three sides. It was a small class, just ten, all boys. An aide and a counselor hovered in the rear. The teacher was young and she seemed calm. During breaks, she allowed boom boxes, but only one at a time. Rap was the music of choice. "I hate that music," she said, smiling. She had gotten her class to make up their own rap song, on the theme of the multiplication tables. She did a verse for the

Kelly School counselor, putting on the emphatic, equally accented syllabication that gives rap music its air of threatening drums: *"Two! Times! Two! Is! I! For! Get!"*

"He is coming into a notorious group of troublemakers," she explained. "We tell them when they go to the cafeteria or out in the halls, 'Don't go out there wearing a sign on your head that says Alpha.' We need to tell them what their reputation is, and we need to get them to work against it." She thought that many had made progress. "Sometimes they'll see mainstream kids running in the halls and say, 'We don't do that.' For all of that, the Alpha teacher thought it would be better to leave the children in regular classes and to use people like her and her aides to help the regular teachers cope.

The teacher had chosen an escort for Clarence, a small, wiry white boy with a crew cut just growing out – it had the look of an untended garden. He showed Clarence the behavior chart, pointing at the various symbols. "That's good. That's good. That's not good." There was a classroom store, stocked according to the children's wishes, budget permitting. Accumulated points for good behavior earned an Alpha student treats from the store. Clarence's escort said he had won a plastic figure of the wrestler Andre the Giant. He hadn't done too well since then. "I had a hundred and sixty-one points? And then I went to zero. Now I got thirty-five points. Say if you get ten points, and you get a check, then you got five points in your bank account."

Clarence nodded. He didn't say much. He fingered objects, such as the passes a student had to get in order to leave the room. "Yup," he said. He followed the white boy around the room. The white boy said, in singsong cadence, "It's *pretty* nice. The teacher gives out crackers and *stuff*. We do a lot of *stuff*. Sometimes we have birthday parties. My birthday's comin'." Then, with adult-looking thoughtfulness, the Alpha veteran said to Clarence, "People don't like us. Because we're special."

"See you Monday, Clarence," said the teacher after the tour.

"Yup," said Clarence.

"I love him already," said the teacher.

There was mud on the playground. Recess was indoors. Returning from lunch, Chris looked at the board. Clarence had written in huge letters: CLARENCE THE BEST!

"Clarence the best, huh?" said Chris.

Robert had a green stuffed dinosaur in his shirt pocket. He'd carried it there all day.

"Robert, put that on my desk. It's starting to get in the way of your learning."

274

He must have been waiting for that command. He said about his stuffed animal, "He's learning, too-ooo."

This was Friday afternoon, when she always anticipated missing them a little over the weekend. She said mildly to Robert, "Well, he can learn as well on my desk as in your pocket."

She read aloud a long time. "Awww"s when she closed the book. So she opened it and read some more. Clarence pulled his chair up tight against his desk, against its bulging contents. He had stuffed his desk so tightly with books and old papers and notes he'd never taken home to his mother, it looked as if they'd need a crowbar to empty it. As Chris read, Clarence watched Mariposa industriously copy over her story. The other day during this quiet time, he had cut a piece out of Mariposa's sweatshirt, just trying out the scissors. (He had said he was sorry afterward and had offered to let Mariposa cut off a piece of *his* sweatshirt.) Now, as Mrs. Zajac read, he drew his sleeves over his hands. He watched Mariposa, gazed at the stapler on her desk, reached over and fingered it, turned it sideways. He watched his fingers stroke the cool gray metal. He opened up the stapler, and Mariposa finally made an angry face at him. He grinned. Now he wanted to go to the bathroom, the game of bothering Mariposa forgotten. His elevated hand yearned toward

Mrs. Zajac. He wiggled his fingers at her.

"We're going to take our journals out. Yes, Clarence, you can go to the bathroom."

Clarence walked to the door, got outside, and started his stiff-ankled, untied-sneakers run.

"Clarence is leaving the class today," she said to the children when Clarence had jogged off out of earshot. She leaned back against the front table, nails drumming lightly on the cover of the novel. "He's going to another class."

Robert applauded briefly.

Chris glanced at him and went on calmly, fingers drumming on the book. "Not for a punishment, but because that's where I think he'll do better. Clarence isn't all that pleased about going, just like none of us would be. I thought it would be nice if we made a little card for him, just wishing him good luck, and signed our names to it."

Mariposa distributed the journals.

"That might be one of the things you might want to write about in your journals," Chris added. "How you feel about Clarence leaving. And when he's leaving today, I want you to make sure that you do say goodbye to him. I don't want to make a big deal in front of the class, because he isn't that thrilled about it."

"He says it's you that he's leavin'," crowed Robert. He grinned.

276

"It's me that he's leaving," she repeated flatly.

"No!" piped up Felipe. "He said the reason he's leaving is because you told them to."

"Well, there were a lot of people involved. We all thought it was the best thing for him. So anyways, that might be one thing you'd want to write about in your journals, about him leaving."

She walked among the desks. She stopped at Juanita's and said to the shy girl, "If you want to complain about what a creep Mrs. Zajac is, you can do that."

Juanita smiled up at Mrs. Zajac.

Chris bustled around, talking fast. Clarence would return any moment. She got Judith to find that good, heavy white paper Chris knew was somewhere in the room. She asked Felipe to design the card.

"Clarence, we're writing in our journals."

He walked in slowly, eyeing the room in general.

Chris went to his desk and, bending over him, whispered, "Since this is your last day, you might want to write how you feel about it." She went back to her desk and watched Clarence.

After a while, he said, without turning to her, "I don't know what to write."

"Come here, dear." She leaned across her

desk and whispered, "You could write about leaving."

"No."

"Then write about why you don't want to. Write that down."

The remedial reading teacher came to the door to pick up some children. Chris called to her, "Can I keep them for today?" The whole class should be here.

Plan book open, pen in hand, Chris laid the back of that hand across her mouth. She stared at Clarence. He had begun to write. She stared over his head toward the door. Only an hour now and the walkers would line up there. Routine would carry her the rest of the way.

"All right, you can put away your journals."

"Ca ca ca can I keep working in mine?"

"Can you keep working in your journal, Clarence? Yes."

Story rewriting time. "I don't got no more paper," said Kimberly.

Chris lifted her eyebrows, smiled, and made one hand into claws. The children cried "No!" covering their ears and grinning as they cried. Clarence dropped his pen and did likewise.

Clarence went back to his journal. "Mrs. Zajac, how do you spell 'through'?" In a little while, he carried his opened journal to her. He

278

sat down at his desk and watched her read.

I'm not going to that school because I
don't like it and I don't think that school is
a good place for me And why did you put
me in that school it is not a good place for
me i now Monday through the whole week
am not going to that school i mean it you
shouldn't said yes now i am not going to
the school I am going to run away?

She took him to the hall. "Give it a chance,
Clarence."
"Nope."
"The teacher seemed nice, didn't she? Why
don't you want to go? What's so bad about that
school? Tell me what you don't like about it. I
think you'll like it. I really do."
He just kept shaking his head.

The children were in story conferences. Felipe said loudly to Irene, "I bet I get a C on this
story. You watch. I bet I get an F." That did it.
Felipe began to cry. "I'm stupid. I'm stupid in
every subject."
Chris watched from her desk. She had no
sympathy to spare for Felipe today. Perhaps,
she thought, that was the problem.
For science, the last lesson, she showed a
film strip on the constellations. That cheered

up Felipe. Clarence was already cheered up. He lay on his belly on the floor to watch the story of how the ancients had laid templates on the wild stars. Mrs. Zajac, at the projector, sang, "I see you, Clarence. Don't think you're getting away with anything."

The clock began to move for her again. The day was almost over. Felipe finished up the card. "Goodbye, Clarence. Good luck, Clarence," it read. It was elegantly lettered. "I could've made a better one if I had more time," Felipe said.

Clarence grinned. He was washing the boards, his back to the class. Children gathered around Felipe's desk and signed their names.

Robert, keeping to his own desk, piped up, "I ain't signin' it. I hate Clarence."

Chris wheeled on him. "Robert, things that we do to others come back to hurt us twice as bad."

Robert wore a faint grin.

"Think about it." Her voice was low and fierce. "That's not a very generous or nice thing to do, and I'm extremely disappointed in you." She took a deep breath. Below her, Robert laid his head to one side and fiddled with a pen. Color rose in his cheeks. It rose in blotches on Chris's neck. "Someday, Robert, somebody's going to make you sad! Right now, I don't like what you just did. At all! I don't think it's funny, cute. Nothing! And I'm disgusted!"

Chris took another deep breath and went back to her desk. She glanced at Clarence, who was still washing the boards. She looked at the children signing the card. She grabbed her pocketbook and rummaged through her change purse. She grabbed the tape dispenser. Inserting herself into the crowd around Felipe's desk, Chris hurriedly taped seven quarters to the card, the children murmuring, "Ooooo." It was a bribe of sorts. She wanted to make sure that Clarence would accept the card.

"Bus one," said the intercom.

Felipe handed Clarence the card. Clarence studied it, standing over near the front table.

From near her desk, Chris called, "Good luck, Clarence. We'll all miss you." She wasn't saying goodbye. This was a cue for the bus students, and they caught it.

Alice, in purple coat and beret, rubbed Clarence's back hard. "Bye, Clarence."

Clarence put down the card and scowled. He shoved it across the front table, rejecting it. He went back to washing the boards. But he started grinning again as the bus students trooped past him, sweet female voices saying, "Bye, Clarence."

Little Arnie said, in a voice too squeaky for the manly words, "So long, old buddy."

Then only the walkers remained. They loitered around the front table. Clarence examined the card again.

Jimmy said, "A dollar twenty-five!"

Felipe said, "Two dollars."

Judith, detaching herself slightly from the throng, said, "A dollar seventy-five."

Clarence put the card in his pocket.

Chris kept busy. "Judith, I need you to do me a favor. These papers are piling up."

Over by the front table, the usual end-of-the-day movie and TV show reviews were being delivered. *"Friday the Thirteenth,* bro. It's goooood!"

Felipe said to Clarence, "You still going to live in the same place? Well, in that case, I'll see you every day!"

"Every day after school," sang Chris. "All right, walkers line up."

"Mrs. Zajac. Mrs. Zajac," said Clarence.

"What, Clarence?"

"Arshhht."

She laughed.

"I got her," said Clarence to Jimmy.

Clarence turned back to the board. He stood next to the spot where she wrote the word of the day for penmanship. He had erased the one for today. Now Clarence took up a piece of chalk and wrote carefully, laboriously, "C-Clarence."

"Look!" said Felipe.

Mrs. Zajac smiled. "Well, at least it's nice penmanship. You all have your homework?"

Clarence stood beside her. He touched her arm, and inclining his head toward his name on the board, he said to her, "Do dat?"

"Yes, Clarence," said Chris. "We'll do that on Monday. I promise."

She led them to the door that opened onto the staircase. The procession halted there to await the intercom, releasing the walkers.

Arabella said, prematurely, since they weren't leaving just yet, "Goodbye, Clarence."

Julio said, "If you see my cousin up there, tell him he's a wimp."

"Yes, Clarence. You have a real nice time. Okay? And you be a good boy there?" Chris grabbed him from behind, in a gentle head lock, and moved him around in front of her. In her faintly mocking voice, which made the children giggle, Clarence grinning in her embrace and looking off to one side, she went on, "Like I know you can be? And work real hard, like I know you can do?" She gave him one more squeeze — "And have fun?" — and let him go.

"Walkers may be dismissed," said the intercom.

Children poured out of adjacent classrooms. Hers raced past her. Then the rest of the mob came by. The staircase rumbled. She stood aside and looked down over the railing. Clarence went right outside.

Chris stayed awhile in the room to read the journal entries. Most of the children had written that they felt sad. Irene had written, "I'm sad, but I'll get over it." Chris laughed. She pursed her lips as she read Juanita's entry:

I think Miss Zajac feels sad today because is the last day of one of her students.

All of Clarence's usual victims wrote that they forgave him. Almost all of them wrote that they thought Clarence needed special help, and a new class was the best thing for him. So she hadn't left them scared that they might get banished, too, and they had believed her when she'd said it was being done for Clarence's own good. Chris wished she knew what Judith thought. But Judith had worked on her *Shana and the Warriors* and had kept her own counsel on Clarence.

Chris locked the journals away in her closet and hefted her bags. At the door, she stopped and looked at Clarence's name on the board, in the penmanship position. The boy had style. He had left his mark. At least he hadn't gone away angry.

When she got outside the school, she said, "Boy, do I feel better than last Friday."

Someone must have used the parking lot as a service station last night. A puddle of oil with an old filter in the middle lay on the sidewalk. Chris stepped nimbly around the mess. There was a touch of spring in the air, and the river's scent.

Recovery

Through the salt-streaked windshield, this grimy part of town looked even grimier to Chris as she drove down to work. It was the season of muddy footprints in the classroom. Outside the classroom windows, the snow had melted. When the sun came out, it shone on brown grass, on the unburied trash lodged against the playground's chain link fence, and on a pile of glossy, bulging green garbage bags somebody had dumped out there over the weekend. Victor, from the bilingual room next door, told Chris that a couple of his students had come to school, eaten the free breakfast, and then split. In Chris's room, another of the pale ceiling lights had started flickering. The smells of packaged onion rings and cheese puffs filled the room at snack time, then lingered. In reading, a child from another homeroom mentioned that he'd found some handcuffs in his mother's bureau. A boy came into reading with snot hanging out his nose. Chris kept handing him tissues while looking away. The things that the children made in art looked discouragingly alike. The decorations in the room – last month's book report projects dangling on clothes hangers and strings of yarn, the once alluring witches' faces on the wall above the closets, the poster of the monkey, captioned "The More I Think The More Confused I Get" – all seemed worn out, like the view from an invalid's window. She cranked the casements halfway open in the morning. Sounds from the factories mingled with the hum of the heater – these were the kinds of sounds a propeller-driven plane makes; you could drift away on them.

Al called Parks and Recreation about the garbage, but nothing was getting fixed. In the Teachers' Room, somebody quipped, "Landfill. Don't you know that's the future of Kelly School?" The Teachers' Room seemed newly grubby, the armrests of the orange sofas patched with tape, the busted stove with insulation poking out, the bathroom's sticky door and its noisy toilet, the sound of which revolted Chris while she ate lunch. Over coffee, a teacher said of their high calling, "Garbage picking is more rewarding." March wasn't over yet.

After school Chris ambled with the other teachers into the too brightly lit, yellow-walled, windowless "cafetorium." She sat with teacher friends at one of the lunch tables as Al, in shirtsleeves, standing before his faculty, voice booming, gave his speech of March. She knew this speech from years past, and she sat with her head bowed, watching herself doodle on Al's handout. Al said that anyone who had finally wearied of this school should think about a transfer for next year.

"Evaluate what you're doing," said Al. "If you're not happy, if this is the most boring job you can think of . . . think about it. I thank the Lord I'm not in the same school where I started out."

"The Lord blesses you, Al," called a female voice. Chris looked up. The quip came from a teacher seated a couple of tables away, one of Al's perpetual critics. Chris went back to doodling.

She felt more dispirited than usual for this dull time of year. So did many others, including Al. The results of a new statewide standardized test had just come in — the Basic Skills Tests, which third, sixth, and ninth graders took. The other night Chris had read about the scores in the *Transcript-Telegram*. Everyone had read the article. On the Basic Skills Tests, Holyoke schoolchildren had some of the worst overall scores in the state. No question on those tests was harder than this one:

Carol can ride her bike 10 miles per hour.

If Carol rides her bike to the store, how long will it take?

To solve this problem, you would need to know

A. how far it is to the store.
B. what kind of bike Carol has.
C. what time Carol will leave.
D. how much Carol has to spend.

More than 30 percent of Kelly School's sixth graders had gotten flunking marks, below 60, on those very easy tests. Almost all who failed came from families below the poverty line, and many were Puerto Rican. Al was very upset. He was trying to buck up his faculty.

"I don't want to hear the test scores anymore. I know what kids we got here," Al declared.

Chris drew some wagon wheels on Al's handout — in social studies, it was almost time for the pioneers.

"We can't bring them all up to grade level no matter what we do," he went on. "But can we improve instruction here? You *bet* we can."

Then Al said, "But —"

Chris looked up. She knew what was coming. She smiled.

"We're doin' a good job. We really are," said Al.

Chris had a dream on Sunday night, the weekend after Clarence was finally sent away.

It's Monday morning. She sits at her desk. In the desk right in front of her sits Clarence! He has someone else's face. She knows that face but can't put a name to it. She also knows that it is Clarence in disguise. First chance she gets, she hurries to the office. "Clarence is back! I know it doesn't look like him, but it is! He isn't supposed to be here." The people in the office smile knowingly at her. She waylays some other teachers, but they just shake their heads and walk away. And then she's back in her room, and Clarence still sits at his old desk, wearing someone else's face. She gazes at him. "Oh, well," she says to herself. "Nobody seems to care. Everyone seems to have forgotten. I'll just keep him."

Chris sat at her desk that first Monday without him. The children filed in: Julio in his long, slow strides like a man on stilts, Pedro in his happy rolling gait, Robert in his heavy shuffle, dragging his heels, *clump, clump, clump.* She half expected to see Clarence dance into the doorway.

Jimmy came to her desk. "Is Clarence comin' back?"

"No, Jimmy. He's at his new school now."

"We should take his sticker off then," said Jimmy, who, with unusual vigor, ripped the name card off Clarence's old desk. Jimmy didn't like commotion. He was glad Clarence was gone.

Chris gazed at Clarence's chaotically stuffed desk. She asked Mariposa to clean it out.

In the Teachers' Room early that week, a colleague asked, "Is your room different without Clarence?"

"Night and day," Chris said.

Her classroom *was* different, wasn't it? It was certainly quieter, she thought. Maybe too quiet. The first days of that week dragged by. She kept imagining Clarence at the Alpha class. She fretted about the Basic Skills Tests. Several of the students from her low math group of last year had flunked. What had she done wrong? She brooded on the general question: why did the poorest children seem to learn the least in school?

But the problems she faced weren't general, and on Wednesday, out on the sofa during art and music, Chris began to take stock. Lifting her eyes from the plan book on her lap, she ran through the faces in her room. She saw Arabella's pigtail, fluffy pompadour, and perfect crescent smile. Arabella had made exceptional progress; if it continued, she should reach grade level in all subjects by the end of next year. Chris saw Alice shaking her head just to watch her silky hair brush across her shoulders. Alice had made progress. Alice did all that she was asked, but Chris thought she ought to start asking her to do more. Dick ought to do more talking, and Mariposa — her latest earrings looked like wind chimes — had to pay attention during social studies. Maybe Mariposa would do better, now that she didn't have Clarence sitting next to her and pilfering items from her desk and cutting pieces off her sweatshirt.

Most had made normal progress. Normal measures would carry them along. But was it just her imagination or had the problems of the ones with big problems gotten bigger suddenly? With Clarence gone, she did see the others' needs more clearly. She felt sure of that.

How many in this class would flunk the Basic Skills Tests next year? Jimmy probably would if he took the test on a Monday, when he was always exhausted. She imagined Jimmy yawning and stretching right in front of her, just like a baby getting ready for a nap. That was one of the problems with tests. They tested things more basic than skills, and one of those was a good night's sleep. Pedro still smiled through the days, still at about second-grade level in every subject except for math: She had gotten Pedro some special tutoring. The testing that she had ordered for him six months ago must be imminent now.

Sitting on the sofa, head laid back and staring at the high ceiling, Chris conjured up the faces of several who had slacked off lately in their work, and she thought, "They don't know it yet, but they're going to miss Clarence." Then she thought of Claude. He had not slacked off. He had never started.

When she contemplated Claude, Chris thought of his school days going slowly by while a stronger current ran beneath. She imagined Claude at his desk, daydreaming about fishing as if he had all the time in the world, and she thought, Claude has only a little more than a year now to start learning how to put his mind to a task and get a little organized. If she didn't help him do that, he would be – she could see Claude there – wandering around lost, picking at his lip, in the halls of junior high.

She knew several Claudes. One of them amused her – the absent-minded boy of many ailments. He came to class once with his hand wrapped like a mummy's in a giant Ace bandage that covered a tiny cut on his thumb. Sometimes he walked past the classroom door by mistake. He would rush to the closet and forget what he'd gone for when he got there, all the while discussing his confusion out loud.

"What was I lookin' for? I know! That paper. It's here someplace. Whew! Here it is."

The sad, lonely Claude wore pants that still had little bunches of thread where the price tag had been. This Claude was so out of touch with what his peers thought was "fresh" or "def" or "toy" that he told the whole class about his imaginary friends, Herbert and Herberta, who kept him company when he was lonely. Claude got laughed at for that, of course. Out at recess he tried to get the other children's attention by taking an old piece of two-by-four he'd found in the grass and swinging it perilously close to their heads. He would step on classmates' heels, and would turn around at his middle-person desk and try to show Julio, who did not like Claude, a card trick that didn't quite work. One time Claude came in from recess and tried to make conversation with beautiful Alice by saying, "I met someone who says he hates you."

There was, finally, the maddening Claude, who was sneaky and quick-witted. He had a perfectly good mind, Chris thought.

All three Claudes came together, almost every day, at homework excuse time. Why hadn't he done his homework again? "The only kind of paper we have at home is the kind where there's no lines," said Claude.

"I did it," he had said to Chris the other

morning. She had asked him for his spelling homework.

Don't ask, she thought. Don't let him get started. But as usual she couldn't resist. Oh, well, she thought, this is some of the most creative work Claude does all day.

"Okay, Claude, where is it?"

"I don't know," said Claude, looking up at her earnestly. "It could be *anywhere.*"

She'd have to get his mother in again. Talk about *basic skills.* She hadn't done enough about Claude. It was high time she had a look inside Claude's bookbag. I'm almost afraid to look, Chris thought. She'd do that soon.

If she could have, she'd have avoided thinking about Robert now, but she saw him all too clearly. Robert was too big for his desk. He sat in his middle-person spot, lifting his desk up and down on his thighs, black hair in a crew cut, a broad white face, his lips very red under fluorescent light. One morning, at the start of math, Robert piped up in his squeaky voice, "Mrs. Zajac, do you want me to go out in the hall while you read the answers?" Robert meant the answers to last night's homework. This was his way of telling her he hadn't done his. He smirked.

She was standing in front of the low math group, ready to begin. Her hands went to her hips. "Robert, I don't think this is any kind of a joke. I think it's kind of ludicrous that by now you aren't doing your homework. If you don't care, I'm on the verge of not caring. I'm sick of babying you."

Robert looked up at her and made a small sound, like a mewling infant. Very bold for Robert.

"Shut your mouth!" she said.

Robert bowed his head slightly but started making little gabbing movements with his lips. Then he lifted his eyes to hers and made his eyebrows bob up and down.

"Out!" she said. The imperious teacher finger pointed toward the door.

"I'm going to leave him out there 'til he rots," she said to herself.

On the blue carpet beneath Robert's desk, items accumulated. One day a myriad of expended staples. On another bits of paper torn from a notebook, and the twisted wire binder of the notebook itself, lying there like a busted spring. Always there were candy wrappers and empty junk food bags from snack time. In the pauses between lessons, Chris would gaze at Robert. He would sit at his desk, his pen poised over work that he would not do. A pensive expression would cover his flat, ample face, and for a moment he would look like a well-fed executive in a photograph by Bachrach. This vision of Robert would pass, without any transition, and he would turn back into an oversized boy with ink-spotted jeans, the cuffs rolled up, the waist of his underpants showing. For no apparent reason, his face would flush red. Then it would grow pale. He'd slap his own face a few times. His face would light up again. He'd wave his hand hard. "Ooo! Ooo! Ooo! Mrs. Zajac! Mrs. Zajac!"

"Yes, Robert?"

"Can I go bathroom?" Just like a three-year-old.

Permission granted, he'd rub his hands together. He'd grin maniacally.

During a health lesson, one of many Chris gave about the perils of drugs, Robert announced, "My mother's old boyfriend had another girlfriend, and she had a baby, and it was addicted to heroin."

"Oh, Robert, how sad!"

Robert grinned.

"Oh, my God," Chris thought. "What a life he's leading."

She had brought him up to the front table to help him work on a story. He said to her happily, "Mrs. Zajac, I have this friend named Crazy Eddie, and a blood vessel broke in his ankle and there was blood all over his bed."

"Why do you call him Crazy Eddie?" Crazy Eddie was probably shooting up, she thought.

"Because he peels in an' outa our parking lot.

He's real crazy." Robert's eyes narrowed, and he grinned, not as he might have grinned if he were happy, but with the exaggerated menace of a cartoon character.

She tried to get him to talk, but it seemed as if his thoughts must veer to the grotesque. The reviews of horror movies that he gave classmates, for example. "I like the part on Jason. Once there was a nail puller. Jason picked it up and slammed it right into some guy's head. Awesome!"

And he often wrecked her chats with the class.

"Does anyone know anything about Japan?"

"Yeah. It's fulla chinks," said Robert.

"He just does that to see what I'll do," she thought.

She still hoped to get his mother to take Robert to a psychiatrist. She had seen his mother several times, a towering figure who usually appeared unannounced at the door. Robert always seemed excited when his mother came to school, and for a while afterward would do some work. Chris had told his mother that her visits seemed to help, and his mother had said she would come to the school once a week, but had not returned since.

Would Robert flunk the Basic Skills Tests next year? Probably, Chris thought. But not because he didn't have a lot of basic academic skills. When, back in the fall, she had administered the California Achievement Tests to the class, Robert hadn't even bothered to read half of the questions. He had simply filled in at random and sloppily the bubbles on the answer sheet. In Robert's case, a standardized test merely measured the child's willingness to take a standardized test. Robert didn't care enough to try much of anything. She guessed he didn't dare. He couldn't fail if he didn't try.

He wasn't as disruptive as Clarence. He didn't spread his problems around as much. When he felt like hitting someone, he hit himself, and when he started squeaking or singing while the others tried to work, a look would usually silence him.

She gathered up her books and headed back to the room. She couldn't think of what to do for Robert, except to try to get him psychiatric help.

Chris knew only one incontrovertibly good reason for Clarence's being sent away: the rest of the class had to benefit. But this first week without him limped along. More and more children who had regularly done the homework simply stopped. On Thursday morning Judith got a 65 on a math paper. It was, for Chris, like going to the bank and finding that she didn't have any money left. She had told herself that the low math group needed the larger share of her time, and that the top group, and especially Judith, could mostly teach themselves. She'd have to distribute herself more equitably.

That morning passed slowly. The room had a rancorous air. She scolded the low math group, and all three reading groups, too, for not doing their work. After lunch and reading aloud, she went to center stage, in front of her front table, to start a grammar lesson with her homeroom class. It was a sunny day. Out the window on the playground, a small group of sixth graders picked through the contents of the garbage bags – the bags had split and the late March winds had lifted pieces of the trash and distributed them along the far fence. Behind Chris's left shoulder on the front chalkboard, the lists of children who owed her work now overflowed the usual quadrant. Chris planned to teach her lesson and ignore those lists for a while longer. She looked at Courtney, though, and she felt a little angry, both at Courtney and herself. She knew that Courtney hadn't done the language assignment. "Courtney, where's your homework?"

"You didn't tell me to do it."

"Courtney! Since when do I say, 'Everyone has to do the homework except for Courtney'?"

Courtney pouted.

The rest of the year turned on that pout. Chris folded her arms. "I think it's time we had a little talk," she said. There was acid in her voice. She looked down at her class, from one face to another, and she smiled at them with most of her teeth.

"What is today's date? What month is it?"

Many little voices helped her figure out the date.

"It is not June," she said. She scowled down at them, but they looked so worried, so many faces seemed to say, "I didn't think I was *that* bad, Mrs. Zajac," that for a moment she felt like laughing. She was losing the edge, she thought. It would have to be all acting now. She felt, really for the first time in weeks, at peace and fully energetic.

The color had faded from Chris's neck. She cried, "Some of you think school has ended!" Two sets of red-painted nails pressed against her breastbone. "I don't know why!" Her teacher finger lifted high into the air. "Some of you think you don't have to do homework anymore!" Her teacher finger came down hard. "*I* don't know why!" Her hands flew up and outward. "Some of you think, 'Yeah, I have to do the work, but who cares what it looks like. The old witch'll accept anything.'" Her hands came back to her breastbone. "*I* haven't changed! I'm not going to accept garbage. Which it looks like I'm getting from some of you people."

She looked at them. She let it all sink in, and then she said, "Because what do you think the old witch is going to make you do if you hand in lousy work?"

"Do it over," said several faint voices.

"Do it over," said Chris, adding, "Do you think we could possibly do quality work this afternoon?"

Every head nodded, except Robert's.

It all sounded like the first day of school, and that was what Chris had in mind.

The next afternoon, Chris went into her classroom closet and came out with a construction paper Easter bunny. It was ragged and creased from years of folding. She said what she usually did when announcing an informal art lesson. They could make anything they liked, but if they wanted, they could make an Easter bunny. This one of hers might give them some ideas. But they shouldn't make one just like hers. Mrs. Zajac was a terrible artist. They were much better artists than she. Felipe cheered, and then Chris said, "But art is only for the people who don't owe me any work."

That got Felipe going. He did the math he owed her fast. Maybe the sight of Felipe rushing to the board, mounting a chair, and erasing his name from the delinquency lists inspired the others. Maybe Chris inspired them, striding from desk to desk, telling the delinquents what they owed. Suddenly, the room was full of scholars. Soon a parade of children approached Chris's desk. They carried papers. Some brought them in both hands, as if carrying little trays to her. "Pretty good, Pedro!" "Very good, Jimmy! Now go to the bathroom, and when you get back, we'll work on the second question." "This is not the best work you can do, Arnie. I'll tell you that, buster. But I'll accept it. Okay, Arnie, you can erase your name." As the afternoon wore on, Julio, Ashley, Courtney, brought papers to the shrine. They rushed away to erase their names. Jimmy came back to her desk with an entire social studies paper done. "Very good, Jimmy! Finally, finally, finally, you gave me something of quality. I knew you could do it. You should be proud of yourself, Jimmy!"

By the time the walkers left, the green chalkboard, drying in streaks, was empty, except for a tiny, dusty patch of names in the upper right-hand corner. Robert's and Claude's stood out, but they'd had more catching up to do than the rest of the class put together, and they'd made some headway. The exercise in housecleaning made her feel that they had confronted the past honestly and had put it behind them. Chris felt pumped up. She couldn't remember when she'd had this much energy, especially on a Friday. The wall above the closet was newly adorned. The witches were gone. A host of Easter bunnies took their place — multicolored, floppy-eared, crazed-looking. Next week new bulletin boards. New campaigns. New everything. She was going to double her planning time starting next week. She had more energy than she knew what to do with. She never would have felt this way, Chris told herself, if Clarence were still in the room, or, to be honest, if she hadn't needed to prove to herself that her room was different without him.

2

Chris often muttered in the room, "Patience, Mrs. Zajac. Patience." She felt especially impatient for signs of progress now.

The next week Chris launched several offensives at once. Too many, perhaps, to fit inside one week. At one moment, she found herself trying to finish up a lesson while outside her door there stood waiting for her: Paul, the vice principal, to talk to her about Courtney; the psychologist, to talk to her about Robert; and Claude's mother, to talk to her, neither for the first nor last time, about Claude.

She saw them one after the other, hurriedly, then faced her class. "Claude, let me see that bookbag." She had just told Claude's mother that Claude had to get better organized.

Claude presented his bookbag dutifully. He stood up at the front table next to Mrs. Zajac. He was being helpful, holding the bag open while Chris groped around inside it. She pulled out of Claude's knapsack a great disordered fistful of crumpled construction paper folders and half-finished homework assignments, some dating from the fall.

"What's all this?" cried Chris. She plunged in her hand for more. Another fistful of papers. Then a bunch of books with papers inserted among the pages and sticking out every which way. She pulled out a store-bought binder of the kind that is marketed as an "organizer." "This is a nice organizer, Claude. Do you know what the word 'organize' means?"

Claude nodded earnestly.

Out came the ancient remains of a sandwich, a test on the Revolutionary War, an Advent calendar. "Claude! Look, Claude, let me give you some advice. Every day you have some papers to show Mom and Dad. Don't leave them in your bag. Use your organizer."

Claude looked at Chris very earnestly and declared, "I got another organizer in my desk, too!"

"It doesn't organize itself, Claude," Chris

said, and immediately regretted it. Several children tittered.

Chris pursed her lips and looked around her. The important thing at that moment was protecting Claude. Any minute, the rest of the class was going to find this searching of the knapsack all too enjoyable.

"Okay, Claude. You're going to organize yourself today."

Chris shoved the boy's desk across the carpet and out the door. Claude followed, hands fidgeting as if he'd like to help. She instructed him in the use of the organizer, and gave him a heap of new construction paper to make new folders, and left him sitting at his desk just outside the door, out of danger for a while.

Claude sat in the hall pulling books and papers out of his desk and his bag, heaping them all into a large, chaotic pile. He sang softly as he worked. *"Doo doo dee doo."*

Al was prowling the hallways. He stopped in front of Claude's desk and folded his arms, ready to dish out some wrath. The boy must have done something serious to be sent out here *with* his desk. *"What* are you doing?" Al asked him.

"I'm organizing myself," said Claude brightly.

Al looked taken aback. Then he said sternly, "Can you do it more quietly, please?" and moved on down the hall.

"Doo doo dee doo," sang Claude as he sorted through most of a year's worth of papers, placing them into various new construction paper folders and into his organizer, though not in any discernible order.

By that afternoon, Chris felt exhausted. The art and music teachers took over. She went to the sofa in the hall and didn't even try to work. "This week I feel like, the harder I work, the deeper the hole," she thought. Claude's problem was much worse than she'd imagined. "I'm disgusted with myself for letting it go on this long. Maybe I should just give up on Claude." Having imagined surrender, she perked up a little. She'd keep after him. Strategies rarely worked at once, and no strategy worked all the time. Little steps, she told herself. Be patient. Just keep on working on him. She'd get his mother to visit again.

Chris sent many notes home with Claude. The mother came in.

"Sometimes," Claude's mother said to Chris, "I want to criminate him."

She had a thick French-Canadian accent. Chris wasn't sure exactly what Claude's mother meant, but understood the general meaning. Chris smiled and said, "To be honest, so would I sometimes."

Claude's mother had a harried, worried air. She said to Chris, "I don't know what to do anymore. We do care what happ-*ens,* but I cannot quit my job."

Chris liked the woman. They had several pleasant conversations. "You a left paw," Claude's mother noted. She marveled at Chris's patience. "When you go to Fleury Funeral Home, you are going to be an angel."

Chris blushed. Then she started trying to reorganize Claude's household. Chris got her hands moving like the wheels of industry and laid out a plan for Claude's afterschool hours: the old homework-signing deal, the time and the place where Claude should study at home, the hour at which his father should check the work.

But his father didn't seem to follow instructions. Claude still came in with the wrong homework, or, more often, no homework. One evening Chris called up Claude's father. "He's just got to organize himself better," Chris said into the phone. "So I'll keep on him, and I'll let you know how he's doing. Okay?"

Claude's father said to Chris, "Claude didn't give you the note, huh?"

"Note?"

"Well," said the father, "I was *supposed* to write a note. I guess I forgot."

Chris laughed and laughed after she got off

the phone. She told Billy, "What's in the cats is in the kittens, as my mother likes to say."

For a time, though, her struggle with Claude grew worrisome. One afternoon, she was trying again to tell Claude that he *had* to start doing his homework. Claude declared that he always did his homework. Then Dick, of all people – kind, quiet Dick – said, "Yeah, sure, Claude."

Claude said he'd do all his homework from now on.

Dick bet him a dollar he wouldn't.

"Okay," said Claude.

From every part of the room cries erupted: "*I'll* bet you a dollar, Claude!" "Me, too!" "Yo, Claude! I'll bet you a quarter!"

Wearing a sickly smile, Claude turned down all other bets. Judith wrote out the terms of Claude's wager with Dick on a piece of red construction paper, which she laid on the counter by the window. But Judith had second thoughts. A few days later Felipe told Claude, "Claude, all you think about is fish. That's all." And Judith spoke up. "So what, Felipe? You're always talking about becoming an astronaut. Why can't the kid talk about fishing?" Now Judith would mutter at classmates who teased Claude, "Leave the kid alone." Once again, Chris thought, "Thank you, Lord, for sending me Judith."

Chris herself sometimes felt a great desire to

glue Claude's glasses to his nose, shake him by the shoulders, and say, "Forget the illnesses, forget the fishing, forget the excuses. Concentrate on what you're doing right now!" She had to keep on him. But she had to do it gently. The boy was enough of an outcast as it was. Chris taped an index card to the top of Claude's desk: DON'T FORGET TO COPY YOUR ASSIGNMENT! Claude was very happy with the card and kept fingering it, but he didn't usually follow its command, at least not yet. Chris kept lecturing him, but she did it quietly and in private. First thing in the morning, she would call Claude to her desk, ask him for the work he owed, and then tell him she was disappointed. He was a smart boy. She couldn't force him to learn. She would help him. But she wouldn't pay any attention to him if he didn't try. Day after day, she issued that threat.

Robert's mother also paid a visit, a couple of weeks after Clarence left. At first the woman balked at the idea of a psychiatrist. Then she declared that Robert had his father's crazy genes. She ended up demanding that Robert see a psychiatrist at once. Chris wished he could, but there was paperwork involved. Robert's mother also said, "This school hasn't done nothin' for him." And Chris, who had gone out to see the woman thinking "she probably had a real bad time in school herself," came away with her neck an angry red. All the rest of that day and that evening and the following morning, too, Chris kept wishing she had said, "At least we've tried, lady!"

The day after that meeting was the worst since Clarence. Robert tried to provoke her all morning, and succeeded just before lunch. Robert had come to school without his books again. All on his own, Jimmy had gotten up and fetched a spare textbook from the cabinet for Robert – maybe Jimmy was trying to head off noise; noise hurt his ears, Jimmy often said. At the end of the lesson, Chris asked Robert to put the book back. Robert, bouncing his desk on his knees, looked up at her with a little smirk and said, "Jimmy got it out. He can put it back."

Chris started yelling, really thundering at Robert. Matters came to rest in the usual way: Robert at his desk, looking down at his lap, his cheeks very red, the suggestion of a small, excited smile on his face; and Chris breathing deeply, glaring down at him, and thinking, "This does *no* good. Yelling at him doesn't do *one* bit of good." She talked it all over that night with Billy and decided that in the end, though he'd given her enough cause by himself, she'd only done to Robert what she had wanted to do to his mother. She'd try not to do that again.

Robert wanted her to yell at him. He wanted her attention. She had to find a way to give it to him for the right reasons. First of all, she had to make herself stop giving it to him for the wrong ones.

A slightly sour smell of sneakers getting heavy springtime use scented the classroom. In the April sunlight that streamed in stripes between the blinds, the room often looked messy, a fragrant pile of pencil shavings under the sharpener and books and papers everywhere. But it had that feeling about it again of the craftsman's workshop. She saw Robert as the biggest problem in her room now. To herself, she said, "If Robert doesn't see a psychiatrist soon, *I'm* going to need one." she decided to isolate him. She had tried this tactic once before, on last year's most difficult student. It had backfired. The boy had liked being isolated. Maybe Robert wouldn't. Deep down, Chris thought, Robert really wasn't an antisocial child. She had misgivings. The tactic was harsh. But she had to do something. She warned him first. "Robert, if you make an effort, I'll give you all the attention in the world. But if you don't, I'm going to isolate you." He shrugged and turned away. She raised her voice. "And what I mean by isolate, Robert – you will not talk to anyone. You'll sit in the corner by yourself. I'm not going to put up

with the behavior I've been putting up with!"
She'd yelled at him again. She'd have to keep
her word.

Chris didn't have to wait long. An hour or so
later, Robert refused to work on the latest story.
She moved a desk under the penmanship part
of the chalkboard, so that it faced the board.
She made sure that desk was empty, so he'd
have nothing to play with. She took away
Robert's pencil and paper. She led him by the
arm to the desk. "There is no way in the world
I'm going to say, 'Everybody has to write except
Robert.' If you won't do it, fine. But you're not
going to waste my time playing with pencils."

The situation was manageable, if a little
nerve-racking. She glanced at Robert occasionally while she helped the others with their
stories. He rocked and rocked in his chair in
the corner. One time when she looked, he was
pounding his thighs with his fists. He didn't
seem any more unhappy than usual. But the
next time she glanced at him, Robert looked
glum. Once in a while, from the corner of her
eye, she saw him looking around at her. He
sneered.

The next day when Robert started misbehaving she put him in the corner again. She left
him in isolation most of that day, too. The class
had begun a new set of science reports. She
took the children down to the library so they

could do research. As the class spread out among the brown-topped tables set up in rows beside the metal bookcases, she took Robert by the arm. His head was bowed. He was almost as tall as she. She led him to the farthest table and left him there alone. She sat down two tables away, her back to Robert, the rest of the class at the tables in front of her and off to her right. Shy Juanita had sat down alone. But Judith arose and invited Juanita to sit with her and Alice and Dick. Juanita smiled.

There was a stillness around Chris, a library stillness that she'd always liked, with a murmuring from the children mixed in. It sounded cheerful and constructive. Good noise, she thought. A happy scene, if it weren't for Robert. Chris could feel him behind her. She was not going to look.

"Mrs. Zajac." Alice stood at Chris's side. Alice whispered that Robert was bothering them. He was, Alice said, "doing something gross" to his hand.

"Just try to ignore him. Okay?"

Ignoring him was hard. "I don't know what to do," she thought. "I wish he'd just let it all out and scream at me.

He was, but Robert screamed in his own way.

Chris hadn't taken everything away from Robert. He had a penny. Alone at his table, he had begun to scratch the back of one hand with the dull edge of his penny.

Robert looked at Mrs. Zajac. He scratched harder. Classmates passed by, going into the stacks. Robert held the hand aloft to show them. Then he went back to work, bending low. He dug with the penny. The copper penny turned red. It was carving a small bloody furrow in his hand. The furrow started at a knuckle. Now it reached almost to the wrist bone. He looked up now and then. He went back to digging. When the class returned to the room, he kept his hand hidden under his desk.

Chris never saw the wound while it was fresh, and later on she never asked Robert about it. Out of her earshot, Robert said he had attacked his hand in order to get sent to the nurse, who might send him home. He had not wanted to show his wound to Mrs. Zajac, though. "I wanted her to see it herself," he said.

The day after his second dose of isolation, Chris sent Robert back to his old desk with his books and pencils. Something quite astonishing happened then — too astonishing to trust in thoroughly. The day after he had wounded his hand, Robert came in with some homework. Then for a stretch of three days, Robert did all of his homework. In math, he got all the problems right. In reading some days, when up at the table with her, he answered her questions to the group correctly and with such alacrity that she had to ask him to give the other children a chance. Chris didn't let herself believe that she had engineered the change in Robert. It had happened too quickly, and she wasn't going to play psychiatrist. For all she knew, isolation and the change that had followed were just coincidental. She would savor the improvement while it lasted.

On one spring Friday morning, Robert's reading group finally reached the end of the dreary third-grade basal reader. Robert had gotten every answer right on the last end-of-chapter test — he had answered every question wrong on the previous one. The other children were reading. The room was quiet. Chris leaned across her desk toward Robert and told him he'd gotten 100 on the test. "I'm proud of you," she said.

"Huh? Who? Me?" Robert shimmied at his desk.

She ignored that. Next week, she told him, they'd start in on the fourth-grade book. "Think you'll like that?" she asked.

Robert looked away from her and toward the window. "I'm happy for me," he said.

"I'm happy for you, too." She wished she could think of a way to make this moment last.

The following Monday she said to Robert, "You're doing much better."

"I am?" He shifted his shoulders around, his belly wobbling.

"Don't you think you are?"

"No." The maddening coyness of that squeaky, clipped no.

"You don't want to hear good things?"

"No." He was playing the burly coquette.

"Just bad things?"

"Yeah."

She breathed deeply and looked away, but a moment later she heard his voice saying, "Mrs. Zajac? Can I come up and work on my story with you now?"

One morning later that week, Robert started stabbing himself with a dull scissors. But she thought his fits had diminished in number and duration. He kept on doing some of his homework. And as for her, she had kept her promise to herself and had not raised her voice at him — except just twice — since he had wounded his hand.

3

On sunny weekends, in windbreaker weather, Chris's infant daughter, Kate, chased robins around the Zajacs' green back yard, Kate hurrying after the birds in a Chaplinesque waddle and Chris laughing as she chased her. It was the loveliest of ages, Chris thought, watching Kate. She was interested in everything, and everything was new.

The Zajacs went, as always, to Holyoke's elaborate St. Patrick's Day parade. The day was blustery, the sky the leaden color of the street down which, the parade wearing on, some marchers came lurching. When Senator Edward Kennedy hove into view, in tails and top hat and jauntily swinging a shillelagh, announced by many female voices up the street crying, "Teddy! Teddy! Teddy!" Chris whispered to one of her sisters, "I'm going to do it." She set her jaw, stepped off the sidewalk, and then she thought, "Oh, should I?" That cost her the chance. She'd just resumed her trot into the street when one of her elderly aunts, not hesitating for a moment, rose from her lawn chair, throwing off her lap robe, and dashed out to the senator. The aunt pumped his hand with both of hers. As the senator received the woman, with a slight bow and then a smile that he threw toward the sky, Chris veered away and trotted back to her place among her family on the sidewalk. She stood there muttering, making angry eyes at her aunt.

Chris and Billy put on their customary St. Patrick's Day party afterward at their house, nearly all of their extended families there, lots of corned beef and cabbage and some kielbasa, too. Billy merely tolerated the parade, and around this time of year if someone asked Chris a question such as, "What does St. Patrick's Day commemorate?" Billy would say, "Beer drinking," and Chris would fulminate briefly. What about the Polish, Billy? she'd say. Was beer unknown to them? The party was wonderful. Her best friend from college came. Chris got her mind entirely off school until around midnight, when she awakened with a start, thinking, "Has Felipe dropped his instrumental music lessons?" No, he hadn't. She went back to sleep.

Rain fell for a week. Sheets of rain swept across the playground, and the wind howled at the windows. A few blocks away the gusts were dislodging several windowpanes in Pedro's grandmother's apartment. The lights in the classroom seemed very bright. The children, Chris told Mary Ann, were "hoopy." "They're all out of it today. If we have one more day of rain, I'm going to kill myself."

Over spring vacation, Chris would visit Puerto Rico. She thought about the trip now and then, a little uneasily, but at least the weather would be fine. She hoped for fair skies and outdoor recess sooner than that. She laughed when they loaded up the erasers with chalk on April Fool's Day, and when Judith squirted her with disappearing ink, and she slipped over her pinkies and wore all day the two rubber spider rings that Alice sneaked onto her blotter to scare her. That was a sight: rubber spiders dancing on Mrs. Zajac's slicing, chopping, circling hands. The days were flying by now, Chris felt. She must be having fun.

The lovely uphill parts of Holyoke began to turn green. Spring travels up the Connecticut River Valley, but seems to skip the lower wards of Holyoke. On the outside walls of Kelly School, down in the Flats, a new crop of graffiti appeared, mostly in praise of rap groups: RUN DMC = FRESH. A new picture on an electrical box on the playground helped to make up for the lack of formal sex education lessons inside. Back in the fall thieves had stripped the hallways of the school's new lithographs of American scenes. The thieves had come out of hibernation. Several mornings Al came in and found the usual trails of wreckage, but, as was also usual by now, nothing of consequence stolen. Everything valuable was securely locked up, except books. "They" didn't seem to be interested in books, but kept coming back as if just for a visit. Some unidentified youths spotted a brand new red car with a high-powered engine out in the parking lot during school hours. They had the door open and were working on the ignition when someone saw them through the school windows and called the police, who chased the young men on foot and lost them in the side streets of the Flats.

The grass on the playground turned green. City workers at last arrived and picked up all the garbage along the fence. The custodians repaired the locks and ceiling panels that the thieves broke, and painted out the swear words among the graffiti (though they failed to recognize the Spanish ones). And the attempt to equip children to express themselves on paper instead of on public walls and to get their money via jobs went on inside, in many rooms, regardless. Heading off for the Flats on fine mornings, Chris might have seemed a victim of bad choices. She should have pointed her station wagon north, toward a greener town where children scored high on Basic Skills Tests in rough proportion to their parents' incomes and years of schooling. But on most of those spring mornings she was eager to get to her room. When she thought of this class now, she saw that many were performing very well, better than ever. It was a good class, all in all. They were kind to each other usually. Nice to look at, too. "My girls are beautiful," she thought. "And the boys aren't too bad either. They're pretty cute." More than ever, she looked forward to them.

She'd come hurrying across the parking lot at a quarter to eight, always a few minutes behind, overballasted and listing slightly under her bookbag, eyes on the front door. The top math group discovered geometry — first of all, at her direction, in the many angles they'd noticed in the room during daydreamy times: the joints in the metal trim around chalk-boards, the intersecting lines of their classmates' legs under desks. The low group had finally finished with division. She had administered a final review test to make sure, and when she had gone over the last of the papers in the Teachers' Room, Chris had smiled and said, "I haven't changed Henrietta's attitude. I haven't changed Manny's. They're still going to be as obnoxious as the day is long. *But they know long division!*"

The low group began to grapple with decimals, with the very question on which the top group had begun the year: "How many parts is this number divided up into?" The children of the low group seemed delighted. No more long division or other stuff for low group kids. When Chris read them the answers to that day's problems with decimals, the children made many exclamations.

"I got a hundred!" said Jorge.

"*I* got a hundred!" cried Felipe.

Manny croaked, "I got a thousand."

Jimmy didn't even look sleepy. "We doin' this tomorrow, Mrs. Zajac? Thousands?"

Felipe, for no apparent reason besides curiosity, looked up the definition of ozone, wrote it out, and brought it in to Mrs. Zajac one morning. He wrote a rough draft of a story about a black hole, and, with many upward puffings at the glossy hair on his forehead, he actually started to rewrite it. There were moments during creative writing when she scanned the room and saw a scene that looked too good to be true, like a Norman Rockwell painting, this one entitled *Children of Many Nations Happily at Work*. Chris sat at her front table, the casement opened wide behind her, her pen poised over a child's story, her head lifted as if to distant music.

Every child worked, even Robert. Some sat in circles of twos and threes, their voices mingling as they read each other their rough drafts. Others bent over their desks, writing assiduously. Arabella giggled aloud at her own story. Now and then a question rose above the serene babble. "Mrs. Zajac? How do you spell 'high tech'?" That was Judith. In the latest crop of stories, Chris thought she saw signs of new progress in grammar, syntax, and consecutive thinking. She sat with Judith for a long time and discussed her latest story, which was marvelous. She sat with Pedro and had him dictate his story, which eventually made sense. Ashley wrote her best so far, about a robber who had barged into her family's apartment, chased by the police. Chris made time for Alice. "Okay, Alice, that was a good story. But remember my poem. Good, better, best. This was *good*, but it could be better. Maybe someone else needs to work on sentences. I want *you* to work on doing a little more. Why don't you write down some more ideas, and I'll help you fit them in."

She told herself that she was witnessing real progress that wouldn't have been possible with Clarence in the room. She hoped that he was doing well, and was glad when she heard rumors that he was. She also felt relieved when she heard he'd gotten into trouble for beating up another child. "If he was behaving perfectly, what the heck was I doing wrong?" She missed him sometimes, but in the midst of missing him she'd recall sitting with him at her table, trying to get him to write a story, his face growing stonier the harder she tried. She'd remember wasting half of the hour of creative writing trying to get him to work, and wasting most of the next half hour trying to regain her composure. She would remember coming back from lunch to find Arabella sobbing, and would remember knowing at that instant that she'd have to lecture Clarence again and that doing so would mean he'd put on the stony face and cause more trouble in the room the next time she turned her back. She'd remember thinking, "All I want to do is teach. I want a quiet afternoon so I can teach." It was the kind of small remembered pain that is encouraging. The children hardly ever mentioned Clarence anymore.

The delinquency lists rarely got very large. The actual number of disciplinary incidents remained about the same, but most didn't last long, most didn't lead to further incidents, and, Chris noticed, most didn't leave her feeling all worn out. Felipe went into an extended math sulk one day. She kept him after school to talk about it. He screamed at her, "You hate me! I know it! Why don't you just admit it!" But she kept calm outside and fairly calm within, and a thunderstorm worked wonders in Felipe. A few days later he remarked that Mrs. Zajac was "the funnest" teacher he'd ever had. On a day not long after that, the intercom announced that recess was outdoors, as it did almost every day now, and Felipe groaned, "Awww!" When Chris asked him why on earth he wouldn't want to go outside for recess Felipe said, "Because we want to work on our spelling."

Inside the room, during social studies, the pioneers drove out onto the Oregon Trail in a station wagon. "Put your heads down on your desks. Jimmy, keep your eyes open, because I'm not sure about you." They were pioneer children, and she was their mother. She wore a short-sleeved blouse and khaki skirt. She walked up and down among the desks of her middle people, hands in her skirt pockets, stopping now and then to bend down and make sure Jimmy's eyes were open. "You come home and your mother says, 'Okay, we're going to a place called Molasses.' And so the first thing you say to yourself is?"

"Where's Molasses?" said Felipe, head still in the crook of his arm.

What was Molasses like? The mother didn't know. Were they ever coming back? Nope, going there permanently. A few worried ohhhs from the children. Chris smacked her lips. "Okay. And your mother says, 'You know, on the way I can't stop at McDonald's or Burger King or 7-Eleven and get some supplies. So, because I need room for the food, we can take very little of your things.' She sang, "Goodbye, stereo. *Goodbye, TV.*" And her hands came out of her pockets and threw those things off the side of the trail.

The bit about the TV brought gasps of surprise and disbelief and a few cries of protest – "No way!" – from the roomful of lowered heads, and, voice cracking on that high but gravelly laugh, Chris cried, "Goodbye, bike!

Goodbye, all those things!"

They climbed the Rockies — she had never seen them, except in photographs — and endured the hard realities of life and death on the trail. Her hands flew out to one side and threw down their Cabbage Patch dolls and all the dishes and the kitchen table by the side of the trail. "Because if you don't drop your stuff out at that point, you are *stranded*. One of our vocabulary words for this morning. You're *stuck* there, and there's nothing around for miles and miles and miles and miles and miles and miles. Finally, you get to Molasses."

"Thank goodness!" said Arnie. He didn't seem to be joking.

And they had to build houses and contend with Native Americans, who didn't want these interlopers taking their land — and they wouldn't have felt any different, would they, if they'd been Native Americans? — and with exhaustion and illness and no hospitals. "I think most of us, including Mrs. Zajac, might pass out and say, 'No way!' "

Most of the children had sat up, and most nodded their heads.

"What you have just experienced in your minds is something not very, but a little similar to what the settlers experienced a long, long time ago. In those days they didn't use a car. What did they use?"

"A wagon," said Dick.

"I'd have an eight-cylinder Peterbilt," said Claude.

"Those people," said Chris. "Why did they do it?" With feeling, she added, "They seem like nuts to me." They spent the next fifteen minutes figuring out why; the answers were in the text. In subsequent lessons, she put on a skit with them, arranged them in study groups, had them write short essays in which they imagined themselves children going west in covered wagons – a lot of the essays were pretty good, she thought – and showed them a movie in which Indians in ceremonial dress did a ceremonial dance, and Dick, the quiet boy who loved social studies, piped up, "Mrs. Zajac, is that a stereotype?"

"It could be, but they did have rituals and dances," she called from her desk, over the sound track. "You should know, though, that not all Native Americans had the same ones." In the darkened room, Chris laid her cheek on her blotter and smiled. At least one child had remembered the academic lessons of September. "*That* makes you feel good," she said to herself.

4

Jimmy, Chris thought, has started spring vacation early. He sat at his desk with his cheek resting heavily on his hand. The skin around his eyes was stretched. He looked Chinese. It was the last day before the April break, and Jimmy was angry at Mrs. Zajac. She had caught him with homework done in his mother's handwriting again, and she had called on him several times, trying to wake him up and to get him to do some math himself. As she walked to the other side of the room to work with the top math group, Jimmy rearranged the hand supporting his cheek. He made it into a fist, but left the middle finger sticking out. Eyes closed and middle finger hanging down, pendant from his cheek, Jimmy defied her, as Roman generals once defied each other.

Chris turned to the window until her smile faded. "Poor Jimmy," she thought. "He just hates to think."

She advanced on the boy from behind. "Wake *uh*-up! Good *mor*-ning!" He leaned away from her but withdrew his middle finger.

Al's voice intoned over the intercom at midmorning: "Attention, staff. It would help me out immensely if you could fill out the census forms before you leave today, so

I can work on them next week."

Chris looked up at the squawk box and smiled. That, she figured, was Al's way of telling them that he would be working over April vacation.

Al's voice again: "Can I have your attention, staff. Please. We have a new vending machine in the office. If you have a chance, go and take a look at it."

Chris looked up at the squawk box. This time she shook her head.

The children gave her a surprise party in the afternoon. During the preparations, hanging crepe streamers while Mrs. Zajac was away at lunch, Judith said to Jimmy, "Do your math and she'll be happier." Jimmy did some of it.

"Ahhh! You little sneaks! Isn't this nice!" Oh, my, didn't Mrs. Zajac look surprised! How had they managed to keep the party a secret?

Judith eyed her from under lowered brows.

Chris wasn't sure she wanted a vacation. Al came by the room while the class was at gym. "Did they give you a gift, Chris?"

"Yes. They gave me a chocolate bunny and a chocolate Easter egg, and they're going right to my hips."

The children came back shouting. She let them. She merely corrected grammar. *"Mine,* Felipe. Not *mines. Mine."*

Saucy Henrietta from math class poked her

head in the door. "Bye, Miss Ajax."

"You're going to be a week smarter. Right, Henrietta?"

Henrietta nodded deeply.

"Bye, Miss Zajac."

Whose voice was that? There was slender Juanita, her lovely frizzy hair and shapely ears, and her dimples. Was this the first time she'd heard Juanita speak out loud voluntarily?

"Goodbye, Juanita. You have a nice vacation."

She said goodbye to Robert and to Claude. She wished them nice vacations, and hoped that something of Robert's new attitude would survive the week off. There'd still be the last of April and all of May to work on Claude.

The walkers had lined up at the door. She went up to Jimmy and cut him out of the line. Tapping him in the chest while he made his low, monotonic laugh, Chris backed him over to the corner where Miss Hunt used to sit.

"Do you think school's hard, Jimmy?"

"No."

"Jimmy, you don't like it when I call on you in math."

"No."

"Why?"

Jimmy was shy now, rolling his head from side to side and looking at his feet. "Because. It makes me feel stupid."

"But you aren't stupid. You have the answers sometimes. Why do you think Mrs. Zajac calls on you?"

"So I'll pay attention."

"Do you think she cares if you learn?"

"Yeah-uh."

"Do you think that might be another reason why I call on you?"

"Yeah-uh."

"But you're right." She took him by his thin shoulders. She turned him around, pointing him toward the door. She hugged him from behind. "I do call on you partly so you won't fall asleep. Otherwise, I'm afraid you might be snoring."

In her grasp, Jimmy smiled.

Isla del Encanto

Sacred Heart, a church of virtual cathedral size, dominates the once Irish neighborhood of Churchill. Driving to Mass with Billy at the wheel, through the now mostly Puerto Rican part of town, Chris huddled in the passenger seat and tried not to let her mind connect the sights of graffiti and litter with the knots of mostly dark-skinned people on the stoops and corners. She could have switched to a Catholic church in a neighborhood that didn't trouble her, but she refused to quit Sacred Heart and her favorite priests. A church is a church wherever it is, she told herself, and besides, going to one in a Puerto Rican neighborhood did her good. She'd gotten to know some Puerto Ricans while serving on parish committees. Leaving church, she usually felt less troubled, and would tell herself that she had to work harder on correcting her own prejudice.

Plexiglass protected Sacred Heart's huge stained-glass windows and lent the inner air the feeling of a garrisoned sanctuary. Parishioners rarely filled even half the pews. Sounds of Latin music, mostly salsa and merengue, came in from the streets outside during the quiet English Mass. Separate services were held at different hours in English and in Spanish. At the English Mass – as Chris's parish priest, Father Joyce, had observed – people stopped talking when they entered the church, they didn't bring in babies, and they spread out among the pews. Many took seats far from the altar. At the Spanish Mass, people came in talking, continuing the conversations that they'd begun outside. The Hispanic parishioners clustered together in the forward pews. The church always sat hushed after Communion at the English Mass, but voices murmured, babies cried, throughout the Spanish. "People clap their hands, and they're not afraid to sing," said Father Joyce. "There's a real noise level at the Spanish Mass that would drive most people crazy at the English Mass." He added, *"Vive la différence.* But it's hard to find ways to bring the two communities together."

Father Joyce had initiated bilingual services. When Chris went to one herself just before April vacation, the idea seemed to have caught on; a lot of people came, both Puerto Rican and white. Chris, the tireless volunteer, was a lector. She was standing up near the altar when the service started and the priests and acolytes paraded in. The church was very noisy. That surprised her, but not nearly as much as the music. Puerto Ricans played on an electric piano, a guitar, and Puerto Rican *cuatro,* and kept the rhythm on maracas and a set of bongo drums. It sounded to Chris like party music.

All the Puerto Ricans were clapping. So were the marching Irish and French Canadian priests. She didn't know what to do. She realized that she was tapping out the rhythm against her leg with her rolled up program. The music sounded lovely. The beat infected her. Finally she, too, started clapping.

In a former butcher shop half a dozen blocks away, on any Sunday, Judith would sit among a very small congregation, about two-thirds small children, the littlest of them gathered around Judith. One sat on her lap. They would sing a lively tune with Spanish words. Jonah being swallowed by the whale was a favorite. In translation, the song's refrain went: "Because he didn't pay attention to the word of God." Judith's brother-in-law accompanied them on an electric guitar, through a crackling speaker. Up at an old wooden lectern, Judith's father kept time on a *güiro,* a gourd with a serrated surface, which one scratches with a stick. A little girl sitting beside Judith, out in the several rows of folding wooden chairs, played adroitly on a tambourine. Judith, singing loudly, held her hands over the hands of the baby girl on her knees and showed her how to clap.

The main room of Judith's father's church was windowless. The linoleum had peeled away near the door, exposing an older floor of small black and white tiles. Half of the suspended ceiling was missing. Above it was the old ceiling of pressed tin. At the front of the room, Judith's father had erected a plywood platform covered with patches of carpet. *"Escapa por tu Vida,"* read a sign on the back wall. "Escape for your Life." An American flag hung alongside. *"Gloria a Dios!"* cried Judith's father.

The church was one of several that had sprung up in the vicinity of Precious Blood Cathedral, the little storefront sanctuaries clustering around the huge, dying Catholic church. These Pentecostal churches existed back in Puerto Rico, too. Protestant missionaries, as well as North American businessmen, had followed the Marines onto Puerto Rico at the end of the nineteenth century. It had been a Catholic island, and it remained one, but Protestantism secured some ground. The Catholic Church had not provided a great deal of secular help to the island's poor. It had not cultivated a large Puerto Rican priesthood; when the

Church in Puerto Rico had begun to replace the priests from Spain, it had brought in mainly North American clerics. The immigrant Poles, Irish, and French Canadians had all come to Holyoke with their own priests. They had erected their own Catholic churches, where they held services in their native languages, with their own customary music. Puerto Ricans coming to Holyoke from their island, by contrast, could not for many years find a local Mass in Spanish. In fact, for a time, a Puerto Rican couldn't even get a proper funeral locally; the white-owned mortuaries refused them.

Father Joyce guessed that most Puerto Ricans in Holyoke remained "cultural Catholics," by which he meant that the large numbers who went to no church at all still called themselves Catholic. Only a small minority of the Puerto Rican community went to the Pentecostal churches, but this group, Father Joyce thought, had a special, internal strength. One local Latino psychologist wondered if some Pentecostals, like some Jehovah's Witnesses, did not take too strict an approach to child rearing. Maybe, he thought, they were only readying children for rebellion. But Father Joyce observed that Pentecostal families tended to remain intact and to be disciplined in their daily lives. At the very least, the little churches like Judith's father's attempted to deter early, out-of-wedlock pregnancies and addiction to alcohol and to the various drugs that frequently changed hands nearby.

After the song and prayers, the congregation split up for a while. Judith taught Sunday School, usually to six and sometimes to eight small children, in another windowless and smaller room equipped with a scrap of carpet, some metal folding chairs, a rickety table, and an old automobile seat propped against one wall. Judith looked very grown up in black high heels and a gray and white striped dress. She told Bible stories, David and Goliath one week, Cain and Abel another. She had a little blackboard on which, just like Mrs. Zajac, she wrote down the facts she wanted her pupils to remember. She walked back and forth in front of them as she told the stories in Spanish, stopping to interrogate them and laughing over childish replies, also interjecting now and then commands to pay attention. She had one difficult pupil, a skinny little boy with mischievous eyes "My Clarence," she called him. When he acted up, she'd make him stand and, standing behind him herself, would envelop him in her arms. He would grin and stop chattering. She looked like a snake charmer then, arms around the rascal from behind, swaying from side to side, and as she talked, reaching around to inscribe an imaginary mark on the boy's forehead to show the rest what God had done to Cain's.

Judith kept her lessons to about ten minutes. Then they'd sing a song or two, and Judith would get out some scissors and a shoe box of crayon remnants. She'd show them how to make bunnies out of the paper shells designed to hold cupcakes, which she'd bought for pennies at a bakery nearby. She watched as her Clarence fashioned an imitation cigarette – or possibly a joint – instead, and made as if to puff on it. Judith put on a sour face. The young teacher reasoned: "A child's behavior in school comes from what he learns at home. And look what *he* learns at home."

After the midday service, Judith's family would go home. The outer doors at the project had lost their locks and knobs. Anyone who wanted to get in could crook a finger through the hole and pull open the door. This was still arson country, and there were drug addicts around. Judith's parents almost never left her alone in their apartment.

They had a Puerto Rican Sunday dinner: roast pork and beans, yams and plantains, spicy chicken stew, *pastelillos*. The apartment, though small, was tidily kept. Brightly painted plaster fruits and vegetables, which Judith's father had made, hung on the kitchen cupboard doors. Many colorful knickknacks covered the coffee table in the tiny living room, among them a *güiro*, like the one Judith's father played in church, except that this one had been cut in half and its handle had been removed. It was now doing service as a vase.

On a spring Sunday afternoon, done with preaching until evening, when he always held another family service, Judith's father sat in an easy chair, holding the *güiro*-vase while the Red Sox played, unwatched, on TV. The *güiro* is one of the traditional instruments of Puerto Rico, made from the gourds of the calabash tree. Turning it over in his hands, Judith's father gazed fondly at it and chuckled.

There was a gentle, easygoing, old-world quality about him. He had first come to the mainland thirty years ago to work on farms. When he had left Puerto Rico, almost everyone in his village had lived in humble wooden houses — some in houses made of hay, he said. Without rancor he blamed the island's famous first governor, Muñoz Marín, for abandoning agriculture, in order, Judith's father said in Spanish, "to put the island on the road to being rich." His grandfather had a farm of thirty acres back then, much of it in sugar cane, and also many animals. But Judith's father couldn't earn much working there. He could make $50 on the mainland for work that paid only $13 or $14 on the island. So he had come to North

America. He had worked on farms in Florida, Pennsylvania, and New England. A recent car accident had disabled him for heavy work, and he had been forced to live partly on public assistance. He believed that Puerto Rico ought to become a state, which explained the American flag at his altar, but he had never really gotten comfortable with life on the mainland. He could understand English fairly well but spoke little. His older children sometimes teased him, saying, *"Puerto Rico me encanta, y welfare me aguanta"* – "Puerto Rico enchants me, and welfare supports me." The saying was popular locally. It implied that going back to Puerto Rico was not a realistic option for a poor islander.

Judith had been to Puerto Rico once, as a baby, and since then only vicariously, via a Spanish-language newspaper called *El Vocero*, for sale at Papote's *bodega* in the Flats. The tabloid's front page often carried a photograph of a bullet-riddled corpse lying somewhere in Puerto Rico. Imagining red blood from the evidence of black and white news photos, Judith had the inaccurate impression that Puerto Rico was a very violent place. She didn't want to move there. But her father, who knew better, had not given up the idea of going home someday.

After the sumptuous Sunday dinner, Judith's

father rubbed his eyes, and in a drowsy voice, gazing at the *güiro*, he began to reminisce about fishing in a Puerto Rican river at night with lanterns and machetes, about hunting birds with a bow and arrow as a boy in Juncos.

One day after school, Chris stood in the parking lot putting her bags in her car, and heard from behind her mingled shouts and a few shrill cries. She turned. Over on West Street, the northern boundary between the school and a no man's land of vacant lots, she saw a large circle of children. It bulged in one spot, then in another. She knew right away that it was a fight. Chris left her car door ajar and ran toward the children.

She wore a pair of slip-on, flat-heeled shoes, so she had to run stiff-ankled, like the boys with their unlaced sneakers. But she didn't go nearly as fast. She felt like a figure in a dream, making lots of furious motion but little headway. The children saw her coming. The circle broke and the children ran, too, in a more or less concerted mass, down across the vacant lots and to the edge of the dingy red apartment blocks, which marked the beginning of the residential Flats. Down on the corner of Center Street, the circle re-formed and the fight seemed to resume.

Panting, Chris stopped at the edge of the

curb beside West Street. She didn't feel safe going farther. She didn't feel she had any real right to. It is often hard for a teacher to know where her responsibilities should end, but at this moment West Street defined the limits for Chris, both of her authority and knowledge. She stood at the curb, and shading her eyes from the bright sunlight, she peered toward the Flats and the fight that was far away now, down on that corner.

Every now and then in uptown Holyoke, Chris got into an argument that went something like this: Some white acquaintance would say, "Goddamn Puerto Ricans." Chris would answer, "Look, I teach them. There are no more goddamn Puerto Ricans than goddamn anyone else." She'd describe radiant Puerto Rican children, such as Judith and Arabella, and the usual response was: "Yeah, but she's an exception. She's a good one." Chris felt uncomfortable in those arguments.

The ignorance of some of her townspeople appalled her. An angry parent visited Kelly School the first year of desegregation and declared, "Look, they even got the Puerto Rican flag here." In fact, the unfamiliar flag he had spotted was that of the Commonwealth of Massachusetts. Earlier this year a white parent stormed into Al's office complaining that his child was being taught some Spanish. While her own blind spots were not as large, Chris knew that she had some. Out in the city alone, she occasionally felt her mind close. In her car, passing by a group of young Puerto Rican men who stood on a street corner on a spring midafternoon, she felt uneasy, as she did sometimes driving to church. She knew that those men might work night shifts, and that most Puerto Ricans who stand on corners are not looking for trouble — for many, especially ones of agrarian backgrounds, conversation outdoors is infinitely preferable to seeing friends in a cramped living room. But Holyoke was Chris's city. She wasn't a latter-day, out-of-town VISTA volunteer coming down to the Flats to do her part for Democracy. She knew, of course, that a few vandals, and not Puerto Ricans in general, were responsible for the graffiti on buildings and on boarded-up storefronts. But she hated the graffiti and the signs of decay and disorder in neighborhoods that had once seemed safe and well kept. And through a car window it was easy to connect sights like those with Puerto Ricans. Driving through a once familiar neighborhood such as the one where her father grew up, she felt like a stranger in her own home-town. She would have felt uneasy getting out of her car.

Chris was born too late to experience any

disadvantage from being Irish in Holyoke. She couldn't imagine how she might have felt if marked as "a shanty Irish girl" in the Yankee Highlands. Last year, though, on the class field trip, she imagined she got a taste of what it must be like to live in a world of hostile looks. Her class had arrived at an exhibit at the same time as an all-white class from a Boston suburb and some elderly white tourists. The white children from the suburb were rude and noisy. Her kids were very well behaved. But those elderly tourists smiled at the white children, and when her gold-skinned Puerto Rican students asked questions, the tourists recoiled, exchanging heaven-help-us glances. She could read their minds. "Ugh, Puerto Ricans. What are *they* doing here?" Her students didn't notice. Something of that maternal instinct that makes a she-bear dangerous swept over Chris, and for just a moment she was Puerto Rican, too. Oh, she would have liked to scold those bigoted old fools. "Look at these kids from Arlington you look at so fondly. They're terrible, *and* they're lily-white," she imagined herself saying. But the tourists didn't actually say anything overtly insulting, maybe because of the looks she gave them. The experience was new for her. She felt glad afterward to have discovered such angry, righteous feelings in herself.

Chris spent her first years as a teacher in a small uptown neighborhood school. Back then she had taught white children, some poor, some fairly well-to-do, many from working-class families like her own. She could easily imagine those children's lives outside school. She always knew some of their parents. She could look out the huge, old-fashioned windows of her classroom and say to some of her students that she saw their mothers hanging up laundry and might go outside right now and have a word with them if those children didn't shape up. She pined sometimes for that old school. These days, Chris would stand at her classroom window in the afternoon, especially on the afternoons before a vacation, and watching her walkers amble away across the playground, she would think, "I don't even know what I'm sending them back to."

And yet in the intimate setting of her classroom, the facts that half her classes nowadays were of Puerto Rican descent and more than half were poorer than she'd ever been did not seem like insuperable barriers. Unlike white parents, Puerto Rican ones tended to bring their children to the scheduled conferences with Chris, and to bawl out their children or praise them right there on the spot. When Chris entertained Puerto Rican parents in her room, no differences seemed much larger than that. She didn't find it hard to talk to Puerto Rican parents, even if an interpreter was needed. They wanted to know about their children's schoolwork and seemed especially interested to know if their children showed her proper respect. The word *"respeto"* means good manners practiced for their own sake. That was the general meaning Chris had in mind when she talked about respect.

She already knew Felipe's father, Eduardo, slightly. She had taught Felipe's sisters, who were good students. She thought Eduardo and his wife must be marvelous parents. Her first conversation this year with Eduardo, at her classroom door, had not altered her opinion. Eduardo had asked her — Felipe was standing there — how the boy was behaving. Chris had said, "Well, Felipe has his ups and downs." Eduardo had gazed sternly at Felipe, who had bowed his head and watched himself shuffle his feet.

Many teachers thought the Flats too dangerous for a gringo to go walking in, but children, including white children, walked back and forth across it every day to school, and dangerous incidents were very rare. Walking home made Judith and Arabella nervous, but not Felipe. He knew all the nooks and crannies of the Flats.

Felipe liked to gaze at the old brick factories, especially the abandoned hulks down near the river. "I just like the way they look," he said. The back sides of the Flats are an industrial boneyard, a greener, weedy world hidden from the streets and full of disused railroad spurs with rusty tracks to balance on, intricate aqueducts to study, concrete walls and steel contraptions to climb. Felipe recycled them, as it were, into playground equipment. He knew a stream bank under the old South Hadley bridge, where he sometimes found shopping carts and remains of campfires. Felipe called that spot "kind of like an adventure." He had a clubhouse — a pair of discarded clothes lockers lying on their sides behind the karate parlor, alongside one of the canals.

Felipe lived in the renovated northern section of the Flats, in an apartment building that had a clean, functioning elevator, carpeted hallways, fire alarms, and an outer door that locked. His parents didn't have to worry about thieves or addicts loitering in the hallways or the elevator. In the afternoon, women stood talking inside the entry door. They'd smile at Felipe and let him in. In the late afternoons, he did his homework on the kitchen table of his family's apartment — very clean and brightly adorned with red curtains — while his father cooked supper. His mother came home from work a little later. His father sometimes taught him Spanish in the evenings. Pictures of Felipe's Puerto Rican ancestors hung on the walls. There was also a snapshot of the infant Felipe in a baseball uniform, his father kneeling beside him, looking at his son as if enraptured and holding him erect gingerly, as if cradling a frail bird. In Felipe's household, as in the one where Chris grew up, youthful ambition was honored. Recently, a few days after his hamster Ralph died, Felipe awoke to find a new one in the cage and a note lying on the table, which read, "My name is Ralphie. Please take good care of me, and when you are an astronaut, I will help you in space."

"I think my father wrote it," said Felipe with a crafty smile.

Before heading home, Felipe almost always said goodbye to Mrs. Zajac, even if he felt angry with her – and Chris realized that his parents had taken pains with his manners. On his way home, Felipe stopped at the drugstore on Center Street and bought two copies of the *Transcript-Telegram,* one for his father and the other for an elderly lady in his building. He stopped, that is, if he had remembered to bring his two quarters to school. If he had forgotten the quarters, he went home, got the money, and returned to the drugstore. More often than not, he had to make the two trips, but he liked doing it. In his mind, going back to the drug-store became a journey. He cast himself in the role of his father as a boy, climbing the hillside to the family farm in Puerto Rico. He had gone there only once, as a baby, riding on his father's shoulders, and he did not actually remember the place. But he imagined it, as he imagined castles in the burnt-out hulks of factories. "My father says he used to walk six miles to school and back," Felipe said. "And he used to get water. He used to get water after school. And it kind of reminds me of getting the newspaper."

Felipe's father, Eduardo, had returned several times to his ancestral farm since it had been abandoned. On winter nights Eduardo would lie on his couch in the apartment in the Flats reading the *Transcript-Telegram*, and sometimes he would drift off and return to the farm in his memory.

It would be February, the orange *maga* in bloom. The two-faced leaves of the *yagrumo*, green on one side and whitish on the other — Puerto Ricans sometimes call hypocrites *yagrumos* — would be fluttering in the warm breezes. In his mind, Eduardo would be back in the outskirts of Cayey, in the gorgeous Cordillera Central, climbing on foot up to the farm. The way to it led up a dirt road, past a huge rock where, Eduardo had grown up believing, a lady, a *fantasma*, would sometimes appear,

356

holding out a cup of coffee. He never saw the ghost himself, but as a boy he always used to *run* past that rock. The road turned into a dirt path and then into the memory of one, choked by bamboo and ferns, out of which butterflies floated. The overgrown path went up past banana trees, mango trees with orchids in the crooks of their branches, orange trees, the *ortiga* that made the skin itch, *tamarindo*, eucalyptus, coffee, and royal palm trees, the *palma de yaguas* – its broad, scoop-like fronds had been Eduardo's tropical sleds for sliding down the hillsides.

On a patch of level ground stood the farmhouse itself, empty, still owned by the family, and still straight and square, but half engulfed by banana trees and ferns and rotting at its footings. The farmhouse was made of wood and was therefore, in Puerto Rican parlance, *una casa humilde*, houses of concrete being much preferred on the island. Eduardo's father, Felipe's grandfather, had built it himself, in large part out of nearby trees – a small, one-story house on stilts, about the size of a two-car garage. The family had cooked, with charcoal that they made themselves, on a *fogón* – a wooden table with stones inlaid on its surface, which was still intact. Eduardo's mother and father had lived in the farmhouse until the early 1970s. Modern times had never really

357

touched that place.

When Eduardo remembered the farm, he remembered his father – a proud man with green eyes, which his children would not dare to look at when he was angry. One of Eduardo's sisters ran off with a boy. Eduardo recalled the evening when her transgression was discovered. His father picked up a set of tableware – a plate, a knife, a fork, a spoon – and threw them one by one out the door, saying, when his wife asked him why he did that, "We don't need these anymore." That sister never entered the farmhouse again. When she encountered her father in the city, she would say, *"Bendicion"* ("Bless me," the request that dutiful Puerto Rican children make of their parents and that dutiful sisters also make of their older brothers). Eduardo's father would answer, in Spanish, "May God bless you," and walk on. Otherwise, he never talked to her again until, when the old man was very ill and Eduardo's mother had died, the wayward and long-repentant sister took him into her own house and nursed him. Even then, she didn't think her father forgave her. *"Pero no me quería* – "But he didn't love me" – she kept saying as she told the story. At the funeral, she said to Eduardo with deep admiration, "But he was tough, wasn't he? Oh, he was tough!"

Eduardo shared her admiration. His father

was a true *jíbaro,* one of the last of a line of thoroughly self-sufficient islanders, who had lived by a strict, old-fashioned code. Eduardo claimed the title, too, but he was a *jíbaro* only by birth and not by practice anymore. It wasn't easy, for a Puerto Rican of Eduardo's generation and experience, straddling not just two cultures but something like two different centuries, to figure out exactly who he was.

According to the only full-fledged history of Holyoke, early Irish immigrants, fleeing the horrors of potato famines, brought pieces of Irish sod with them as keepsakes. In Chris's family, legend did not reach that far back. (The only vestige was a story Chris's mother told about one of her own grandmothers: someone told Chris's great-grandmother that she looked like Queen Victoria, and with some heat the elderly woman said, "Don't *ever* say I look like *her.")* But Chris had read a little about the Irish immigration. She knew firsthand about homesickness. Immigration for her ancestors, she thought, must have resembled migration for Puerto Ricans.

In the quarter century following World War II, about 750,000 Puerto Ricans, nearly one-third of the population, left the island for the mainland, the majority going to New York City but enough to other places for the emigration to rank as a diaspora. The U.S. Marines had taken the island from Spain in 1898. They secured the ground for American corporations. The American-style colonization that supplanted the Spanish had everything to do with Puerto Ricans leaving home. The United States transformed the island, not exactly into an image of itself but, it seems fair to say, into a servant of mainland interests. American rule brought a declining death rate but also, in the long run, the sort of selective, capital-intensive development that destroyed small farming, to name just one important sector of the old economy. The population began to soar, and so did unemployment rates.

After World War II, both the federal and Puerto Rican governments encouraged people to leave the island. Chris's teacher friend Victor Guevara remembered jeeps with loudspeakers that advertised jobs on the mainland driving down the streets of his little coastal hometown when he was a boy. Of course, the advertisements didn't say that many islanders who followed the call would end up working for the minimum wage and living in tenements in places that have winters. For mainland employers, especially in agriculture and in the hotel and garment industries, Puerto Rico became a source of inexpensive, unorganized laborers, the more powerless because they were in a strange place and didn't speak the language. And the Puerto Rican government was only too glad to see depart a class of citizens who might otherwise have drained the island's resources and stirred things up politically.

A Puerto Rican who lived near Chris in Holyoke explained the migration to her this way: "We shoved out the people least equipped to deal with the hardships of immigration." Accounts of the Puerto Rican diaspora maintain that most emigrants were poor, had little schooling, and had not been trained for industrial jobs that paid decent wages.

At times of high unemployment on the mainland, significant numbers of Puerto Ricans have, at least in the past, gone back to the island. In Puerto Rico, poverty has not traditionally been regarded as a sin. The island doesn't suffer from a racism anywhere near as widespread or virulent as the mainland's. Emigration is easily reversible, because of numerous and inexpensive airplane flights to and from San Juan and because Puerto Ricans are U.S. citizens. Going back, however, doesn't look realistic or inviting to many of the children and grandchildren of immigrants.

Holyoke's first five Puerto Rican families came to town in 1958. The men had contracts to work on Connecticut River Valley tobacco farms. They lived together in the Flats. A fellow parishioner and friend of Chris's was a member of that tiny incipient community. She remembered her first years in Holyoke as very hard, at least as hard as Florida had been for Chris, but unlike Chris's short exile, hers was enduring. "It's awful when you come to a place for the first time," Chris's friend said. "For a week I was crying. 'Take me home.' I still find I'm not welcome here. You never feel like you're at home. Even people from South America, they can't understand our culture. It's something that you miss so much. People look at you and make a judgment about you. It's something you always have to fight and always have to lock inside you. And the children lose their identity. They don't know they're Puerto Rican, and they don't feel American."

Those first five families had each other, at least. Felipe's father, Eduardo, when he finally decided to emigrate for good, was essentially alone. Traveling with his father to the Connecticut River Valley at the age of fourteen, Eduardo entered a mainland school in the old mill town of Westfield, not far from Holyoke. Bilingual programs didn't exist then, so Eduardo learned his English by the method now formally known as "immersion." That is, he had to teach himself. The first English word he learned was "hi." He remembered trying it out on a girl in a school hallway. She said "hi" back to him. "I was so happy. It worked!" He stayed behind with relatives when his family went back to Puerto Rico. At sixteen, he doctored his birth certificate and got a job in a bicycle factory in Westfield. Not long after that, Eduardo got laid off and went back to the island. On that return trip, he felt as if he saw his homeland clearly for the first time, both its splendor and the ironic fact that most of the people with the money to enjoy it were not Puerto Ricans. "I lived in a paradise, and it didn't mean anything to me," Eduardo said. "I went and lived in Westfield and came back, and I thought, 'How come these gringos have this, and I can't?' " When word came that he could have his job in Westfield back, he left home again. He did not imagine he was leaving the island forever.

Jíbaros tell jokes that they would not like to hear from other mouths. One of Eduardo's favorites, a Puerto Rican version of a classic immigrant joke, went like this: A *jíbaro* has heard that in New York City there is so much money that you find it lying on the ground everywhere, and you have to kick it out of your way. Sure enough, when he arrives at Kennedy Airport, at the Eastern Airlines terminal, this farmer of the hills sees a fifty-dollar bill lying on the ground right in front of him. "Already you're starting to bother me," he says. "Get out of my way." He kicks that fifty-dollar bill aside. "I got plenty of time for you." At the punch line, Eduardo would laugh and say, "He never sees a fifty-dollar bill again!"

Realism came to the *jíibaro* Eduardo on a lonesome New Year's Eve when he was in his early twenties and living alone in a small apartment above a hardware store in Westfield. He had some money in his pocket and no place to spend it. He was hungry, but he didn't have a car, and there wasn't an open restaurant or even a grocery store within walking distance. He stared out the window of his room at the snow in grimy piles on the street outside, and he thought of his father's farm and of the green bananas in the trees. If only he could have one now! "What am I doing here?" he asked himself then. "Why not go back to the island?" He remembered a period that followed, during which he asked himself again and again, "Who am I? I know this body. But who is Eduardo?" Immigrants, even such a hardy one as Eduardo, have to ask themselves questions that children ask. He told himself repeatedly, "You got to be realistic. If you want to dream, okay. If it comes true, it comes true. Beautiful. But tomorrow you got to go to work. That's reality."

He worked, and finished high school on the side. He picked tobacco. He learned to be a machinist, and, unhappy with the policies of his union local, he put himself up for president and won. He also worked as a disc jockey on a Spanish-language station in Hartford. Along the way, at a softball game in Chicopee, he met a lovely countrywoman who, as it happened, came from Cayey, too — he'd had to come to Massachusetts to meet her. He had settled down to raise a family.

The Puerto Rican community of the Flats was not, of course, a monolith. Eduardo divided the Puerto Ricans he knew into several groups. These days far fewer newcomers arrived directly from the island, but there were still a substantial number of people he called "old-fashioned," who didn't want to speak English and held tightly to old island customs and traditions. Some cosmopolitans — he counted himself one of those — spoke both languages and traveled in both worlds and might even eat in a fast food restaurant now and then. "And," he said, "there are a few rotten potatoes, who are involved with drugs and will rob your apartment and break into your car." He liked to point out, though, that he never locked his car in the Flats and had never yet been robbed.

Finally, there were the children. "They are going to be doctors and lawyers," he said. The high school dropout rate among Puerto Rican children was alarmingly high, but his own children did well in school. They would go to college, he hoped.

Speaking of the children and of the Puerto Rican community of Holyoke in general, Eduardo said, "We are here to stay." He guessed that statement applied to him, although he still dreamed of retiring to the island.

At home in Holyoke, Eduardo might say mockingly and affectionately to his wife, if she was acting shy, "Oh, you *jíbara*." But on the surface, anyway, there was no shy farmboy left in *him*. He had a ready smile, like Felipe, and he was quick and easy making friends. He had Puerto Rican friends, South American friends, white and black North American friends, and though he had no interest in being a boss of any sort and mainly kept company with working men, he could travel easily in most of the worlds of balkanized Holyoke, including that of the country club — he was a marvelous, mainly self-taught golfer. He could wear an oxford shirt and necktie and speak the local language, in every sense, and never act obsequious or look as though he felt out of place. And yet this upwardly mobile and versatile traveler — skilled in all ways of contending — still had some *jíibaro* in him. He had a good job, and so did his wife. He could afford to live elsewhere. He *chose* to live in the Flats. When puzzled friends asked him why, he said, "I want to know what's going on with my people." He could afford a telephone, of course, but he thought phones were a nuisance. It bothered him that his hometown in Puerto Rico seemed more Americanized each time he visited – in shorthand he'd explain that his hometown in Puerto Rico had *two* Burger Kings now, whereas Holyoke had only one. He thought the island ought to gain political independence, and he had no use for *independentistas* who took welfare. "Puerto Ricans between thirty and forty, we like to be Puerto Ricans when it's convenient for us," he once said to some North American friends. "I feel I am a Puerto Rican American, and I feel, really, I am an American. You people took me over. *You* made me American, not me." He didn't always hold his tongue when, for instance, white acquaintances told him they'd just met a nice Puerto Rican. "How come you act so surprised? You never met one before?" he'd say. But he had swallowed his share of dirty looks and slurs while learning how to get along on the mainland.

Old injuries welled up. Sometimes when he thought he could hear white people thinking, "Goddamn Puerto Rican, what's he doing here?" Eduardo would go back in his mind to his boyhood in Cayey, and tell himself those people knew nothing about him at all. Lying on his sofa, putting the *Transcript-Telegram* aside to climb in his mind back to the old farm, he'd feel his eyes getting misty. He'd remember the taste of the green bananas and of the oranges in his father's groves — he'd never found an orange anywhere as sweet as those. But even at those moments he would recall that it is possible to feel homesick for two places. He'd remember how on short trips back to the island, a few days would go by and he would find himself thinking, "It might be nice to see a little snow."

2

Just before April vacation, another child had left Chris's class for parts unknown. His name was Alejandro. He had come into her room at midyear from Victor's bilingual class, the only boy "mainstreamed" from that room so far. Mary Ann had arranged for Chris to get Alejandro. He was a gift — small and black-haired and glittering, with a movie star's clarity about his looks, and on top of that, very bright and very interested. Alejandro had just begun to get command of English. Unlike most of the children, he actually seemed to enjoy the basal reader's workbooks. He liked any chance to strut his stuff. Chris often found excuses to put Alejandro in bear hugs.

But his father was taking him back to live in Puerto Rico. Alejandro said he felt scared. "Changing schools, that's the worst thing for me. You know the first day, when you go to school and they always stare at you? You don't know nobody, and when you go outside, there's nobody to play wit' you. That's the worst thing, the feeling you have. You all hot inside, and everybody lookin' at you like who's that new kid, I never seen him before." He couldn't do his homework lately, Alejandro said. "I *want* to do it, but something happens to me. I get dizzy, and I fall asleep."

Chris thought, "I never experienced that myself: I always lived in the same place." She got Victor to try to talk the father into letting Alejandro finish the year with her, but the boy's father said they had to leave town. She spent a long time bucking up Alejandro on the days before he left. On his last day she kissed him goodbye and told him he'd do fine. She thought he probably would; he had so many gifts. But when she wondered what it meant for a child to be transplanted to Puerto Rico, she couldn't conjure up any pictures at all.

Now she was going there herself. Now, she thought, she'd have *some* idea.

A year ago, a Holyoke teacher named Efrain Martinez had arranged a tour of his native island for other teachers over April vacation.

Efrain had figured that many of the faculty would want to go, since nearly half their students these days were Puerto Rican. The school department had given its blessing; the superintendent of schools had gone on the first trip. But teachers had to pay their own way, and the ones who had the most to learn didn't want to. Several white colleagues had told Efrain to his face, "I wouldn't go to Puerto Rico if you paid *me*."

An islander who emigrates from an outpost of empire to its mainland stands an excellent chance of being far less insular than many mainlanders. From an early age, Efrain had immersed himself in the art and history both of Puerto Rico and the world. He had come to Massachusetts for graduate school and had settled in Holyoke. He had landed, it didn't take him long to discover, in one of a parochial nation's bastions of parochialism. The sort of Holyoker who wanted to speak respectfully of Efrain's origins, he noticed, would refer to him as Hispanic. The sort who wanted to insult him called him Puerto Rican. He found that a social studies text in use in the city's schools designated Jamestown as the first settlement in the new world, and he wondered, "What happened to St. Augustine? What happened to California? What happened to San Juan?"

Efrain didn't get paid for his arduous work as

a tour guide. Local ignorance, more than an islander's pride, caused Efrain to launch his one-man campaign to edify the educators of Holyoke. This year not enough teachers signed up for the tour, and Holyokers mainly interested in a vacation, including a number of Puerto Ricans, filled the vacancies. Among others on the tour were the assistant superintendent (a native Holyoker of Irish descent who spoke fluent Spanish), several teachers, and the Zajacs — Chris, Billy, and their son. Kate stayed behind with Chris's mother.

The bus had just dropped the group at their hotel in San Juan, in the tourist quarter, when Chris said to Billy, "It's nice, but I couldn't live here." She felt silly saying that, as if Billy might decide to move to Puerto Rico, but the need for reassurance doesn't follow logic.

Billy laughed. "That's because you couldn't live anywhere but Holyoke."

"Well, maybe when all our friends and relatives are dead," Chris said, still feeling a little silly but comforted.

The next morning, on the way to Easter Mass, Chris told the Puerto Rican taxi driver that she came from a place where a lot of Puerto Ricans had settled. The driver said, "People go there to be on welfare. They don't want to work," and for a moment she felt as if she really were at home. But the heat, the tropical breezes, the palm trees, the musty smell in the hotel room, all made her feel too far from home. She missed her daughter. She kept comparing what she saw to things back home, as tourists do and immigrants must. She had a hard time relaxing. The second day, during the tour of old San Juan, inside the second oldest church in the western hemisphere, Chris separated herself briefly from the company and, kneeling in a pew, prayed that everyone get safely through this trip and that they have a safe flight home. After that, she felt readier to enjoy the holiday.

Efrain was the sort of tour guide who makes it easy to learn something. The story of the island's colonization reminded Chris of her unit on the American Revolution. "I think they should have a San Juan Tea Party." She felt worn out from the last weeks of school, and she skipped the trip to the city of Ponce. But San Juan was too hot for snoozing, and a lot of the American tourists around the hotel pool spoke rudely to the Puerto Rican waiters, so she felt uncomfortable hanging around there. "I've got to get out of my little cocoon," she kept saying to herself.

They took a trip around the island. At a seaside restaurant on a cliff, looking out the window at the rolling blue Atlantic, Chris said,

"Thank God." She'd begun to think she didn't like Puerto Rico, because she didn't really care for what she'd seen of hot San Juan. They stopped in Cayey to visit some of Felipe's relatives. The conversation didn't go beyond pleasantries, but just to be behind the private walls of another culture, in a living room as neat and cozy as her own, felt like enlightenment.

The best part of the trip for Chris was the visit to the mountain town of Comerío. Efrain had gotten the island's school authorities to provide the transportation. A school bus picked up the group at the hotel in San Juan. The bus bounced along into the mountains, Chris, sunglasses perched in her hair, bobbing in her seat like a posting horseback rider. "No wonder my kids are bouncing off the walls when they come in to me."

An official from the Puerto Rican Department of Instruction was on board. He identified himself as a "curriculum advisor." ("Oh," thought Chris, "a coffee-drinking job.") She changed seats so she could talk to the official. Maybe he could tell her something about the fate of Alejandro, which was, in a way, what she'd come here to find out. She told the official about the handsome little boy. "What will happen to him?" she asked.

The official said that Alejandro's new classmates might shun him for a while, but would probably accept him once he had his Spanish back. Returning Puerto Rican children created problems, the official said. Many needed bilingual programs in reverse, to relearn Spanish. Some were known as *calientes* – "hot ones" – and posed the threat of infecting classmates with mainland ways. Other children teased repatriated kids sometimes, calling them "*newyorquinos*" and "*newyorricans.*" Chris looked off into the middle distance. Poor Alejandro. But anyway, she told herself, the girls would like him.

About a dozen people rode on the bus into the mountains. Hundreds welcomed them when they arrived in Comerío. The town describes itself accurately as *montaña en flor* – "mountain in bloom." Banners hung across the streets around Comerío's village square: WELCOME TO TEACHERS FROM HOLYOKE. The place amazed Chris. Craning her neck at the bus window, she saw green hillsides rising at impossible-looking angles on all sides above the buildings of the town. From the windows and doorways around the square many curious faces peered at the bus. A throng of citizens stood in the shade in a corner of the square. A grade school band in red uniforms struck up the Marine Corps hymn, hitting many sour notes on the way from Montezuma. (Was some gentle

374

irony intended in the choice of music?) "This is their first semester, and they are learning," explained one of the speakers. There were many speakers. Too many for Chris.

The dignitaries, the uniformed chiefs of police and the fire department among them, sat out in the square in a row of folding chairs, removing their hats now and then to mop their brows. Another row of folding chairs, also in the blazing mountain sunshine, awaited the honored guests. The local priest, a local school principal, Comerío's mayor, and Holyoke's assistant superintendent, Tim Barrett (who had brought gifts of T-shirts that said, "Holyoke, Birthplace of Volleyball"), all took turns at the podium. Chris sat in the sun, listening. Her face started growing ruddy at once. She could feel it — instant sunburn.

Politicians everywhere like to talk, Chris thought. That one now returning to the microphone for a second time, for instance — he had many counterparts in Holyoke. Each speaker, when finished, headed for the shade, Chris noticed. She looked around. Most of the other honored guests had fled for the shade, too. Only she and another Holyoke teacher remained out in the sun. She would not get up and follow the others. The comerieños might think her a rude gringo if she did. She would see this through, even though most of the speeches were in Spanish.

Later, Chris asked Tim Barrett to translate. Tim said the mayor had spoken yearningly of the prospect of a highway that would bring new jobs to Comerío and with them perhaps an end to the shuttling of children between Comerío and Holyoke. That was a good speech, Chris thought.

The day's schedule had already slipped, and now their hosts debated a new change in plans. Why didn't they hurry up? She'd like to see the schools. Nobody around here seemed to keep schedules. "Me and my precious schedules," she thought. "I've got to lighten up. Chill out, Mrs. Zajac, as my kids say." Finally, back on the bus. The road was narrow, twisty, winding upward. The driver honked at every turn. Chris clutched the handrail on the seat in front of her. "I'm glad I went to church on Easter Sunday." At last they arrived at an elementary school, a collection of red and yellow barracks-like buildings up on a breezy, lofty mountain-top. Evidently, the wealthier *comerieños* lived up here. "It's just like Holyoke," said Billy to Chris. "The higher the ground, the more money."

The school was in recess. Again, banners hung everywhere: WELCOME TO OUR SCHOOL. DISTINGUISHED GUESTS, WE FEEL HONORED. PEOPLE FROM HOLYOKE, WELCOME. Chris checked out the playground first. Standing in grass near a swing set, she gazed out across the peaks of the Cordillera Central, every imaginable hue of green before her, the colors shifting with the fluttering of two-sided *yagrumo* leaves across the peaks and valleys, and a brisk wind in her face. "Mr. Barrett," she said to the assistant superintendent, "can we do something about improving the view from the Kelly School playground?"

Tim Barrett gazed out at the shimmering mountains, too. "We'll need some earth-moving equipment."

Now, for the first extended period of the trip, Chris felt fully at ease She had her son in tow, and a crowd of uniformed schoolchildren followed them around, staring openmouthed at their small North American counterpart. One little girl, who kept following them, caught Chris's eye. The child had freckles and flaming red hair. Chris waylaid Efrain and asked for an explanation. He said that slaves had been clustered near the coasts and that lighter-skinned Spanish coffee growers had gone into the mountains. "So it's not uncommon to see redheads here. But," Efrain added, "we come in all shades and sizes."

Many children asked Chris for autographs. A blond-haired girl pursued her ardently, and in just the same easygoing style she employed for

Friday chats up at her desk, Chris questioned her. The girl had grown up in Miami. She told Chris that when she'd come to Comerío, she hadn't known Spanish and had been kept back a year. "I had a boy like that," Chris said to her. "I'm afraid that's going to happen to him." She lowered her head a little, to get her eyes close to the girl's. "But that doesn't mean you're not smart." The usual pep talk ensued.

Chris ambled around, visiting classrooms. The first-grade teacher wrapped her arms around Chris's son from behind and introduced him to her class, and Chris decided right away that this teacher passed her test — Chris would feel comfortable having her son in this classroom.

"Think they have Judy Blume?" said Chris, exploring the library. "Oh, look. Laura Ingalls Wilder. Here's *David Copperfield.* By *Carlos* Dickens." Chris chuckled to herself. Many little faces peered in through the library's louvered windows. Chris peered back at them and, smiling, said, "Hello. What are your names?"

The fifth-grade teacher wasn't in his room. "I can tell it's a man," said Chris, looking in the door. "There isn't very much junk on the walls." She stepped inside the classroom.

For a moment, it seemed as if Mrs. Zajac would take over and start a lesson. The children were all hooting and hollering. She eyed them with a knowing and slightly sardonic smile, then lifted her voice above the babble. She asked them what they were studying. Although they evidently didn't understand her question, they did understand her voice, and they quieted down directly.

The Science Fair

You're wearin' jeans!" said Jimmy to Mrs. Zajac.

"And Reeboks!" said Arnie.

"Even old ladies wear Reeboks," said Chris.

"You're wearin' jeans," said Jimmy again.

"You're not the same," said Arnie.

"I am the same."

"You look about twenty," said Arnie.

"I am about twenty," said Chris.

Her Puerto Rican sunburn had faded. It was a morning in early May. She smiled as she led her class down the hall. But when she got near the office, Chris frowned. Robert's mother was standing there talking to Al. Chris moved on briskly, averting her eyes. She would deal with Robert again tomorrow. Robert wasn't going on the class trip to Old Sturbridge Village. Al had said he couldn't − Robert had been misbehaving again, and besides, he hadn't brought back the permission slip. Chris wasn't entirely sorry. She wasn't going to have to raise her voice once today, not even in her thoughts.

The class, in shirtsleeves, walked out into sunshine. A couple of the girls skipped. They climbed into their bus. Chris spied and eavesdropped on the children for a while. Jimmy took a seat by himself and promptly fell asleep. She peeked around her seat at him, she smiled, and she left him alone. The boys sat in the back, of course, except for Felipe, who sat among the girls. Felipe, she thought, would not lack for girlfriends in junior high. She listened, smiling, as several of the children made the astonishing discovery that there were faces of other children from Kelly School in the windows of another bus. Someone made a crack about Claude and fishing, and Judith dealt with that. "It's America," Judith said loudly. "You're allowed to be whatever you want to be."

Felipe spotted a McDonald's and cried out, "Take us there! It's better than the school food!"

"Manure is better than the school's food," said Judith's voice.

Chris heard Judith say to Arabella, "My mother gave me the *tenth* degree. Don't talk to any strangers and stay with the teacher and if you can prevent it, don't go in any bathrooms."

Chris had a cozy feeling about Judith's future these days. Obviously, Judith's parents had done well by her. Chris thought of how hot the

Flats would be in another month or so. She wished she had it in her power to move Judith's family out of there. Anyway, Chris was moving her class out of there for today. The bus was peaceful, the children in a holiday mood. Back in the room, the boys rarely gave her a chance to spend much time with her girls. She got up and sat down across the aisle from Judith and Arabella. Mariposa and Judith sang jump rope songs for Chris most of the rest of the way.

At the orientation, the guide explained to all of the fifth-grade classes that in a moment they would walk out into Sturbridge Village and travel back to the year 1830. "We're English," the guide said, to get them in the spirit. Chris remembered vividly her own fifth-grade trip here, and how transported she'd felt. The guide released them. Chris gathered her class around her outside, at the edge of the bridge into the village, and reminded them that they had already studied this era. Now they would see it come to life. They should stick close to her, she added.

Claude looked up at Chris and declared, "I'm with you ninety-five percent of the way!"

Claude looked earnest. Had he just misspoken, or did he mean that? Chris looked down at him. Then she took him by the hand. For most of the expedition, Claude ambled happily along holding hands with Mrs. Zajac.

Woods surrounded them, inviting groves with orangey, pine-needled, fragrant forest floor. They strolled down neatly bordered paths in the shade of tall white pines and soon found themselves beside a lovely village green, all set about with maple trees. Sturbridge Village is a village that never was. Buildings of the 1830s were reconstructed here in a forest in central Massachusetts. How lovely the buildings looked now, reconstituted straight and square, in coats of white paint that would never grow old and peel. The Towne house, a white federalist mansion that once belonged to a successful New England merchant of Charlton, Massachusetts, sits at one end of the green. At the other, on a little rise, the tall, porticoed Center Meetinghouse, a Baptist church in its former life, presides over the town common.

The village gleamed in spring sunshine. The hardwoods were in leaf, the flowers blooming in the gardens behind white picket fences. People in period costume, the living mannequins of the village, passed by Mrs. Zajac's class. A young man in a straw hat and breeches with suspenders walked along an edge of the common beside a pair of perfect oxen, groomed as if they were racehorses. Young women walked by in long dresses and white bonnets. Judith gazed after them. She looked down at the wool tights she wore under her skirt — the nearest thing to pants she was allowed to wear, being a proper Pentecostal daughter – and, laughing, Judith said, "I got these at K Mart." All the children were smiling, chattering happily. Mrs. Zajac was smiling. At the tinsmith's shop, Felipe just had to touch some of the authentic items on display, in order to make them real. Alice told him, in a whisper, that he wasn't supposed to touch. Felipe yelled out, "She's always yellin' at me!" And Chris turned back, still holding Claude's hand, and said, "Okay. No grouches."

They stopped in at the handsome little Greek Revival Thompson Bank, and the elderly guide in his banker's frock coat talked to them about old currency and commerce. Dick asked hopefully, "Did they have bank robbers?" Chris took them on a short detour to the bakehouse, where they got tollhouse cookies, the treat that she remembered best from her own schooldays. A few of the children had no money. Chris got out her purse so that everyone could have a chocolate chip cookie. She gave in to their request that they stop at the souvenir and candy store, and she regretted it a little. Ashley bought a bag of candy that must have weighed a pound. Chris told the chubby girl please not to eat it now, but the next time Chris looked, Ashley had devoured it.

Chris kept an eye on Ashley during a lot of

that springtime ramble through the model village. The girl troubled her. Ashley hung back when the others crowded up to the edge of an exhibit. She wore a pair of dowdy brown double-knit stretch pants, clothes that had long since fallen out of fashion among her peers, who preferred blue jeans. In her mind, Chris fumed at Ashley's mother: "What does it cost to buy her a pair of jeans?" (Chris had not quite realized her special objective of the fall. She had now managed to meet every child's parent, except Ashley's. She had tried. She'd asked Ashley to tell her mother it was very important that she come to the last parent conference. The next day, Ashley had sidled up to Chris's desk and said, "My mother may not be able to come. She says it depends on what kind of day it is, or whether she has something else to do.")

The class filed into the reconstructed one-room District Schoolhouse, where a young and rather nervous-looking woman was playing teacher. The school had wooden desks with inkwells but otherwise looked familiar. The class sat down. Felipe, wondering just how much the past resembled the present, shouted a question at the young play-teacher: "Do you put anybody outside if they're bad?"

"I might," said the scowling young woman. "Or I might try to embarrass you. Or I might bring you up here and make you hold logs for a while."

Victor had arrived at the schoolhouse with his class at the same time. "I'll have to try that," he whispered to Chris.

"And I might use this," said the teacher, holding up a short rod, an authentic ferrule, "on your hand or your bottom."

"Where can I get one?" whispered Victor to Chris.

"Anybody ever take you to court for hitting a kid?" called Felipe to the teacher.

The class crowded up to the edge of the visitors gallery inside the potter's shop. Their eyes grew wide, their mouths hung open, as they watched a pot emerge from a spinning lump of clay under the hands of the neatly costumed potter. "That's *fresh!*" said many voices.

The academic objective of this expedition was, of course, to have the class glimpse a time that seemed primitive compared to their own. But no nineteenth-century village could ever have looked so thoroughly kempt, serene, and civilized as this one. The mud and blood of everyday life were not displayed. In Sturbridge Village on that sunny day, the past looked like a vast improvement on the present that most of the class came from. Then again, even a more accurately harsh version of this village might have looked like an improvement.

Judith and Arabella, the class's two most religious girls, stuck close to each other. They held hands now and then. They walked together down the tidy paths, across the covered bridge, which was fragrant with the smell of old wood, past the wonderfully costumed guides. They stopped to listen to the birds singing in the trees. The village inspired the two girls. Arabella, who lived in the mostly rebuilt section of the Flats, remarked, "I'd like to leave Holyoke. People walk around with big radios, and they're always yelling."

"I'd like to leave, too," said Judith. Both girls' voices were happy. "But the radios don't bother me."

The class circled back, walking beside the mill pond. Claude stopped to gaze into the waters, wishing he had brought his fishing gear. Chris took him by the hand again. Their last stop was the Freeman Farm, a little farmhouse painted brick-red, with a gambrel roof of cedar shakes. They poked around inside awhile, then came to rest outside, a band of now weary travelers on a dreamy springtime afternoon. They clustered around Chris beside a split rail fence, Mrs. Zajac and her class gazing out on a patch of plowed ground. All around they saw neatly fenced-in pastures, cultivated fields and hayfields, and beyond, horizons of tall trees.

Sounds of traffic from the Massachusetts Turnpike drifted through the woods. A rooster crowed from the barnyard.

"Where the horses are?" Pedro asked Chris.

Judith stood beside Chris at the fence. Judith, from a family of Puerto Rican farmers who had lost their land, gestured at the field before them, its new corn crop sprouting. "My father would love this," she said to Chris.

Time to go back, and Chris calling loudly from the front of the bus, "I want to congratulate my class. You behaved very well." Chris ambled down the aisle and sat on an armrest among the girls. They sang while the boys snickered and listened intently. The girls broke into "Miss Suzie":

> ". . . And broke her little —
> Ask me no more questions . . ."

Hysterical laughter.

> ". . . The boys are in the bathroom
> Zipping up their —
> Flies are in the meadow . . ."

"Let's sing it again!" said Kimberly.

Chris rolled her eyes and tapped her own breastbone. "*I* know that one. That's as old as I am. Wait a minute. Wait a minute." She sang, on key and sweetly, to the tune of "Molly Malone":

> "In Holyoke's fair city,
> Where girls are so pretty . . ."

Other girls gathered. "Want to sing, Ashley? Want to sing, Courtney?" asked Chris. She said, "When I was in grade school, my friends and I used to have a song we'd sing and kick our legs out." Looking at Judith, Chris added, "I grew up in a part of Holyoke called the Highlands." Then Chris sang:

> "We are the Highlands girls.
> We wear our hair in curls.
> We smoke our sisters' butts.
> We drive our mothers nuts."

And Judith and Mariposa sang more jump rope songs for Mrs. Zajac, including some in Spanish:

> *"Tu madre, tu padre*
> *Viven en la calle*
> *De San Valentine . . ."*

The girls sang:

"Shake it, shake it, shake it,
Shake it all you can,
So all the boys around the block
Can see your underwear."

Courtney did the shimmy in the aisle to this tune, her blue eyes looking old and sad. Chris watched her and felt a little sad, and worried, too. They sang for Mrs. Zajac, who shook her head, a satire of a TV ad that was going around Holyoke:

"Come back to Jamaica,
We'll hijack your plane,
We'll steal all your money,
And feed you cocaine."

The class re-entered Holyoke on the Willi-mansett Bridge. By the time they got there, the bus had quieted. Chris and most of the children gazed out the windows. The old bridge, made of steel and painted green, looks as if it were constructed from a grown-up version of an Erector set. To the right is a dark railroad bridge and the tail of a rapids below. Down to the left the brown river grows lazier. It flows south beside brick mills, between muddy banks. A couple of discarded fuel tanks, half rotted now, sat in the shallows. On the far river bank, on the Holyoke side, garbage decorated the few trees.

Up ahead loomed the vast complex of brick mill buildings where Chris's father spent most of his working life. Chris used to pick him up here, when she was in high school and her father had lent her the car. The sooty bricks of industrial Holyoke seemed to stain the air on that sunny afternoon. There was litter on the river banks, litter in the weeds entwined in the metal fences along the roadway, litter down side streets and in vacant lots.

The bus crossed the bridge and carried the class back through the lower wards. They had left a village that tried to re-create the mid-nineteenth century. They came back to a city that had in fact been founded then, and might still serve as a model of a nineteenth-century industrial town. The bus passed some new stores and a couple of apartment houses with the soot removed and solid-looking front doors, buildings renovated by a nonprofit organization called Nueva Esperanza – "New Hope." But all around those few examples of real human progress stood buildings with windows boarded up in plywood and covered with graffiti. The bus passed lots made vacant by old and recent fires. If one looked closely down side streets, one would have seen, here and there, pairs of sneakers hanging from the wires.

Heading back to Kelly, they went down Cabot Street, then past streets named Franklin and Sergeant, names that honor some of the city's founders and their invested capital, long since returned many times over and withdrawn. For the most part, people with Spanish surnames now live on streets named for New England Yankees. But in this part of town street and surnames have never coincided. Some people say that the lower wards were beautiful back when O'Malleys and Fleurys lived on Cabot Street. This was a fine part of town, some people say, before the Puerto Ricans came. The delicate brickwork around the windows and along the eaves of many grimy tenements suggests that once the lower wards looked comelier. But probably the lower wards have always looked better just a while ago. They did not look like model neighborhoods one hundred years back, when the city was still growing. In 1875, a report of the Bureau of Labor Statistics described the worker housing of Holyoke as follows:

Holyoke has more and worse large tenement houses than any manufacturing town of textile fabrics in the state, and built in such a manner that there is very little means of escape in case of fire. The sanitary arrangements are very imperfect, and in many cases, there is no provision made for carrying the slops from the sinks, but they are allowed to run wherever they can make their way. Portions of the yards are covered with filth and green slime, and within 20 feet, people are living in basements of houses three feet below the level of the yard. There are also quite a number of six and eight tenement houses, with only one door at front and none at back, over-crowded, dirty and necessarily unhealthy. . . . It is no wonder that the death rate, in 1872, was greater in Holyoke than in any large town in Massachusetts, excepting Fall River, and if an epidemic should visit them now, its ravages would be great.

Citing this report in 1939, the author of the only full history of Holyoke wrote without irony: "The squalor and filth in which Irish and French Canadian immigrants lived in these years is partly attributable to their lack of any knowledge of the most elementary rules of sanitation."

The tired children smiled out the windows of the bus. They passed by Judith's father's church. Judith spotted her sister in a window in the apartment above and waved. It was a warm day in the lower wards, and many women sat by their windows, looking out.

Chris sat at one of the empty children's desks, shoulders rounded, sunglasses resting in her hair. "Well, did you all enjoy yourselves?"

"That was the best trip I ever had!" shouted Felipe.

"Besides having fun, I hope you learned something about American history."

They crowded around her, showing her the presents they had bought for their parents at the gift shop.

"I got this wine jelly for my mother," said Claude. "It tastes just like wine."

"Claude! You're going to give that to your mother, and you just stuck your finger in it." Chris's voice contained no vehemence. She sat and smiled toward the window. Claude froze, the jellied finger in his mouth. Arnie showed her a ring he had bought, one fashioned from a flat nail. "It's *real* metal," he said.

"Oh, Arnie, that's nice."

Ashley stumbled over a chair, and Chris went to her, helped her up, and sat by her for a private conversation. Chris called her "dear heart." "It's usually Claude who has something happen to him. *You* can't do this, Ashley."

Ashley shook her head with mirth, her glossy, long black hair swaying and her lips sealed, looking at Mrs. Zajac. It was nice to see Ashley looking happy for once.

Teachers often console themselves with thoughts such as these: "It's just a bad day, It's just a bad year," and "There's a full moon this week. That's why the kids haven't been doing their homework." Chris half believed in the power of the moon. She strongly believed in the power of the season now upon them – Little League baseball and the warm, long evenings of daylight savings – to bring on academic decline. She fumed at the class a few times during May, and one day when almost no one had done the homework, she went to the Teachers' Room and declared, "I hate them right now. I'm going to the Golden Lemon and start drinking *now*." One day she actually had to tell Judith twice what page to turn to in math – the closest she'd ever had to come to reprimanding Judith, who said, "I don't know what it is. I just can't shake the tiredness away." Sweet-smelling rain fell on many mornings and the sky lightened by the end of math. Gradually, moist heat began to fill the room. It was still there the next mornings, not unbearable but ominous heat, like heat at dawn in August.

Chris had come back from her vacation in Puerto Rico thinking, "I need a vacation from a vacation," and for a few days felt as if she was floundering. She rummaged through her chaotic closet and couldn't find her materials on the Civil War. "Mariposa? Could you look for them, please?" The little girl with the corkscrew-curly hair stood at the closet door, shaking her head at the mess inside. "*Miss*-is Zajac!" Mariposa said, and she clucked. Then Mariposa went in there and found all the materials, and Chris spent a long evening at her dining room table outlining her lessons for the rest of the year. She felt much better afterward.

When Chris had returned from Puerto Rico, her heart had sunk at the sight of Juanita's empty desk. Shy, blossoming Juanita had been moved away to some other town. Chris asked the counselor to make inquiries. Evidently Juanita's relocation had less to do with her than with a fresh argument between her divorced parents. Inside the girl's workbook was a fragment of a year's collaborative effort, a record of real progress, now aborted: the girl's careful answers and Chris's bold, red-penciled comments: "Excellent!" and "Good work, Juanita!" The workbook was just detritus now, awaiting year-end clean-up. Chris hoped Juanita was all right. She thought, "So much is out of your control. So much!"

Some children had changed markedly. Kimberly, for instance, the tall girl with the lazy-sounding voice and myopic eyes. In September everything about her — the whiny voice, the sour expressions on her face, her habit of turning her shoulders away from Chris when Chris spoke to her — had seemed to say, "I don't care if you don't like me. I don't care if I get answers wrong." Kimberly now seemed willing to try. One day Chris heard her say to Ashley that if Ashley's spelling partner was out, Ashley should work with another group — she could work with Kimberly's. Chris thought, "I'm seeing little sparks out of Kimberly. Now if I could just grab them . . ."

And was something like a change coming over Claude? He had lovingly fingered the index card Chris had taped to his desk top, the one with the message DON'T FORGET TO COPY THE ASSIGNMENT! The card had peeled up. Now it had vanished — to where, Claude couldn't say. The red piece of construction paper on which Judith had recorded Claude's bet with Dick still lay on the counter under the window. The spring sunshine had drained the paper of most of its color. Claude had long since lost the bet — that he'd do all his homework from now on. Dick hadn't tried to collect. But one spring morning, after the usual lecture from Chris, Claude got almost all of the questions right on a science paper. A few days later, Claude asked Chris if he could collect the spelling homework – a request never granted to a child who hadn't done his, and in Room 205 a customary way for a child to tell her that he had. Then Claude actually finished a story. Chris read it at her desk. "Its about fishing again. But it all makes sense for once!" And on top of that, Claude, with a solid F average in social studies, did quite well on a social studies test.

Claude stared at the paper when Chris handed it back at the end of the day. His eyes went wide. "Eighty?" he said. "That's the best score I ever got!" He wanted to show Julio, who wasn't interested. He showed Judith, who was. The intercom called Claude's bus. He dashed to the door, the test paper in hand. He stopped. He remembered he'd forgotten his bookbag. He dashed back into the room. Dashing one way, then the other, Claude kept declaring, "That's the best score I ever got!" Chris watched the performance from her desk. She shook her head slowly. She let herself smile. Was something like organized academic desire stirring in Claude? It was too soon to know for sure.

"I love math," Jimmy said one morning a few days after the class trip.

Chris thought, "Pick me up off the floor."

"Me, too," said Manny.

"Me, too," said Jorge.

"Ugh," said Felipe. "I hate math."

"It's my favorite subject," said one of the girls.

"I like math and reading," said a boy in her low math group who came from another homeroom.

Chris looked at the child who had uttered that last sentiment. "Thank you," she said. "You have me for both."

She was the same old Mrs. Zajac, who wasn't born yesterday and was an old witch. She was an old-lady teacher who didn't fall off the turnip cart yesterday, and meant business, and who knew she had repeated the assignment fifty thousand million times, and, disgusted as you were about having to do your work over, was twice as disgusted herself that you didn't try to do it right the first time, who hoped you never had a doctor or mechanic who didn't check his work, who made lots of mistakes herself, was a terrible artist, unlike you, and knew how smart you really were, and said, at least three times between 7:45 and 1:45, "Pedro, do you understand?" "Mariposa, dear heart, stop writing letters and pay attention," "We're working. Right, Felipe?" "Claude, I don't want to hear it," and "Robert! Stop slapping yourself." When Jimmy once again avoided his classmates' suggestions by reconstructing his whole story, so that it no longer made any sense, the same Mrs. Zajac as the one of September said, "Okay, Jimmy. We'll start again."

She didn't use the threat of Mr. Laudato anymore or keep anyone in for recess, except on one bad day when many came in without homework and she delivered what she called "tirade number six sixty-six" about diligence. She said to the class, "I corrected these papers last night. Mrs. Zajac almost took the gas pipe."

The yearly ritual of the class trip now successfully completed – Claude hadn't gotten lost – the Science Fair loomed for all of the fifth-grade classes at Kelly. According to the rules, the children could form teams of their own choosing or work alone. Each team or child would choose a topic, such as dinosaurs or water power. (No earthquakes; after last year, the fifth-grade teachers had deemed models of exploding mountains too dangerous and messy.) Each would write a report on the chosen topic. Finally, each would construct a demonstration, to fit on a table in one of the gyms for the climactic event, the Fair itself. Part of the plan was to get parents involved. Chris sent home letters, in English on one side and in Spanish on the other, asking that the parents help their children with the demonstrations. Every day of the three weeks after the class trip, Chris gave them an hour or more to get ready for the Fair. Many early signs weren't good.

During an early rehearsal, Kimberly, who teamed up with Courtney, told Chris, "We're gonna put these foods on the table and tell 'em what the things are."

"Okay. You have foods on your table," said Chris to the two girls. "Someone comes by at the Fair. What are you going to tell them?"

"Like this is a potato?" said Kimberly.

"Everybody's going to know what a potato is!" said Chris.

"Like what foods nourish your body?" said Courtney hopefully.

Chris questioned Ashley, who was working alone on a water wheel. "Okay, what will it do?" Chris asked.

"Maybe it will turn," Ashley whispered.

"*Maybe* it will turn?" said Chris.

"Probably," said Ashley.

"No. No probably. It *has* to work, Ashley."

Chris questioned the team of Irene and Mariposa. "Are you just going to have a bunch of rocks in front of you?"

"We're going to get a lot of rocks from around my house," said Irene. "And figure out their environment. Like whether they came from a desert . . ."

"Their environment? Rocks don't have an

environment, and I doubt any around your house came from a desert." Chris's eyes got very wide. "You're going to have to be more specific."

But there were exceptions, and the most exceptional was Claude. Chris was astonished. Claude joined up with Pedro and Jimmy. Chris had to insist that Claude's partners do some of the work. Claude was clearly the leader. She asked the three boys to describe their project, and Claude piped up "It's gonna be like on streams and rivers and how they form. How they move." Talking fast, shaking a hand furiously, Claude described all this while Chris ran her tongue around the inside of her mouth, suppressing her smile. "That's very good, Claude! I like what I'm hearing!" They were down in the library. Chris turned to the aide there and said, "Would you help these boys find some more books on streams and rivers?"

"And ponds and lakes!" declared Claude.

Later, she overheard Claude say to a classmate, "I'm gonna work on my science project every night!" The next week, he described again for Chris, in remarkable detail, the birth of rivers. To the class in general, Chris said, "I hope some of you are as well versed on your projects as Claude." For a moment, Chris wondered, "Did I really just say that?"

This was the boy who, a month ago, when

Mrs. Zajac was putting the heat on him, said he felt mixed up and wanted to go home. Now he raced around, making a chart for his project. The chart was incredibly neat.

Among a generally disappointing bunch of written science reports, Claude's looked pretty good. Only Felipe did a really first-rate job, a report full of accurate facts about dinosaurs, and unlike many others, not copied right out of books. Felipe had written, for instance:

I imagine animals like Elephants with fur coats. I imagine trees like giant featherdusters. That's what some animals and trees looked like millions of years ago.

High-pitched voices echoed in the gym. The end of May had arrived, and the Fair had begun. The noise was like one unremitting, collective scream, which could only get worse, because to converse in the gym one had to add to the clamor by shouting. "Today," Chris predicted, "will be a four-Tylenol day." Leading her class down the corridors to the Fair, she had followed a couple of thin trails of dirt, spilled no doubt from some child's geology exhibit. Chris hoped there would be no larger mishaps.

All the fifth graders had assembled in the gym. They stood in little groups behind tables, which were arranged in a large rectangle along the walls. The tables were laden. Chris decided to look at the projects from other classes first. She found a pretty good water wheel on one table; it was better than Ashley's, in that it contained some water. At the next table a boy from another class sat, looking hopeful, behind an exhibit that consisted of a rose, still encased in cellophane and planted in the top of an empty soda can. "What's your project on?" shouted Chris. She leaned across the table, cupping an ear to catch the reply.

"Flowers," said the boy, nodding earnestly.

She visited another boy, from another class, who said his project was on electricity. "It comes from plugs," he explained. Another had a store-bought model of a human eye on his table. He said, "It's an eye. It sees." One group from another homeroom stood behind a store-bought plastic robot and explained, "You push this button, and it goes left."

Chris felt a secret relief. She had awakened one night not long ago imagining children from other classes standing behind wonderful home-made rocket ships and expounding on physics, while her students explained to fairgoers, "This is a potato" and "These are rocks." Chris told herself now, "At least I don't feel too embarrassed. Mine aren't any worse than anyone else's." But then she stopped at Jorge's table, and her amusement began to wane.

Jorge, from her low math group, often looked exhausted. He had tried to do a science project, a model of a laser made out of colored paper, an electric light, and a cardboard box. Jorge had gotten the idea from a book. He'd followed all the instructions, he told Mrs. Zajac. "But it doesn't work," he said. Jorge had been heard to say a few days before, "I can't get too much help at home." An understatement. The floors of his family's apartment were covered with their dog's excrement. He wore the same clothes day in and day out, and even now, standing across the table from him, Chris could smell the sad odor, like rotting fruit. Jorge and his partners — two other boys who couldn't get much help from home either — sat behind their table and their inoperative cardboard box, looking glum.

Chris told Jorge he'd done well, not to worry, and she moved on. Jorge wasn't in her homeroom. But Ashley was, of course.

Ashley sat alone at her table. She hadn't wanted a partner. Now Chris wished she'd assigned someone to Ashley. The girl once said she had only three friends. "That's all the people I know." Ashley lived in the Flats with her mother and stepfather. Her real father had visited her last weekend. Ashley had told Chris all about it. Her real father had helped

Ashley make her water wheel. Ashley had brought it to school a few days ago. As the girl had carried it up to Mrs. Zajac's desk, Chris had noticed Ashley's hands shaking. Her water wheel was made of cardboard and paper plates. An electric motor made it turn. She had surrounded it with sprigs of greenery. The plastic figure of a Dutch girl stood beside the wheel. "Where's the water?" Chris had thought to herself when she'd first seen Ashley's project. Chris had said to her, "Oh, look at this! Very nice, Ashley!" Now Ashley sat behind the contraption, looking frightened and, as always, as if she'd like to hide, and Chris told herself that the lack of water didn't matter.

Chris cupped an ear and leaned toward Ashley, who said, "It's an overshot water wheel, and when water hits it, it turns." She didn't have much else to say.

Arnie's father had arrived. Chris smiled broadly. She extended her hand. Arnie's father clasped it shyly. Chris noticed that his pants were torn and dirty. An unmistakable, sweetish odor of liquor came from him. It was only about ten in the morning. Chris visited Arnie's table. On it lay a storebought example of an electric switch. Arnie smiled at her. He looked especially cute to her now. He knew something about how the switch worked. Chris was writing grades in her book, grades based not on the projects but on what the children had learned. She wrote *B* beside Arnie's name. Then she paused. The grade meant nothing, she thought. She hadn't based it on what Arnie knew. She'd based it on Arnie's father. She might as well stop grading this event.

Other parents had arrived. There behind her homemade model of the solar system sat Arabella, smiling sweetly, looking chipper and healthy and confident, telling the judges all the names of the planets, their approximate distances from the sun, the main characteristics of each. And there, in his electrician's uniform, moving from table to table and correcting the mistaken notions of the various children who had done projects on electricity, was the explanation for the care behind Arabella's project and for the progress that Arabella had made this year – Arabella's father.

Alice's father wore a necktie and blue blazer. The team of Alice, Judith, and Margaret had done electrical generation. Alice's father had taken them to the Holyoke water power plant a few days ago. Through a friend he'd arranged a special tour for the girls. Afterward, he'd bought them all ice cream cones and taken them back to the Highlands to help them finish the project. Their display, a model town on a large piece of plywood, didn't show how power got generated, but it was the nicest-looking project in the gym. Chris questioned them. The girls knew their stuff. Chris chatted briefly with Alice's father. She thanked him for helping his daughter and her friends so much.

She meant those words. But she couldn't look around the gym now without feeling sad. The children whose parents had come to the gym — for the most part neatly dressed, confident-seeming adults — had the best projects and knew the most about their subjects. In general, the forlorn projects belonged to the children with no parents on hand, such as Courtney and Kimberly, who stood behind a table displaying a box of oatmeal, a hamburger bun, a piece of white bread, a carton of milk, an egg, two potatoes, and a remnant of iceberg lettuce growing brown.

Chris wished she could call a halt right now. The whole event looked like a rigged election, distressingly predictable, as if designed to teach the children about the unfairness of life. She saw one bright spot, though. There was some room in an unfair world for individual achievement. She walked up to Claude's table. She questioned his partners, Jimmy and Pedro, first. Claude said to them, "Come on, guys. Don't let me down." Pedro and Jimmy still couldn't tell Mrs. Zajac much about rivers, even though for weeks she had been opening books on the subject for them. But she felt rescued from this day, for a brief time, when she looked at what Claude had done: on the table, his thorough and neat diagram of a river rising in mountains and flowing to the sea; and behind that, Claude's model river. He had built his model on a metal serving platter. Little stones were piled up at one end, from which a chute of aluminum foil descended, depicting a waterfall, which led to the river itself, which had banks described by more small stones and a bed of aquarium gravel, and water, too. In the water lay a little rubber crayfish and a little rubber fish, which if you squeezed it (as Claude would for fairgoers) spawned several smaller rubber fish from its nether end. She'd never dared to hope for this much from him. And the best was still to come.

"All right, Claude," she shouted over the din, "tell me about rivers."

And Claude, who for six months hadn't managed to complete more than a few homework assignments, delivered a lucid description, even better than during rehearsals, of the birth of rivers. "Ice melts, see. It comes down the mountain into a brook, and the brook makes a river. It flows into the ocean and the whole thing starts over again because of evaporation which makes, like, clouds." As he expounded, talking fast, his right hand flapped, as it used to when he was concocting one of his

loony homework excuses. "Sometimes a waterfall gets worn away," he went on.

He seemed to know enough to talk all morning. Chris had to move along. "Okay," she said.
"Thank you, Claude."

Claude's mother had arrived. Chris spotted
her in the crowd and went up to her. Now at
last Chris could give that likable, worried parent some good news.

"Any improvement?"

"Yes!" cried Chris. "His science project is
pretty good! He's still not getting *all* his work
in, but he wrote a pretty good story. And he did
well on a social studies test."

Chris had a slightly somber thought, which
she kept to herself: "Maybe all my being on
Claude these last weeks has made some of the
others slip."

An island of chairs had been set up for
teachers in the center of the gym's blond floor.
Chris retreated to one of those chairs. She
needed a break. In spite of Claude, this was the
worst Science Fair she could remember. Or did
she think that every year? No. This really was
the worst. Maybe Science Fairs worked in other
schools. But this kind of event had no place at
this school anymore. She'd go to Al afterward
and tell him they *had* to rethink the whole
thing.

Hazy sunlight filtered through the gym's

413

high, frosted windows. The noise, sharp and concentrated, made her feel as if her hands were vibrating, like tuning forks. Chris looked around. Where was Robert?

Robert had come to school this morning without his science project, saying that he had left it at a convenience store. The counselor had taken him to fetch the project. Chris had told Robert that when he got back, he should come down to the gym right away. But he was nowhere in sight.

Chris sent Courtney back to the classroom to see if Robert was there. Courtney returned in a few minutes. "Robert says he's not comin'," she said.

Chris lowered her eyebrows. "Oh, he isn't, isn't he?"

Chris strode down the corridor toward her classroom. The halls were wonderfully quiet. Her skirt rustled. She quick-marched, hands swinging high. Her mind was filled with heated, exasperated thoughts about Robert. Weeks ago Robert had said he wouldn't do a project for the Science Fair. She had tried to talk him into it, and finally, he had agreed. Overall, he had improved since that day when she'd isolated him, but plenty of the old Robert remained, enough to make her think that, when it came to his science project, he just wanted to get a rise out of her. Or just wanted once again to keep failure at bay by embracing it right from the start. He'd settle for the easy distinction of being weird.

Robert was one of those children who make it hard for a teacher to like them. Not quite consciously but on purpose. She had kept telling herself that she admired his boldness and his outspoken hatred of school. But then he'd start gurgling over the idea of a baby being smothered or refuse to do a science project and shrug his shoulders when she asked why.

Chris stopped in the doorway to her classroom. Robert sat at a desk near the door, his broad back toward her.

"You! Get over here!" she said.

At the sound of Mrs. Zajac's voice, Robert ducked his head. What lay on his desk was hidden from Chris for the moment.

"Pick yourself up and get to the office," she said.

Robert stood up. His arms hung limply in front of him. His chin was pressed to his chest. His broad face was bright. He trudged, listing to one side, toward Mrs. Zajac in the doorway.

Chris looked at him. Something was wrong. He wasn't smirking. He was clearly upset. She looked at his desk, and then the tightness left her jaw. She let her shoulders sag, and her face turned as red as Robert's.

On Robert's desk she saw a weathered scrap of two-by-six with raggedly cut ends. On each of its longer edges was a flashlight battery, precariously secured to the board by a profusion of bent and twisted nails. A tangle of wires, twisted around other nails, covered the surface of the board. An attempt had been made to tape the ends of the wires to the batteries and to a small light bulb. The bulb had a broken filament. A hammer and some outsize nails lay on Robert's desk next to his project. He had tried to make an electric light. It suddenly looked like a very difficult thing to do.

Chris looked at the project and she saw all at once a Robert slightly different from the one she thought she'd known just a minute ago. All year long she had tried to get Robert to take a chance and make an effort. Now he had. He had tried, and he had *sincerely* failed. And she had rewarded him with humiliation. How many times had something like this happened to him in his life already? Was this the reason Robert behaved as he did? Is self-inflicted pain better than sadness and despair? She looked at the lashed-up wires and bent nails on the dirty scrap of wood, and it was all there in front of her: the dead, undeliverable letters that Robert had written to the father he'd never met. He had no one at home to help him make an electric light. That was why he'd said he didn't want to do a project. He wasn't just being perverse. "How stupid I am!" she thought. She should have bent the rules and given him more help. She should have arranged a success for him. "How stupid I am!"

"Sit down, Robert," she said softly.

He sat down at the desk and wouldn't look at his project. He looked at his feet instead, arms dangling down between his legs. She sat next to him. "Why aren't you coming to the Fair?"

"Doesn't work." His voice was a squeak. He stared at the floor.

"When were you supposed to figure that out, Robert? Before now. Right, Robert?" But her voice was very gentle. Not much of the year remained, but enough for her to make a change in herself, too. No matter how infuriating he might be tomorrow or next week, she wasn't going to let herself feel truly angry at him again. He had let her see the wounded little boy inside the fat would-be comedian. She felt like crying. At last, he had let her like him.

Robert made a series of little shrugs and began picking at the wads of black electrical tape on his project.

"Can you explain what it's supposed to do?"

"No."

She knew that he could. He had explained it very well last week, after she had directed him to books about electricity. The project showed that he did know how an electric light works. He just hadn't been able to make it happen. Maybe, she thought, she could help him now.

"Robert, if you took a little longer now, it might work."

"No," he squeaked, still looking at the floor.

His jeans looked dirty. The sleeves of the heavy sweatshirt he'd begun wearing since the onset of warm weather were too long. The cuffs half covered his dirty hands.

She didn't have time now to work with him on the project. She had to get back to the gym. Anyway, the light bulb was broken, and she didn't know where to find another in a hurry. She'd take him to the office and leave him there and try to forget about him for a while. No, she couldn't do that. She'd take him to the gym and let him join his classmates and hope that the rest of this day would pass quickly.

Robert seemed to recover fast. He ambled around the gym, making snaky movements with his hands in the manner of the dancers in a then popular TV video, done to a song called "Walk Like an Egyptian." Chris's recovery took longer.

The Fair ended with a ceremony after lunch. The parents had departed. The children sat in a huge, disordered phalanx on one side of the now dusty floor, and the teachers sat on chairs facing them. It was almost over. Al roared for quiet. Chris started giggling behind her hand. "Oh, God. Our leader," she murmured to another teacher. Finally, the wave of giddiness passed and she wiped her eyes.

The team of Alice, Judith, and Margaret got first prize. Arabella got the third-place ribbon and came bouncing up to get it. Chris felt glad that those children's parents had helped them. Claude's team got a ribbon for special effort. That was even better, because Claude had earned it all by himself.

"Oh, my God!" said Claude, receiving his ribbon.

Chris watched, and she smiled. She imagined Claude thinking, "I can't believe this! I got a prize!"

But Chris stopped smiling when she turned her eyes toward Felipe. He was scowling. Felipe's team hadn't won anything. She glanced at the faces of Jorge, Ashley, Kimberly, Courtney. The faces of the losers looked not exactly sad but distant. As more fortunate classmates took the ribbons, many of the losers watched with slightly opened mouths, like children gazing through the window of a toy store. If she could, Chris thought, she'd give them all prizes. She'd go to Al tomorrow. They couldn't let this happen again next year.

Chris once heard a veteran colleague say, "I'm not interested in impossible cases anymore. I'll teach the kids who want to learn." The strategy had an allure. "But," Chris told herself, "some kids don't know they want to learn until you put it in their heads that they do." *I'll teach the ones who want to learn.* She would turn those words over in her mind and answer back that her own son might not get taught if his teachers followed that strategy. And still, it was alluring. You can't fail if you don't try.

If all of life is like a rigged election, there is no point in teaching. Only the surprises prevent boredom and despair. Surprises happened every year, and Claude was one of this year's best. She'd nearly given up hope for him. On a morning a little while ago, she'd substituted him in her imagination for that rather "simple" but sweet old neighbor of her childhood, the one she saw sweeping the sidewalk in front of a store every morning. "Claude could do that," she had thought. She could see him differently now. Claude could become a game warden, a tradesman, maybe even a wildlife biologist. Whatever he did, he'd probably always be about eight weeks behind schedule, but now she knew he could do a lot more than sweep a sidewalk.

Chris spent an unhappy weekend after the

Science Fair. She kept picturing Robert and his failed electric light. She kept asking herself why she hadn't realized that Robert had been asking for help. She washed windows furiously all weekend. Why hadn't she listened to Robert? Why hadn't his mother helped him? She imagined the face of Robert's mother in the glass, and that made her rub harder.

Robert was a boy for whom life certainly looked rigged. But he had let Chris see him in a new way. He had turned out to be willing, in the face of long odds, to try to do a project. That was not cause for despair. This boy was salvageable. Now more than ever, she had to get Robert to a psychiatrist.

As she scrubbed windows, Chris decided to force the issue. The paperwork to get Robert free counseling was completed. His mother had no excuse now. Imagining the woman's face in windowpanes, Chris thought, "If you don't take him, the way you promised, I'm going to file a 51A." That official document has a longer name: "Report of Child(ren) Alleged to Be Suffering from Serious Physical or Emotional Injury by Abuse or Neglect." Anyone could file one of those, and do so anonymously. "She's not going to be allowed to sit back and do nothing," thought Chris. Ah, righteous wrath. She felt a little better.

Laying out her plans for what remained of this year, Chris had figured they'd get through the Civil War's aftermath, just barely. They had to get to the end of the war at least, she thought. "God forbid they don't find out who won."

The Civil War for Chris meant many lessons about slavery. A while back, as she had done every year since desegregation, Chris had directed the class in a slave auction down in the library. She assigned the parts. She gave some children the role of abolitionists, who would watch and afterward make reports. Some would play slave buyers, others slaves. She made Judith the auctioneer and equipped her with a gavel and a set of note cards that described the slaves. Studying those descriptions before the auction, Judith said, "God! They make it sound like these people are animals!" Before the auction, Chris explained for the others' benefit, "The point is to realize what it must've felt like to be a piece of goods. To be like a dress on a rack. Oooo, I don't like this dress. I think I'll buy that one. The slaves were human, but they weren't *thought of* as human beings."

Down in the library, Judith stood at a podium, half a dozen "slaves" lined up facing her. Claude was a slave. He was grinning when the auction started. Chris sat nearby. She called, "Claude, I thought I explained. You're *not* happy to be a slave."

Judith read from the index cards. She giggled when she read about skinny Jimmy. "What do I hear for this big strapping man?" But gradually, Judith and the others began to get into it. The slaves looked crestfallen, the buyers greedy and nasty. Judith raised her voice. She chanted like a real auctioneer.

Margaret was led to the podium.

"Okay, this is important," called Chris. "Here's a healthy young woman. She can give you lots of kids. Are her kids your slaves, too?"

Several of the children cried, "Yes!"

Julio was led, struggling as instructed, to Judith. "This is a male, age thirty," declared Judith. "Married. Can do jobs around the house. A great help. What do I hear for him?"

"Seven-fifty!" called the buyer Felipe.

"Come on. Look at him! There's lots of hard work left in him. Now what do I hear for this hard-working man?" said Judith.

The auction lasted about fifteen minutes. The buyers were cruel to their new property. Felipe wouldn't let his slave sit or talk. Judith banged her gavel down one last time and said, "Thank you for coming to the auction, and I hope they serve you well."

The class filed back to the room. Chris

423

questioned them. What did it all mean? She got most of the answers she hoped for. She asked the class in general, "What are some of the bad things about being treated like property?"

"You can't do nothin'," said Felipe.

With feeling, Judith declared, "They're real humans, not just pieces of garbage, and they're supposed to be treated like people."

"Right," said Chris. "And if our society says there can be slaves, who's to say someone can't turn around and say, 'All people with brown hair can be slaves'? So if some people have slaves, it hurts all people. Also, some slaves could have been great inventors or artists, but almost no slaves were allowed to be those things. When you don't allow people to be themselves, they don't have the opportunity to invent things or write beautiful songs or paint beautiful pictures. That's another way slavery hurts all people."

The class lined up for lunch. Judith moved out of line and said to Chris, "I felt *terrible*, Mrs. Zajac."

The next day Chris elaborated on how slavery hurts everyone, including auctioneers.

Now in social studies, in Room 205, civil war loomed. On the bulletin board near the door, paper letters announced DARK CLOUDS OVER OUR

NATION. Beneath the sign Chris had stapled paper clouds, which read: "John Brown," "Missouri Compromise," "States' Rights." Chris had offered rewards for children who wrote explanations to attach to those clouds. Every day after lunch Chris read to them from *To Be a Slave*, by Julius Lester.

Chris sat on her spindly-legged front table, smoothed her skirt over her shins, and read aloud this line: " 'No other country destroyed African culture as thoroughly as slavery did here." The casements were opened wide. Shouts and laughter of sixth graders at recess drifted in. The voices sounded distant. A soft breeze came in, too, and made the various hanging things flutter and sway – the art projects and book report projects and stories stapled to strings of yarn. Now and then Chris's voice died out in the midst of a sentence and resumed at the start of another. She was censoring the parts about rape. But plenty of horrors remained. She wondered, as she read, if maybe these children were too young for this book. She paused and looked at the class. "Can you imagine walking home from school and someone grabbing you and taking you as a slave to another country?"

Most of the children looked up and then, as she read on, went back to their penmanship or spelling or window gazing. Arnie tapped his pen on his desk, trying to hit the end of a staple, so as to get it airborne. Chris glanced at him, and he stopped. She didn't want to terrify them. Her lively voice, rising and falling, suggested that they would get safely home themselves. Imagined horrors are not horrible in such a setting. There is, after all, something comforting about history, no matter how vividly rendered. Slavery had ended long ago. In the little fluorescent-lit oasis, a person could feel indignant and also glad for having been born into a better age. It was easy to forget for a moment that in the city outside people still called each other "nigger," "spic," and "whitey," and that in the little slum nearby, real estate speculators made fortunes while children lived in squalid fire traps that were fouled by dogs and so infested with rodents that some preschoolers lapsed back to bedwetting rather than risk encounters with rats on the way to the bathroom at night.

How much of Julius Lester's book did the children understand? Did they know that Mrs. Zajac was reading to them about the ultimate rigged life? And that they lived in a rigged world, too, where it's still hard to overcome the accidents of birth? Robert seemed to have an inkling. He had asked Chris recently, apropos of nothing, "Mrs. Zajac, is it true that in the old days, what your father was you had to be?"

426

The remark was one of those which left Chris thinking, "The boy's so bright! If only I could change the circumstances of his life . . ." As she read now, worried looks from Dick, Irene, Alice, Arabella, and some others suggested that they could imagine something of the lot of slaves.

In the book, a slave was getting whipped. Side by side at their desks, Judith and Alice looked at each other. Alice nibbled a fingernail. Judith went back to looking at Mrs. Zajac. With steady, solemn brown eyes, Judith watched Chris read. Judith was listening hard.

"Why do you suppose prices for slaves went up in autumn?" Chris asked.

"Because they could work harder?" suggested Irene.

"Because they had to pick crops then," said Judith softly. She looked in repose, her cheek resting on a hand, but her eyes hardly wavered from Mrs. Zajac and the book.

Judith understood the potential disadvantages of being Puerto Rican. She said that she never felt prejudice from Mrs. Zajac, but had from one or two other teachers – nothing overt, no ethnic slurs, but a pattern of favoritism that seemed to coincide with a "white" surname and the right address. Occasionally, a kid from another class – it hadn't happened in this one since Clarence, who had sometimes made remarks about Puerto Ricans — would use the term "pork" for "Puerto Rican." Sometimes kids of Puerto Rican descent would refer to children in the bilingual rooms, disparagingly, as "those Spanish kids." Judith thought that was pretty stupid. She could more than hold her own among other children. One time, down in the library, working there with Alice during spelling, she actually went looking for a little trouble. Judith and Alice were shelving books. A white sixth-grade boy stood nearby in the stacks. The boy asked the girls where they lived. What boy wouldn't try to make conversation with girls as pretty as those two? Judith put a hand on her hip and pushed the other one out. "I come from the Hispanic ghetto," she said.

The boy grinned uneasily.

"I *do*," said Judith. She turned to Alice. "He doesn't believe me." Judith went on, moving down the stacks, "I've come a long way. At least I'm not flunking, like kids from good neighborhoods."

The boy started to pretend that he was busy.

Judith went on airily, laughing now and then. "Hispanic kids are smart. We had to overcome obstacles. Our ancestors were slaves. That doesn't bother me. I don't care. I wasn't there. I'm one of the lucky ones. When I grow up, I'm going to live in the Spanish ghetto."

428

Having said all that, Judith turned her attention to the boy again. "When you were born, did they take you out the wrong way, or just throw away the wrong thing?" She grinned.

The boy muttered under his breath.

"They shot him in the head," said Alice. She and Judith giggled.

The boy, who hadn't deserved such harsh treatment, but apparently was wise beyond his years, didn't try to fight back. He moved away out of earshot.

Judith and Alice had tried eating lunch together, first Alice at Judith's table of Puerto Rican girls, and on another day Judith at Alice's table of blond girls from the Highlands. But each had missed her other friends, and they'd agreed to eat lunch separately. Judith had gone home with Alice to the Highlands several times, much to Chris's delight. But Judith had never asked Alice over to her apartment in the Flats.

One time, at Alice's house, Judith asked Alice, "Do you like my neighborhood? You want to live down there?"

Alice looked at Judith and said softly, "Not really."

"I live down there," said Judith. She laughed. "I know the streets and the situation and the people. It's not a gold mine." She laughed again, that laugh she offered Mrs. Zajac to say she was just joking. "Maybe copper," Judith added.

Alice said, "My mother used to drive kids down there who didn't have a ride, and —"

"Don't say any of them looked like me!" Judith interrupted, laughing. "Don't say anybody down there looks like me!"

Judith thought Alice's house was pretty. She didn't think that she felt envious. "I have everything I need, and I'm satisfied with what I have. I think I got a great . . . a great future, and I don't really care about material things." Judith remembered fondly her early years in Pennsylvania. Her family had lived in a quiet neighborhood in a small, neat house. There were many children on their street. Judith thought Alice's neighborhood suffered by comparison. The Highlands was too quiet, Judith thought. She often spoke mordantly about the Flats. "Where I live is exciting. You can look out the window and see people coming down the street, fighting and shooting each other." In a more serious mood, she would say that at least the Flats was lively. If there was defensiveness in Judith, it took an extremely intelligent form, and was infinitely preferable to the pathetic shame of the Puerto Rican boy at Holyoke High — the story was well known and true — who had told everyone that he was Samoan, and had begged his teacher not to reveal his true nationality when she'd found him out.

In about two hours, two hours after Mrs. Zajac finished reading aloud, Judith would return to a barren, littered street where she played Double Dutch by the hour; to a housing project where insecurity took the manifest form of front doors without locks; to her family's cramped apartment where summer had already arrived. Judith had an older sister who took her on car trips, but she didn't regularly go farther than the K Mart and Ingleside malls. She shopped there with her parents and interpreted for them at the cash registers. At home, when she got tired of TV and reading, Judith amused herself by making scrapbooks of clippings about movie and rock stars. Volunteers from other parts of town showed movies for the children of the project down in a basement room. Judith said, sardonically, that the end of the movies was exciting, when the lights came on and the rats and mice scurried for cover.

Occasionally in her neighborhood Judith saw sights that troubled her much more than rodents and roaches. One morning this spring, she had come out of her apartment in the project, heading off for school, and found a family on the stairway — a mother, a father, and several small children. The family had been evicted from their apartment and had spent the night on the landing, without blankets. They had managed to save some bowls and spoons, a box of cereal, and some milk, and when Judith came past them, the family was gathered on the filthy staircase eating breakfast.

That sight had inspired Judith's latest essay, which was about the homeless. It began, "I live in the Hispanic ghetto, and I've seen people sleeping on the stairs." In it, she scolded Ronald Reagan. The other day Judith had read the rough draft aloud to a couple of classmates over near the social studies bulletin board. This was what, in Room 205, was called an "editing conference." Claude served as one of Judith's editors, and Claude seemed to understand the irony of his situation.

"That was so great!" said Claude when Judith finished reading. "She didn't get nothin' wrong! Hey, Judith, if you ever become a businesswoman, you could use that in your speech. You could run for President with that thing."

"Claude!" Judith said. She smiled, the sick-looking smile that Claude himself wore when classmates teased him.

Claude didn't seem to know that he was mocking his best friend and protector for being smart. He just thought he was having fun. The idea of Judith's being President pleased him.

The hyperbole must have diminished for him the distance that he felt between him and Judith. Claude couldn't stop. He turned to a classmate. "She could run for President." Robert walked by. Claude said to him, "Oh, man, you shoulda been here when Judy read hers. It was awesome! She could run for friggin' President!"

It is dangerous to be smart. Still wearing that sickly smile, Judith reached out with both arms toward Claude, hands opened as if to shove him away, and Claude desisted.

A few days earlier, Chris had read the rough draft of Judith's essay, and had chuckled over it.

Judith had lowered her eyebrows. "What's funny?" she had asked Mrs. Zajac.

"Oh," Chris had answered. "It's wonderful, Judith. It's just that I don't think I could have written anything like this at your age."

Perched against her front table now, springtime at the window of her classroom, Chris read aloud a passage about slave traders wrenching children from their parents. It was exciting to feel Judith's eyes on her. Chris had a recurrent fantasy about waking up one day to find that a former student had become an admirable and famous personage. She felt ready to settle for something less grandiose. She hoped for confident, "well-adjusted" children. But Judith gave her one of the best feelings she had experienced in her fourteen years of teaching, the sensation that came from knowing that she had a child in the room who, with a little luck and guidance, would certainly surpass her.

June

Thomas Jefferson imagined an aristocracy of intellect, made up in part of "youths of genius" who would be raised by public education "from among the classes of the poor."

Horace Mann, the great spokesman of the Common School Movement, imagined in the mid-nineteenth century a system of universal education for America, which would make "the wheel of Progress" roll "harmoniously and resistlessly onward."

John Dewey imagined schools that would provide for every child "an embryonic community life" and, for the nation, "the deepest and best guarantee of a larger society which is worthy, lovely, and harmonious."

W. E. B. Du Bois imagined that education would someday help to bring about "the treatment of all men according to their individual desert and not according to their race."

James Bryant Conant, the president of Harvard and a leading voice for educational reform from around the end of World War II until the mid-1960s, imagined that public schools would answer the threat of Soviet Russian competition and "secure the foundations of our free society."

What great hopes Americans have placed in formal education. What a stirring faith in children and in the possibility and power of universal intellectual improvement. And what a burden of idealism for the little places where education is actually attempted.

The history of education in the twentieth century presents a picture of a nation perennially dissatisfied, for one reason or another, with its public schools. But maybe if less had been asked, less would have been done. America has greatly increased the quantity of education. When Horace Mann got started, only a small percentage of American children finished grade school. Now virtually every child *has* to go to school until the age of sixteen. In the 1980s, about a quarter of all Americans, adults and children, are actively engaged in education in one way or another. The nation spends about $150 billion a year on public elementary and high schools. America spends a larger percentage of its gross national product on education than Japan, Germany, France, and England, and a slightly smaller percentage than Canada. Many state governments have at least begun to try for a rough equality in financing between poor and wealthy districts. (For the first half of the 1980s, Holyoke ran its schools entirely on state money; on occasion, a former mayor used some of the funds for fixing potholes, too.) Against long odds, school districts all over the country have been desegregated.

And yet while public schools have always helped a relative few rise out of poverty, they have not proven to be the "great equalizers" that Horace Mann dreamed of. Many schools, of course, remain desegregated only in theory. Many high schools are segregated internally, thanks to "tracking," a system Conant helped promote, which in theory sorts students according to natural ability, and in practice most often sorts them along lines of race and economic class. John Dewey did more than any other individual before or since to bring new air and light into classrooms, but the deep changes he dreamed of never came to pass, and he lived to criticize pedagogical practices carried out in his name. Some commentaries from the left doubt that idealism has ever been much more than a cloak for darker purposes in educational reform, such as the production of a tranquilized workforce that would learn enough but not too much in school.

The history of education in America is the history of attempts to reform it. The latest movement deplores high dropout rates and declines in the College Board scores of new teachers. Many tests and surveys show that large percentages of American youth come out of high school and even college incompetent in the three R's and ignorant of basic facts about history, geography, science, and literature. The bad news has inspired many commissions and from them many reports that make use of the word "crisis." As in the late 1950s, these reports often invoke an external threat – not Soviet competition now, but Japanese economic power. "Public education has put this country at a terrible competitive disadvantage," a corporate leader was quoted as saying in 1987. "They're the suppliers of our workforce, but they're suppliers with a fifty percent defect rate."

On the whole, the reform movement of the 1980s has lacked the moral and emotional force of the movement of the late 1960s. The cries of alarm from that earlier campaign still echo, particularly from one group of books that comprise, collectively, a literature of rage.

In an often used metaphor of the 1960s, children were dying in their schools. Changes weren't just desirable; they had to happen right away. Yet to the critics, change seemed impossible within the walls of urban public schools. Ivan Illich's *Deschooling Society*, the manifesto of the movement that called for the dissolution of all institutions of formal education, was published in the early 1970s. It nicely caps the literature of rage. A number of books in this genre were firsthand accounts by reform-minded teachers. Most could have been written in the late 1970s or the 1980s – conditions in many urban school systems have not improved, and in some have gotten worse. A surprising number of the writers were men. According to one view, they'd never have written their books if there hadn't been a war on with draft defer-ments for teachers, but that overlooks the genu-ine strength of feeling in many of the books.

In *Death at an Early Age*, published in 1967, Jonathan Kozol describes a year of teaching in Boston, in a school where children were beaten in the basement, and the students were black and the teachers white and, by Kozol's account, deeply racist. Kozol got fired for having his class read a poem by Langston Hughes.

According to the era's "free school move-ment," public schools were prisons; no change was possible within them; a different sort of school was needed. In *The Lives of Children*, George Dennison describes a "free" school that he helped to create in New York City. Denni-son writes with an enormous certainty, and, in keeping with the temper of the times, he gets carried away when describing the enemy. Dennison holds that public school teachers, even ones he's willing to assume are "fine," can't possibly avoid hypocrisy in imposing discipline on their students. "On the contrary," he writes, "it was only too evident that in accepting their jobs they had given away their integrity, for the truth was that they could not make moral judgments and implement them."

Herbert Kohl (*36 Children*, also published in 1967) makes it plain that he at least did not give up his integrity during the two years he spent teaching in a public school in Harlem. But during his second year, Kohl received discouraging news about students from his first class. He began to feel that other teachers and omnipresent racism had started to undo whatever good he'd done. He writes, "I was no longer sure of the value of my work to the children. That it helped me was undeniable." He felt that teaching had forced him to confront the worst parts of himself, and had helped him to improve: "I fought to be more human and feel I succeeded."

By the end of his second year, Kohl writes, he lacked "perspective": "The thought of twenty-five more children the next year, twenty-five that might have a good year yet ultimately benefit little or nothing from it, depressed me. I wanted to think and to write, to discover how I could best serve the children."

More than poor pay and lack of status make teaching hard. Kohl did what many teachers would always like to do:

> I decided to take a year's leave and go to Europe. As hard as it was to part from the children, it was necessary, and so I spent a year in Spain, thinking, mostly, and writing, avoiding until the last moments the decision to return to work with the children and still remain outside of the system. I have never stopped teaching, but I no longer have a classroom.

2

Chris made up delinquency lists over Memorial Day weekend, which followed the Science Fair, and on Tuesday she got right back to work. "Ashley, you owe me a story. Kimberly, you owe me social studies. Claude, come here, please. Claude, you got a twenty-five on the last spelling test. Claude, I thought you were on a roll. I don't think it's too much to ask that you study your spelling every night." She interrupted the Civil War when half the class could not explain what she had just taught, that the Emancipation Proclamation was partly a political act and not something humble Abe Lincoln did just because it was right. Chris said cheerfully, "In case you people haven't noticed, I'm not letting you sit here for the next four weeks. I'm not letting you come with your bodies and leave your brains behind. So remember to pack your brains when you come to school."

The North, they figured out, had strategic advantages. And it was on to Bull Run. "People with picnic baskets! To watch people going to war! They were going to have a picnic and watch people get killed!"

"People got killed?" asked Robert.

"Robert, in a war, people get killed," said Chris.

"My grandfather was in a war, and *he* didn't get killed," said Robert.

"Did I say that everybody in a war got killed?" asked Chris. Afterward, she resolved, "I'm not going to let my little fifth graders leave me thinking war is fun, like on TV."

She didn't want them to leave ignorant about the future either. She wanted to tell them that their lives did not have to include welfare. These lessons sprang from local reality; they would never have occurred to her if half of her class hadn't come from families on some form of public assistance.

She started the story of Reconstruction, and then for several days in a row she got waylaid by the subject of school segregation, which led her and the class to muse on why, in a segregated system, most of the money for education would go to all-white schools. "What was wrong with that?" she asked. "Why is it important that everyone get a good education?" They talked for a long time on that subject.

Irene said, "My father quit high school and now he's going back to college."

"My mother, too," said Claude.

"My father dropped out in tenth grade," said Arabella.

"I bet, Arabella, if you asked him, he would say he regretted it," said Chris. "If Jimmy goes for a job, and Jimmy has a high school diploma and Claude doesn't, the person with the diploma almost always gets the job."

"That's not fair!" said Claude.

"It's very fair," said Chris.

During the ensuing argument, Alice leaned toward Margaret and said, "I want to go to Smith or Mount Holyoke."

The next day, digressing again from Reconstruction, Chris asked them what they wanted to be when they grew up. She would ask them that question many times, in the midst of other lessons and in between lessons, throughout the last weeks of the year. "You should never sit there and have no idea what you want to do in life," she said. "It might be one week you want

to be an astronaut and the next week a paleon-
tologist, but you should have *some* idea. I think
you should start to think about that. Arnie,
what do you want to be?"

"A policeman."

"A hairdresser," said Arabella.

Lots of chatter followed about who was going
to become what, while Claude advised Arnie
on the sort of handgun he should carry as a cop
— a .357 Magnum would be best, Claude
thought.

Claude said he wanted to be a professional
fisherman.

Chris smiled. "Oh, Claude, you'd be a *very*
good one."

She turned to Jimmy. "Jimmy, what do you
want to be?"

"I dunno," said Jimmy.

"Jimmy, you know, you should want to be
something."

"I do," he said.

"What?" said Chris.

"I dunno," said Jimmy.

She carried on with Jimmy. Getting him to
write his last story of the year became the battle
now. She didn't really win. She brought Jimmy
up to her front table. She tried to coax ideas
from him. She teased him, saying that she
hoped she had him in her class next year,
because now she knew how smart he was.

Jimmy sat with his head on his arms and gazed toward the windows, his flourishing, healthy-looking curly hair surrounding his delicate but ashen face. She lifted him by a skinny arm and said, "Think, Jimmy, think." When she let him go, he collapsed again. She lifted him and said, "I'm going to ask for you next year, Jimmy, and boy, are you and I going to go places!" "He's such a sad case," she thought. "It's like I'm sticking a needle in him when I ask him to think." She did get him to finish the story finally. Jimmy sat right up then, all by himself, to copy it over. Then he looked alert. He looked undistractable, aiding his pen with many twistings of his mouth.

A "pull-out" teacher, one who taught English as a second language and seemed to have a lot of spare time now that the year was winding down, had come to the door in search of some adult conversation. Chris, busy and preoccupied but ever polite to her colleagues, was standing in the doorway with the other teacher, but was looking back into the room and watching Jimmy copy his story. "He loves to copy," Chris said in a low voice to her colleague, nodding toward Jimmy. "As long as he doesn't have to think."

"Well," said the other teacher, "he'll work at Ampad and be happy as a clam." (Ampad was a paper company with a factory nearby.)

"It's too bad, though," Chris replied in a low voice, "because he has potential."

"Just think," said the other teacher. "If we did our jobs the way we're supposed to, there wouldn't be anyone to do the menial jobs."

The other teacher laughed heartily, but Chris didn't seem to hear the remark. She stared at Jimmy, the scrivener. He was one of those children, she thought, who was probably behind from the moment he'd set foot in kindergarten. She didn't think she had helped him much. But maybe she really would have him next year. There wasn't time now for a fresh start.

The Famous Patriots still looked down from over the window, anachronisms that had long since receded into the realm of the unnoticeable. Chris didn't have time now to bring decorations up to date.

The class in Room 205 had come to seem like a combat infantry platoon, full of ghosts and replacements. The ghosts materialized in the form of old papers and books when, for instance, a child came in without a social studies text and Chris got one from the cabinets by the window and, opening it, found on the inside cover the name of Lisette, Blanca, Juanita, or Alejandro. Or when she went looking for an extra spelling book and, finding none, thought of Clarence — for a moment she'd gaze out the window at nothing and think, "I wonder how he's doing."

Now, the year nearly over, another replacement arrived.

Paul, the vice principal, led into the room a slightly chubby boy dressed in dark clothes and dark glasses with straps that dangled from the earpieces. The boy looked at first sight like a sinister eleven-year-old librarian.

"Hello! What's *your* name?" said Chris.

"Miguel," whispered the boy.

"We'll get you settled right away," said Chris. She gave Miguel the books that had belonged to Juanita and, before that, to Blanca. Miguel took to the room within minutes. He wrote in his journal that afternoon — his spelling and punctuation were impeccable: "My new teacher is Mrs. Zajac, and so far I think she's the best teacher I ever had. She doesn't talk mean to anybody in the room."

Snatches of information that Miguel let drop about his family made Chris think he probably came from an unstable household. One day he told Chris, "I'm the first one in my family who *is* smart." The boy was, in fact, very intellectual. He soon began asking her questions out of nowhere, such as, "Mrs. Zajac, how much is a thousand yen?" She asked him, too, what he wanted to be when he grew up.

"A physician," Miguel replied.

"A physician? Would you take good care of me, Miguel?" She smiled, then said earnestly, "Miguel, if you come to school and work hard, you could be a physician." (Miguel, she'd discovered, was in the habit of skipping school from time to time.)

But Miguel was not as smart about being smart as Judith. He didn't hide his good grades, and could not hide his academic curiosity. In the room, the other children were friendly to Miguel, but when at the ends of bright June days Chris stood at her window, watching her children from the Flats head home across the playground, she saw that Miguel was the only walker who walked home alone. She tried to cultivate a friendship between Felipe and Miguel, but the match failed.

She had gotten a piece of good but disquieting news: Pedro had been tested at last. On an inspired hunch, the psychologist had given Pedro a test often administered to stroke victims who have lost their language, a sophisticated test involving pattern recognition. Pedro, the boy who could hardly read or speak, had scored in the near-genius range.

Told for perhaps the first time in his life that he was smart, Pedro said, "Sometime I know things and I can't say them."

Chris had stared at the doorway. "What have

I done for him? He just vegetated in my room." She had flexed the muscles in her jaw. "But I've done a hell of a lot more than anybody else ever did."

Now word came from the office that there would be a special class next year for children who had formidable language problems. Pedro would be enrolled. Chris asked that Julio be enrolled, too. While she was at it, she had the office call up Mental Health once again to see if Robert's mother had taken him to a psychiatrist. His mother had not. Chris filed the 51A, saying again, "She's not going to be allowed to sit back and do nothing." She was cleaning up loose ends.

One morning, Chris made it official – she told the class that she was going to teach sixth grade next year. A cacophony of voices, Felipe's the loudest, cried, "Can *I* have you?"

Robert blurted out, "I want you," and then Robert tried to take it back.

Robert said, "Miss Zajac's mean."

Julio retorted, "Miss Zajac's mean? You wish."

"I don't wish. I know," said Robert. "Every teacher in this school is mean."

Chris sat at her desk, smiling faintly. She felt like a schoolgirl, flattered by the attentions of a boy but not sure she really wants them. One year of being responsible for Robert would suffice, she thought.

Arabella said to Chris, "Robert said he wanted you."

Robert turned around at his desk and yelled at Arabella, "No, I didn't! Liar! Liar!" Then, cheeks flushed, he stared at his desk top. "I'm never gonna have her again in my life! She's a witch!"

"Okay, Robert," said Chris softly. "That's enough."

The school ran out of pencils. Chris bought some with her own money. This happened every June and was as sure a sign as grass stains on the children's sneakers that the year, too, was running out. But she hadn't lost them yet, and she didn't feel like letting go. More than ever now, she felt she had to make every hour count. The top math group had nearly finished with their text. She'd made it through the Civil War. "The Civil War is over. Who won, Jimmy?" she said. Jimmy knew, but it took him a while to say so. She did not want to stop there, or stop trying to lead Jimmy to an acquaintance with the world of deliberate, active thought. On a Friday, however, all efforts halted. The weather stopped her. August came to Room 205.

Chris awakened at dawn with a headache. The day was already sultry when she got to school. The windows of Room 205 caught all of the morning sun. Through them, that Friday morning, the trees on the Chicopee bank of the river, over the factory roofs, looked green and cool. Sunshine sparkled for a while on the dew in the grass on the playground. Inside, though, the heat gathered. She felt it first in her ears. Warmth seemed visible. Its color was gray, approximately the color of the plexiglass in the scratched windowpanes and in the dome above the library, which, seen from the doorway, now looked like a huge eye radiating heat. By midmorning, the air in the room was at least fifteen degrees hotter than the hot air outside. By afternoon – maybe it was the combination of hazy sunlight and smoky, scratched windowpanes – the landscape seemed drained of color. At a distance, everything looked woozy. The children's faces were all moist and flushed. They stood in long lines at the water fountain at the sink. The girls plucked at their blouses, as if removing burrs from them, and everyone, even the boys, fanned themselves with spelling books and pieces of construction paper.

"All right," said Chris. "I know it's hot."

She shut off the lights and sat down beside Claude's desk to read aloud from a new novel about some children who get locked up in a museum at night. Afterward, she did not feel like moving.

"Can we do social studies now?" asked Miguel.

"No!" yelled the other children.

Miguel cowered, smiling.

This time, she would let the majority rule. She had come to a dead halt. Even her breathing was measured. She let them talk to her, and as they did, the children seemed to experience again that alteration of perception that had hit them when she'd come to school in jeans and sneakers for the trip to Sturbridge Village. She remembered this happening to her long ago, when she saw one of her elementary school teachers in a grocery store and felt bowled over — it had never occurred to her that teachers went shopping just like other people. Now the sight of an immobile, exhausted looking Mrs. Zajac, sitting among them and in a child's chair, chatting with them in the overheated gloom, seemed to make the children bolder than they'd usually been with her. Many of them told her that back in September they'd heard that she was mean. They'd heard she was the witch of Kelly School.

"Let's talk about the Civil War," said Miguel. Another chorus of "No!"

Chris smiled. She asked the children, "Who else said I was mean?"

"Everyone," said Miguel. He grinned.

Finally, Chris told them that they could get

games from the cabinets by the windows, and she wandered back to her desk and sat as still as she could.

At the end of that hot Friday Chris gave her pitch for reading over the weekend, but it came from a Mrs. Zajac who pleaded, not demanded. The heat on Monday was, if anything, more intense. Over the weekend, two children from the lower wards but from another school had drowned in the Connecticut River. Chris gave the class a lecture about the perils of the river.

She sent Courtney and Kimberly outside to look for a shady place where they could hold the class. But the only trees around the school were saplings, and her scouts found only a few little pools of shade, sufficient for no more than three children. So class continued inside, in slow motion, without the lights.

3

Near the end of a year, a teacher can't help facing the fact that there's a lot she hoped to do and hasn't done, and now probably never will. It is like growing old, but for teachers old age arrives every year. Sitting at her desk during math one hot day in June, Chris looked at Felipe and said to herself, "He hasn't mastered fractions yet. He won't do that 'til next year."

She looked at Pedro and thought that she had done something for his future, at least, and maybe for Julio's, too. Contemplating Jimmy, though, the boy's head lying on stick-like arms on his desk top, she felt that the changes she had hoped to make in him just hadn't come to pass. He looked like a porcelain figure. He gazed toward the window, evidently lost in something emptier than daydreams. She thought of the children who had been snatched away from her this year. Handsome Alejandro didn't worry her as much as the fetching, shy Juanita, or nearly as much as Blanca. She remembered Blanca's frightened eyes, and re-proached herself. That girl was probably a victim of sexual abuse, Chris decided. She hadn't done enough, she thought. But there had been no evidence. There almost never was.

Some years ago, Chris had acquired the mor-bid habit of reading the police reports in the paper, hoping not to find the names of former students there. Many years she did find one or two. Every year she also heard good news about some children she had taught, but the bad news, when it came, always felt like it weighed more. It left her wondering if in the end she'd done anything for the child. She could imagine finding Robert's name in an unhappy context in the paper someday. She looked at her class now and thought, "How many backgrounds they come from. How many different sets of problems. Even if I had them for three hundred and sixty-five days, would I meet them all?" She used to believe in miracles. Now she tended to believe only in mysteries. "I guess I used to feel I could really rescue kids, that if they had a good teacher, everything would be fine. It's not that I try less now. I'm just more aware of my own limitations." Forlornly, Chris said, "But I don't think I've ever taken a really good student and wrecked him."

She should have been more generous with herself. Teachers usually have no way of knowing that they have made a difference in a child's life, even when they have made a dramatic one. But for children who are used to thinking of themselves as stupid or not worth talking to or deserving rape and beatings, a good teacher can provide an astonishing revelation. A good teacher can give a child at least a chance to feel, *"She* thinks I'm worth something. Maybe I am." Good teachers put snags in the river of children passing by, and over the years, they redirect hundreds of lives. Many people find it easy to imagine unseen webs of malevolent conspiracy in the world, and they are not always wrong. But there is also an innocence that conspires to hold humanity together, and it is made of people who can never fully know the good that they have done.

4

Chris sat in a lawn chair, her students around her on the playground grass. The fifth-grade classes had assembled for Field Day on that greensward surrounded by factories. The sun shone. The day sparkled. Racecourses were in place. A volleyball net had been erected. The gym teacher presided with his megaphone.

The class had lost the first heat of the balloon-popping relay. Felipe and Dick blew an early lead in the water-fill relay. "That's okay," called Chris. "We got the brains, not the brawn." She called through cupped hands, "Felipe, take it slow! The object is not how fast you go . . . Oh, never mind." She laughed.

"We're last in everything," said Chris under her breath. Then in a loud voice she said to the children around her, "Hey, we're slow, but good-looking."

Time for the dress and undress relay. The class's hopes rested on Judith, Alice, and Claude. "Come on, we've got to win *something*. You girls always look nice when you come in. You must know how to dress and undress." The children cheered, and then they groaned as

Claude got hopelessly entangled in the clothes, inserting legs in sleeves, during the dressing part. Robert sat apart, plucking clover, then coiling the stems over themselves and flicking the tops at the backs of classmates. Without turning around, Chris said, "Robert, stop that."

"Me? I wasn't doin' nuttin'."

Robert and Ashley had declined to participate in Field Day.

"Okay, gang, the water balloon throw. We're gonna win this one!"

And a while later: "Oh, well."

The long-distance run began. Chris looked up and saw that she had invested the class's honor in Jimmy and Pedro, who even at rest had difficulty breathing. "Now why did I do that?"

Amazingly, Jimmy led his heat all the way down to the end of the playground, but then he stopped. Jimmy crossed the finish line walking.

"Ashley, don't you want to be in something?"

Ashley shook and shook her head.

"Come on, Ashley," said Arabella.

"Yeah, Ashley, come on," said Felipe.

A little later Ashley whispered in Chris's ear.

"You want to be in the volleyball, Ashley? Good."

They lost the sack race. They lost their volleyball match.

"Oh, well. We can write paragraphs around

them, right?" Chris sat in sunshine. Arabella had made sure to sit right beside Mrs. Zajac's feet. Robert had made sure to sit near Mrs. Zajac, too.

"Mrs. Zajac, why did you become a teacher?" Arabella asked. "You like kids?"

"I like kids."

"You like to punish kids?" asked Miguel, and he made a loud laugh.

"*There's* a theory," said Chris.

"Were you a student teacher?" asked Robert.

"Yes."

"Like Miss Hunt."

"Yes."

"Robert, don't you want to be in the tug of war?"

Robert shrugged.

The tug of war was about to begin. "Do it for Mrs. Zajac!" cried Alice.

At that last minute, Robert decided to lend his bulk to the contest. He took the end of the rope.

They won a heat. They won another. And then they won the finals.

"You may not be fast, but you're strong," Chris told them.

The front chalkboard, after lunch, recorded the triumph in excellent spelling: VICTORY AT LAST ... TUG OF WAR CHAMPIONS ... WE ARE THE BEST ... WE CAN PULL!

★ ★ ★

460

Neither Chris nor the class was quite the same after the heat wave. It had forced her into conceding the reality of June, and there was no going back. Chris held one more session of recess detention, but it really was June now, and she was letting go.

In the room, Chris allowed new liberties. She would lean her elbows on her desk and say, "What happened then?" when a child introduced a digression into a lesson. The last two weeks went on like one long Friday afternoon.

She remarked to Felipe one morning that he often talked loudly.

"And *you* talk loud when you're mad," Felipe shot back.

"Oh ho! He got you there!" said Miguel.

Chris smiled, elbows on her desk, the lesson at a halt, and she listened to them talk.

"My last teacher?" said Miguel to Mrs. Zajac. "He used to make us write out of the dictionary after school."

"That's what I call not a teacher," said Felipe.

"That's what I call a child molester," said Miguel.

She looked at the boys. She wore the faintest of smiles.

Pedro came up to her desk to brag. "In Mrs. — I forget her name — in her class we were studying body parts, and I got the mostest right."

"Good for you, Pedro!"

"I know about that!" said Miguel. "At my last school I went to classes about puberty? And they gave us pamphlets. *I'm* in puberty! We're *all* in puberty!"

Chris shook her head. "My little Einstein," she thought. She wished she'd had him all year long.

She sat at her desk more often than before. While sitting there one day, she noticed Claude go out the door toward the bathroom and then turn right. Minutes later, she got a glimpse of him on the other side of the balcony. He had taken the longest way to the bathroom. When he returned, she said, "Claude, you took the route to Tokyo."

"I always do," Claude said.

In fact, he had been taking that route, making those trips to the bathroom *last*, ever since September. Claude. He was still disorganized, but Chris saw method in it. She wasn't worried about him anymore. She couldn't say exactly why. She just wasn't. Introducing the final story of the year, she had suggested various topics, and turning to Claude, she had said, "Or you could write about why hunting is bad or good," and Claude's face had lit up. It was a going-away present to him.

The maples on the far river bank, billowing green clouds, made a new and lumpy horizon.

Out on the playground on a mild, sunny June afternoon, all the regular recesses had ended and loud children's voices had died away. A little, quiet group of children, the variously handicapped ones, came out and some played jump rope on the cement pad below the window. Inside, Chris's class worked on a social studies assignment. The room was still, and from outside came the drifting-away sound of the ventilators. Chris turned her chair to the window and watched the long rope arcing, a child skipping.

"I loved jump rope," she said aloud after a while, still staring out the window. "Double Dutch and Scotch. Scotch was reverse Double Dutch. What do you call it now, Judith?"

Judith looked up from her social studies paper, a little startled. She glanced over her shoulder at Mrs. Zajac, who, without turning from the window, repeated her question. "What do you call reverse Double Dutch? We used to call it Scotch."

"Oh," said Judith. "Irish." Judith went back to work.

Chris laughed. "Do you sing songs?"

"Mmmm-hmmm," said Judith over her work.

"Do you play high low medium wavy walky talky slowly Pepper?" asked Chris, still looking out the window.

Judith looked back at her teacher again

with narrowed eyes.

"Is Pepper still fast?" asked Chris.

"Yes!" exclaimed Judith, whether in amusement or exasperation wasn't altogether clear until Judith turned sideways in her chair and faced Mrs. Zajac with a wry smile. Judith seemed to be thinking, "Might as well let her get this out of her system."

"Ever play Chinese jump rope?" asked Chris. "I was very good at one rope, not so good at two."

Those conversations with Judith were precious to Chris. They became more precious at the end of another day, when Judith announced that her father planned to move the family back to Puerto Rico.

"Oh!" Chris blurted out, "I don't want you to leave!"

Chris knew that going back home would be wonderful for Judith's father. But Judith had become her shiniest hope. She was one Puerto Rican child who could certainly succeed on the mainland, and on mainland terms. Chris had counted on seeing Judith next year. She'd hoped to have her in class again. She'd looked forward to following Judith's career through teacher friends at junior high and high school. Chris thought about the girl from Miami whom she'd met at the school in Comerío, the one who'd had a hard time adjusting to the island. But then she thought, "Judith is accepting this better than I am."

Judith shrugged. She said she had to take things as they came. "I've got to, if I'm going to live in this world," Judith said.

And Chris thought, "Well, I guess I ought to take this like an adult, too."

The last music lesson came. The music teacher took the class outside. The children marched behind the music teacher, who strutted soldierly around the playground, playing on a set of bagpipes.

"Well, thank you," Chris said to that cheerful, enthusiastic, permissive soprano when the music teacher and the class returned to the room. "The class really enjoyed you this year. Didn't you, class?"

The children gave each other sneaky looks. They emitted one soft, collective *"Yeahhhh."*

Al had ordered almost every teacher to move to a new room for next year. In the halls, where bulletin boards were turning blank and corkbrown, many little Sherpas, laden with cardboard boxes, passed to and fro. Chris had not thrown away much in her fourteen years on the job. Now she was reforming. The piles that she pulled from her desk drawers, cabinets, and closet were impressive in their volume: folders full of old dittos and forgotten lesson plans and old sign-up rosters. "Look at this," she said to her helpers – Judith, Irene, Arabella, and, of course, Mariposa. "That class was so bad, I had to have them sign out for the bathroom." She found old letters to parents and the sheaf of bank books she once had to keep for students and her college paper on the purposes of education. 'Personal Philosophy of Education,' she read. "What a lot of bull. I didn't have a philosophy." There were perhaps a thousand dollars' worth of store-bought idea books for practically every contingency. Now and then she lingered over a discovery. " 'Chris Padden, Elementary Games,' " she read aloud, her helpers all around her. "Mem-o-ries!" she sang. "A flash from the past," she said. Old plan books made a pile two feet tall. "They're going to bury me with my plan books."

"Dump," said Chris when Irene showed her a collection of dittos about birds. "Dump," she said to a folder full of math games.

Jimmy, of all people, retrieved that folder from the discard pile.

"What do you want that for?" asked Chris.

"For some time when I get bored," Jimmy said, and Chris paused a moment, head cocked to look at him.

She had all but emptied her top right-hand desk drawer when she came upon a folded slip of lined white paper. She opened it, and at once she knew the handwriting; it was still as familiar to her as that averted, stony face and those amazing dimples. She read silently awhile about her own demise:

There once lived a witch her name was Mrs. Zazac and she was a very bad witch and never like no body there was a boy name Clarence she didn't like and she lived in a hunten house . . .

"Oh, I've got to save this." She put the story in her box of things to keep.

5

Gertrude Harty is invariably remembered by her former students as "little Miss Harty." She was tiny, and she seemed as fragile as a bird, but even in old age and retirement she had a presence. Receiving visitors, she still dressed as if for school, in a tweed suit and thin gold necklace, which she fingered now and then.

Almost all of the school buildings where Miss Harty taught had been torn down. The site of the first, a one-room schoolhouse in a little western Massachusetts town, had long since vanished under the waters of the Quabbin

Reservoir. Miss Harty remembered the day when the town's graves were transplanted. After the gates of the dam had shut and the site of that first school of hers disappeared under the flood, Miss Harty had gone back to Holyoke, where she was born and raised, and had spent forty-two years teaching grade school. She could conjure up many of her students as readily as if they were all members of an extremely fertile, gigantically extended family.

"She's one of the ones I remember," Miss Harty said of Chris. She said she pictured Chris Padden in third grade, wearing a pink and white checked dress, sitting alertly with her books and pencils neatly arranged in front of her. The girl Miss Harty called to mind was very serious and often raised her hand. But only when she knew the answer — standing up to deliver it, as Miss Harty wished schoolchildren were still required to do. Miss Harty figured Chris had parents who listened to her.

Miss Harty remembered the first day of snow that year long ago. She had put on the Victrola a recording of Robert Frost reading "The Runaway." She remembered Chris listening intently, brow wrinkled. She could see that Chris and most of her classmates were worried about the little colt in the poem, who is afraid of snowflakes. "I tried to take the essence of the poem and engage them. I remember Chris and

Chris's class. They were so receptive and responded so to the poem. It was fun for me, and I hope it was for them," Miss Harty said.

Robert Frost was what Chris remembered best of that year's lessons, too. Miss Harty had died this spring, during the third marking period. Standing over the coffin at the wake, Chris, who at most wakes felt mainly an overpowering urge to get outside, had this time allowed herself some nostalgic thoughts. "A little bit of Robert Frost died with you, Miss Harty," Chris had declared in her mind. Miss Harty had been a teacher of the quiet variety. When her students had gotten noisy, she had made her own voice softer until they got curious and had to ask what she had said. Chris had not been able to copy her favorite old teacher in that respect, but as much as anything else, the year in Miss Harty's room had made Chris want to be a teacher, too. Chris wished that she had visited Miss Harty years ago to tell her that. But Chris had never forgotten little Miss Harty, and Miss Harty had never forgotten Chris. "She was a very bright child and very dependable," Miss Harty said a few months before she died. "I don't remember her as an apple polisher. She was just one of the children you like to remember."

Chris herself now had an extended family of former students whom she liked to remember.

The one who had been her all-time highest achiever was now a very pretty young woman with blond ringlets surrounding her face, like an elaborate picture frame. Her name was Suzanne. She had been living this year just a few miles from Kelly School, at Mount Holyoke College, where she was studying history and literature and still getting mostly A's. Suzanne was working hard for those grades but thought she could do even better. That year back in sixth grade, Miss Padden had made her feel that she could do anything. Suzanne remembered other lessons: Miss Padden deftly handling a fight Suzanne had with a classmate; Miss Padden trying to teach her not to be arrogant about her academic gifts; Miss Padden always making her feel that she could tell Miss Padden anything; Miss Padden instructing her to be cautious on the matter of boyfriends. "I had a massive crush on this guy who's now a waste case," Suzanne said. Miss Padden had warned her, with a look Suzanne could still remember – Miss Padden's head cocked, her tongue clucking once softly – when Suzanne was about to expose her unrequited affections for that boy one day in the room. Suzanne remembered thinking Miss Padden was beautiful. That year Suzanne, a seamstress as well as a student, made imitations of Miss Padden's outfits and wore them to school.

Suzanne remembered that Miss Padden had a boyfriend. (Billy had sometimes called on Chris during the school day back then, when he and Chris were courting.) "She'd excuse herself from the class," Suzanne said, "and we'd all whisper about it. I liked her so much I kind of felt jealous when she left to talk to him. And then she would come back in, and we were all happy she was there again. I think we all didn't like that, because she had affections elsewhere."

There was a difference between the way Miss Harty had inspired Chris and Chris had inspired Suzanne, a generational difference. When Chris was growing up, teaching was still one of the best jobs available to a bright, ambitious woman, especially one with working-class parents. That, of course, was no longer true. Chris knew Suzanne wouldn't become a teacher. "Suzanne's too smart." In fact, Suzanne was hoping to go to Harvard Law School. But the transactions, between Miss Harty and Chris, and Chris and Suzanne, were similar. Suzanne had one overriding memory of Chris, and it was of a person who had helped her once and who, by doing that, had helped her all along the way.

"She's, like, my most memorable teacher," Suzanne said. She kept meaning to visit Miss Padden and tell her that, but hadn't yet.

6

On a sunny afternoon the last week of school, on the grounds in front of another, older elementary school, under one of several large maple trees, Clarence sat designing a tattoo, with felt-tipped pens, on the bared chest of an Alpha classmate. The friend he was tattooing was a huge twelve-year-old Puerto Rican boy, nearly six feet tall, nicknamed Little Richard by his Alpha teacher. He leaned against the tree trunk, a beatific smile on his face, while Clarence drew a huge eagle on his chest. The small, wiry white boy who had shown Clarence around the Alpha class some months before watched Clarence draw. Clarence had already tattooed himself: a big red eagle on his chest and a swastika on his right forearm.

In a little while, Clarence and the white boy began to tussle in a friendly-looking way. Clarence quick and lithe. Then the white boy plucked some grass and threw it in Clarence's face. And Clarence, his jaw suddenly fierce, ripped up some grass and rubbed it hard in the white boy's face. The white boy went limp and when he got the chance, scrambled a little distance away. Little Richard laughed serenely, and Clarence sat down again beneath the tree. Then Clarence said, "Girls. Check it out."

Of course, he was the first to notice a change in the landscape. Four schoolgirls, with neatly coiffed hair and in designer clothes, had sat down under another maple, about twenty yards away. "They think they're high-class prep," said the white boy.

Clarence called toward the girls, "Tell that girl in green pants to come over here!"

The girls elevated their chins and looked away. They were probably telling each other, "Those are Alpha kids. Just ignore them."

"Kiss mines!" Clarence yelled at them.

One of the girls turned an angry face toward the boys. "I'm not yours!" She must not have been accustomed to that idiom.

The white boy made a wolf whistle.

Little Richard yelled, "Fuckin' bitch!"

"He called you a fuckin' bitch!" called the white boy toward the girls. "That's what *he* said."

"*I* didn't say it!" called Clarence.

"Gimme that ass," murmured grinning Little Richard.

Clarence looked at Little Richard. Clarence smiled. "Go say somethin' to them girls," said Clarence to Little Richard.

Little Richard grinned more broadly then. He got up and walked in a wide, slow circle around the girls' tree.

Clarence laughed behind his hand as he watched.

Little Richard returned from his threatening promenade to the Alphans' tree and made as if to hump its trunk.

"They're so gross!" said one of the girls' voices, and once again the girls all turned their faces away.

And the three Alpha boys sat down together again.

"I wish I had a soda right here, man," said Little Richard.

"I wish one of those girls wanted to get popped," said the white boy.

Clarence plucked at the grass.

Clarence's teacher said that at first she had wondered why he had been sent to Alpha. It had been weeks before she had caught him breaking any rules, but the first time she had, a couple of her other charges had told her they were glad, because Clarence was always doing bad things she didn't notice. She still hoped to get him back in the mainstream soon. "I don't think he should stay long in this group," she said. But she allowed there was some question about who was a bad influence on whom. She had begun to notice a pattern. Her room was often divided into groups for various activities. Clarence would sometimes wander from group to group, and as he did, fights would erupt in the group that he had just left. "I can't nab him," she said. "And then, there's that adorable smile."

It was the next to last day, of school when Clarence returned to his old class. Chris and the children had moved downstairs to the room that Chris would occupy next year. They'd cleaned up all the desks and put them in the hall, per Al's decree. Only a couple of chairs and Chris's gray metal desk, just the same as her last one, remained. The class had lined up against the wall beside the doorway, and Chris sat facing them. They were having a spelling bee. The children were laughing. It was peaceful in the room.

The windows to the playground behind Chris opened at ground level, within the reach of spray paint. These new windows were almost entirely opaque under a coating of white and green graffiti, which from inside looked like several years of accumulated bird droppings. This room also had a back door, which opened directly on the playground. Chris had propped it open with a chair to let in the breeze and sunshine. Past the doorway, behind her and to her left, figures of boys on bicycles flashed by — older-looking boys, perhaps playing hooky from junior high. Passing by, the boys left snatches of conversation behind. "Motherfuckin'. . ." Hearing those words from outside,

Chris stiffened. "Lovely," she muttered to herself.

The spelling bee had come down to Miguel and Judith, and now Miguel had won. Judith laughed. The children lounged on the carpeted floor. Chris was sitting at her desk, watching them. She was thinking how small and cute they all suddenly looked. This always seemed to happen. In September her new students would walk in and right away become people whom she had to try to motivate and mold. Now that she was about to lose responsibility for them, they turned back into children, and she started missing them. In the midst of this reverie, sudden, untoward motion on the perimeter, that sense of something out of place, made Chris turn her head, and there in the opened doorway to the playground stood the familiar figure of Clarence. Brown-skinned and wiry with huge eyes. The knees of his jeans had holes in them. He wore a dirty white T-shirt. He stood there, dismounted, holding on to the handlebars of a ten-speed bike, and gazed in at the children with his mouth slightly ajar.

"Hi, Clarence!" said Chris. "How *are* you?"

He looked at her and smiled. Those dimples! And he looked so small! In her mind, he had grown much larger. Could this have been the most difficult student of her career? He was only four and a half feet tall.

"Come on in!" she said to him.

Clarence, she noticed, still stuttered sometimes at the starts of sentences. "Nuh nuh no I can't. Gotta go someplace." But he lingered in the doorway, and his mouth came ajar again as he gazed at his old classmates. They were all looking back at Clarence now.

"Oh," she thought. "I feel bad for him."

"Don't you want to come in and talk to any of them?" asked Chris. It would be sweet and fitting for him to pass the last of this afternoon with them, as if perhaps he'd never been sent away.

"Did you pass?" said Robert.

"I don't know," said Clarence.

Chris sat in her chair, turned toward him. She smiled at him. Probably he wanted to join them, but was feeling shy. Maybe she could coax him. "Don't you want to come on in?" said Chris again.

"No," said Clarence. "Not today." He smiled at her, and again he went back to gazing at the children while Chris gazed at him.

"Oh, well," said Chris offhandedly. But she had to try once more. "Sure you don't want to come in?"

"No. Bye," he said.

He turned away and sped off on his bike, so quickly she hardly saw him go. It was like the time, months ago, when Clarence was supposed to stay after school, and she turned her back for only a few seconds and turned around again to find that he had vanished. The doorway was empty. She turned back to face the room.

On the last day, Chris handed out the report cards. It was a solemn moment, mostly because the report cards named each child's teacher for next year. The children studied their cards silently. Several would have Mrs. Zajac again. They were smiling. Most didn't have her, and they looked pensive. Now they'd have to wonder what next year's teacher would be like. Alice, who had left a few days ago on a vacation with her parents, had Chris. Her parents had requested it. So had Margaret's. Chris had Courtney again — by lottery, as it were, and not by parental request — and she had Felipe, whose father had also requested her. This was notable, the first instance in Al's experience of a Puerto Rican parent asking for a particular teacher. But Arabella's mother hadn't known that one could do that. When Chris ran into her later, that handsome woman said to Chris, "She doesn't have you next year? Oh, she was hoping she would!" Chris was sorry, too. She'd have liked to keep Arabella for another year.

Jimmy stared at his report card. He looked up at Chris as she passed by and said, "I thought I was gettin' you."

He sat for a while with his head resting heavily on the heel of his hand, staring off glumly.

Chris pursed her lips. "Oh," she thought. "I shouldn't have teased him about getting me next year."

A few of the children had brought her presents. Irene gave her a very sentimental card, delivering it on Chris's side of the big desk. Irene lingered next to Chris. She wanted Chris to kiss her. Chris did, and said, "Oh, Irene, thank you!"

Ashley offered her present. It was a sprig of flowering privet that she must have broken off a hedge on her way to school that morning. Ashley delivered it from the other side of the desk. She was afraid of being kissed. "Oh, Ashley, thank you! That's very nice." Ashley, lips fastened tight, slowly backed away and sat down among her classmates.

Chris had told them they could bring in records. "But no Beastie Boys," she'd added. They had put on a record and had hopped up to sit on the counter by the window. Now they sat there, legs dangling, their arms around each other's shoulders, swaying in concert, and singing along to a song called "Talk Dirty to Me," which in this setting seemed innocent enough. Chris joined them for a moment. Wrists cocked and eyebrows raised, she danced out across the carpet. She stopped. Ashley was the only one not sitting on the counter. She was standing off to one side, watching her classmates. Chris went to her. "You want to hop on the end there, Ashley?"

Ashley shook her head, black hair swaying across her cheeks. "I don't know the words."

Eventually, Ashley changed her mind. Then the whole class was sitting in a row on the counter. Chris leaned against the jamb of the inner doorway, arms folded on her chest, and gazed across the deskless room at her class, watching them sway to their music in front of the vandalized, half-opaque windows. "I'm going to remember them this way," Chris thought.

Looking at them gave her a familiar empty feeling in her stomach. She heard herself thinking, once again, "My chicks are leaving me." But most of them would do just fine, she thought. Judith, sitting on the windowsill, looked beautiful. Chris hoped that Judith wouldn't meet too many handsome men too soon. She still felt uneasy about Pedro. "I guess the neighborhood is what scares me, and the grandmother. I mean, I know she takes care of him as best she can and she loves him and that's nice, but she's old. I mean, you can't expect an older woman to do discipline and all this stuff that goes along with bringing up an adolescent. Pedro's immature right now." She worried about Jimmy. But then again, Jimmy had given her a few tiny reassurances. First, a couple of days ago, he had asked for those math games, and then earlier today, Jimmy had come up to her and said, "You know, Mrs. Zajac, you didn't finish that book." Jimmy meant the last novel she had been reading aloud, the one about the children hiding in the museum. At least, she thought, Jimmy had not slept through all the hours he'd spent with her.

After a while their chorus line disbanded. Claude dozed in the sun, sitting in the chair that propped open the door to the playground, and Arnie did some handstands on the carpet in the mostly chairless room.

"Arnie, stop acting so crazy," said Chris.

"It's the last day of school," he said.

Chris fingered her gold necklace. "What can I say?"

The children were dismissed early. Soon the intercom said, "Bus one," and the usual commotion ensued, Claude scrambling for his bookbag, Chris crying out, "Wait! Margaret! Oh, well." That was all right. She had Margaret next year.

"Dick, I just want to say have a nice summer, okay? Everybody have a nice summer. Okay?"

Many voices called back to her from the hall, "Have a nice summer, Mrs. Zajac."

"I'm not," Claude said, looking up at her in the doorway. "I'm gonna have a *great* summer."

"Good, Claude."

"Lots of fishin'. Yup. Monday fishin', Tuesday fishin', Wednesday' fishin' . . ."

"How about some readin'?" said Chris. She had to bite her tongue for the last time over Claude.

Chris stood at the door to the hall, watching the last of the bus riders vanish around the corner.

"Ohhh," she murmured after them. "I feel a little sad."

As usual, the walkers took a more leisurely farewell, but soon they were filing out the door to the playground. Chris put an arm around Judith's shoulder, but Chris, seeming suddenly shy, didn't try to kiss her, and Judith, who looked serene and happy, smiled and walked away. Chris followed her outside. A child from another class must have pulled a fire alarm. Over its bleating, Chris called, "Take care, you guys! Have a nice summer! Be good!" The walkers waved without turning back. It seemed altogether too casual for the disbanding of a village.

She stood outside, watching as her walkers got lost among the others. "Ahhh," she said. "I'm losing them back to their environment for a summer. It's sort of sad. Well." She walked back into the empty room with pursed lips, and made as if to busy herself at her desk. She muttered over Ashley's piece of privet, "This is from one of those hedges." She took up tissues. She sniffled, and took up more tissues. "Ahhhh. I feel bad about 'em. Some of them. Judith. Mainly her. Because I don't think I'm going to see her again." Chris went to the sink and started cleaning it, still sniffling, and then she looked up toward the door to the hall, and she smiled with wet eyes. "And then again . . ." she said aloud. Summer beckoned. She did some thinking about next year. She had a lot of work to do over the summer. She told herself that teaching sixth grade would be like starting a new life.

Al convened a farewell faculty meeting. He said, "I have to thank all of you for this year. It's the best year I had in twenty years." He didn't say why. Al was Al. He went on for a few minutes, and closed by saying, "But . . . we had a year."

An hour later she was driving under the railroad bridge. She crossed the first canal, which marks the edge of the Flats. She probably wouldn't see this part of town again, or any of her walkers, until September. Within a few weeks this year's disappointments would begin to fade. Now they were still fresh. She thought about Robert. "He's my failure, I guess. Him and Clarence."

Even the most troubled children had attractive qualities for Chris. Even the most toughened, she always felt, wanted to please her and wanted her to like them, no matter how perversely they expressed it. She belonged among schoolchildren. They made her confront sorrow and injustice. They made her feel useful. Again this year, some had needed more help than she could provide. There were many problems that she hadn't solved. But it wasn't for lack of trying. She hadn't given up. She had run out of time.

Acknowledgments and Sources

My thanks above all to Christine Zajac and to her students and their parents. My thanks also to Billy Zajac, Mrs. Padden, Jimmy, Mary, and Peggy. I owe many thanks to Barry Werth and to Tim Barrett, George Counter, and Jim Newton. John Clark, Gail Furman, David Grosbeck, Blanca Ortiz, Kate Dean, and Tommy Philpot were gracious and helpful, and so were many others in the Holyoke school system, especially my friends at Dean Vocational. For their help and kindness, my thanks to Al Laudato and Paul Mengle. Everyone at Kelly School was kind to me, and I wish to thank the staff, faculty, and administration, including: Elaine Baskin, Diana Brown, Carol Burke, Doris Cruz, Joanne Devine, Debbie Drugan,

Laura Dupont, Larry Duprey, Roberta Duprey, David Edson, Mark Fournier, Victor Guevara, Millie Hannigan, Ellen Jackson, Liz Jazab, Mary Kane, Barbara Keane, Ellen Keefe, Joe Kendra, Peter Kennedy, Chris Leary, Nancy Logan, Candy Leydon, Mary Ann McDonough, Gwen Morrissey, Terry Mykytuk, Pat Petite, Pat Redfern, Marisol Rexasch, Mel Rivera, Lourdes Ruiz, and Linda Washington.

Stuart Dybek did a great deal of work on early drafts of my manuscript. Mark Kramer did heroic work on a late draft. Mike Rosenthal, Jonathan Harr, Fran, Nat, and Alice all listened ad nauseam and gave good advice. For counsel and encouragement, I have also to thank Benjamin Barnes, Ed Etheredge, Jon Jackson, John O'Brien, Tim Rivinus, Ginny Sullivan, and Sam Toperoff. My thanks to Georges Borchardt and to Larry Cooper, Sandy Goroff-Mailly, Bob Kempf, Steve Lewers, Austin Olney, Joe Kanon, John Sterling, and Barbara Williams.

A number of schoolteacher friends helped me, including Martha Batten, Elizabeth Cooney, Caren Dybek, Susan Etheredge, Margie Riddle, Faith Toperoff, and Joanne Wilson. Susan Todd and Sandy Warren suggested that I write about their occupation.

John Graiff helped me in innumerable ways. I am indebted as usual to Jamie Kilbreth, and irretrievably indebted, once again, to the very patient Richard Todd.

Of all the books about education that I read, my favorite is *Schoolteacher* by Dan C. Lortie (University of Chicago, 1975).

Larry Cuban's *How Teachers Taught: Constancy and Change in American Classrooms, 1890–1980* (Longman, New York, 1984) is a fine and temperate examination of change and the lack of it inside classrooms.

For me, the best current survey of public schools is *A Place Called School: Prospects for the Future* by John I. Goodlad (McGraw-Hill, New York, 1984).

For the history of corporal punishment, I relied on an unpublished paper by David Rempel, provided by the author. The sociological study I refer to in that part of the book is *Schoolteacher.* I also used the following books:

Compayre, Gabriel. *Compayre's History of Pedagogy.* Translated by W. H. Payne. Heath and Co., Boston, 1886.

English Pedagogy, Old and New, 2nd ed. Brown and Gross, Hartford, 1876.

Monroe, Paul, ed. *Cyclopedia of Education,* vol. 5. Macmillan, New York, 1914.

A Pedagogue's Commonplace Book. Sought out

and arranged by Edith Rowland. A. M. Dent and Sons, London, 1925.

Efrain Martinez lent me several books about Puerto Rico. He showed me around the island and reviewed parts of the manuscript. Victor Guevara was a wonderful guide to local Puerto Rican culture. I also relied on the following books and articles for the history of Irish immigration and for glimpses of Puerto Rican history and culture:

Berg, Ronald H. "The Socioeconomic Exploitation of Ethnicity on a Western Massachusetts Tobacco Farm." *Dialectical Anthropology,* vol. 5, no. 3, November 1980.

Fitzpatrick, Joseph P. "Puerto Ricans in Perspective: The Meaning of Migration to the Mainland." *International Migration Review,* vol. 2, no. 2, Spring 1968.

Handlin, Oscar. *The Uprooted,* 2nd ed. Atlantic Monthly Press, Boston, 1973.

Lauria, Anthony, Jr. " 'Respeto,' 'Relajo,' and Interpersonal Relations in Puerto Rico." *Anthropological Quarterly,* vol. 37, no. 2, April 1964.

Lopez, Adalberto, and James Petras, eds. *Puerto Rico and Puerto Ricans: Studies in History and Society.* Schenkman Publishing, Cambridge, Mass., 1974.

Macisco, John J. "Assimilation of the Puerto

Ricans on the Mainland." *International Migration Review,* vol. 2, no. 2, Spring 1968.

Maldonado, Edwin. "Contract Labor and the Origins of Puerto Rican Communities in the United States." *International Migration Review,* vol. 13, no. 1, Spring 1979.

Maldonado, Rita M. "Why Puerto Ricans Migrated to the United States in 1947–73." *Monthly Labor Review,* September 1976.

Martinez, Antonio. *Family and Migration: A Systems Analysis.* Doctoral dissertation, University of Massachusetts, February 1984.

Poblete, Renato. "Anomie and the Quest for Community: The Formation of Sects among the Puerto Ricans of New York." *American Catholic Sociological Review,* vol. 21 (1959), pp. 18–36.

Wagenheim, Kal. *Puerto Rico, A Profile,* 2nd ed. Holt, Rinehart and Winston, New York, 1970.

Woodham-Smith, Cecil. *The Great Hunger: Ireland 1845–1849.* Harper and Row, New York, 1962.

Young, Bruce M. *New England Farmworkers' Council: Case Study of a Community Service Organization.* Unpublished doctoral dissertation, University of Massachusetts, May 1975.

Many people gave me tours of Holyoke,

including Tim Barrett, Barry Werth, and Chris Zajac. Miguel Arce of the admirable organization Nueva Esperanza gave me a tour of residential South Holyoke. Tom McColgan explained the recent history and the inner workings of the local real estate market. The written history of Holyoke is scant. The history to which I refer in the text is *Holyoke, Massachusetts: A Case History of the Industrial Revolution in America* by Constance McLaughlin Green (Yale University Press, New Haven, 1939). *The Parish and the Hill,* a novel by Mary Doyle Curran (Feminist Press of the City University of New York, 1986), offers a vivid and rather dour view of growing up Irish Catholic in old industrial Holyoke. Ella DiCarlo's *Holyoke – Chicopee: A Perspective* (Transcript-Telegram, Holyoke, 1982) was also useful. An interesting case study of religious controversy in Holyoke is *Protestant and Catholic: Religious and Social Interaction in an Industrial Community* by Kenneth Wilson Underwood (Beacon Press, Boston, 1957). For background on the schools of Holyoke, I read a number of old annual reports: *Annual Report of the School Department of the City of Holyoke, Massachusetts* for the years 1899, 1900, 1901, 1902, 1903, 1904, 1905, 1906, 1908, 1910, 1911, 1917. The schools that these reports describe seem quaint in many particulars. Take, for example, the report of the Supervisor of Writing in 1908: "Writing requires a free movement of the pen, therefore many exercises have been given to insure correct pen holding, with the result of great improvement along this line." But reading these reports, I got the feeling that a child transported back to the turn of the century would not feel lost in the schools of that era. Indeed, to most modern American schoolchildren, the schools of the early 1900s would not seem nearly as different as the towns and cities around those schools.

For information about the history of educational reform and for valuable advice, I am grateful to Robert Hampel and to Theodore Sizer. I am grateful to the historian Bill Mc-Feeley for conversations about educational history. Lynn Cadwallader also gave good advice and lent me several books, including her doctoral dissertation, *Nathaniel Topliff Allen, 1823–72: A Case Study in the Professionalization of Nineteenth Century Teaching* (University of Massachusetts, February 1983). Al Rudnitzky of Smith College advised and encouraged me.

I found the following histories of education useful:

Bowles, Samuel, and Herbert Gintis. *Schooling*

in Capitalist America: Educational Reform and the Contradiction of Economic Life. Basic Books, New York, 1976.

Button, H. Warren, and Eugene F. Provenzo, Jr. *History of Education and Culture in America.* Prentice-Hall, Englewood Cliffs, N.J., 1983.

Butts, R. Freeman. *A Cultural History of Education: Reassessing Our Educational Traditions.* McGraw-Hill, New York, 1947.

_____. *Public Education in the United States: From Revolution to Reform.* Holt, Rinehart and Winston, New York, 1978.

_____, and Lawrence A. Cremin. *A History of Education in American Culture.* Henry Holt, New York, 1953.

Cremin, Lawrence A. *Public Education.* Basic Books, New York 1976.

_____. *The Transformation of the School: Progressivism in American Education, 1876–1957.* Knopf, New York, 1961.

Hampel, Robert L. *The Last Little Citadel: American High Schools Since 1940.* Houghton Mifflin, Boston, 1986.

Katz, Michael B. *Class, Bureaucracy and Schools: The Illusion of Educational Change in America,* expanded ed. Praeger, New York, 1975.

_____. *The Irony of Early School Reform: Educational Innovation in Mid-Nineteenth Century*

Massachusetts. Beacon Press, Boston, 1968.

Ravitch, Diane. *The Troubled Crusade: American Education, 1945–1980*. Basic Books, New York, 1983.

Tyack, David B., ed. *Turning Points in American Educational History*. Xerox College Publishing, Lexington, Mass., 1967.

____, Robert Lowe, and Elisabeth Hansot. *Public Schools in Hard Times: The Great Depression and Recent Years*. Harvard University Press, Cambridge, Mass., 1984.

Warren, Donald R. *To Enforce Education: A History of the Founding Years of the United States Office of Education*. Wayne State University Press, Detroit, 1974.

For statistics on education I drew from:

Snyder, Thomas D. *Digest of Education Statistics, 1987*. Office of Educational Research and Improvement, Washington, D.C., 1987.

The Statistical Yearbook, 1987. UNESCO, Paris, 1987.

Many books have something to say about women in teaching. Here are some that deal with the subject in detail:

Donovan, Frances R. *The Schoolma'am*. Arno

Press, New York, 1974.

Hoffman, Nancy. *Woman's "True" Profession: Voices from the History of Teaching.* Feminist Press, Old Westbury, New York, 1981.

Sugg, Redding S., Jr. *Motherteacher: The Feminization of American Education.* University of Virginia, Charlottesville, 1978.

I found several sociological studies of teaching to be engaging. I relied especially on *Schoolteacher,* by Dan C. Lortie, and on the following:

Jackson, Philip W. *Life in Classrooms.* Holt, Rinehart and Winston, New York, 1968.

Lipsky, Michael. *Street-Level Bureaucracy: Dilemmas of the Individual in Public Services.* Russell Sage Foundation, New York, 1980.

Rist, Ray C. *The Urban School, A Factory for Failure: A Study of Education in American Society.* MIT Press, Cambridge, Mass., 1973.

Waller, Willard. *The Sociology of Teaching.* John Wiley and Sons, New York, 1932.

I read several books about high school. Two good ones are:

Powell, Arthur G., Eleanor Farrar, and David K. Cohen. *The Shopping Mall High School:*

Winners and Losers in the Educational Marketplace. Houghton Mifflin, Boston, 1985.

Sizer, Theodore. *Horace's Compromise: The Dilemma of the American High School.* Houghton Mifflin, Boston, 1984.

For guidance in how to observe in a classroom, I used *Looking in Classrooms* by Jere E. Brophy and Thomas L. Good (Harper and Row, New York, 1984).

For information about tracking, I relied mainly on *Keeping Track: How Schools Structure Inequality* by Jennie Oakes (Yale University Press, New Haven, 1985).

Harry S. Broudy's *The Real World of the Public Schools* (Harcourt Brace Jovanovich, New York, 1972) provides a wonderful and mordant critique of public education and of critics of public education.

The following are a few of the well-known critiques of education from the late 1960s and early 1970s:

Dennison, George. *The Lives of Children.* Vintage, New York, 1969.

Illich, Ivan. *Deschooling Society.* Harper and Row, New York, 1970.

495

Kohl, Herbert. *36 Children.* New American Library, New York, 1967.

Kozol, Jonathan. *Death at an Early Age.* New American Library, New York, 1967.

Silberman, Charles. *Crisis in the Classroom: The Remaking of American Education.* Random House, New York, 1970.

The brief observations and quotations that begin the last section of this book are taken from:

Conant, James Bryant. Introduction to *General Education in a Free Society* (Harvard University Press, Cambridge, Mass., 1945). I also perused Conant's *Shaping Educational Policy* (McGraw-Hill, New York, 1964); and Conant's *The Child, the Parent and the State* (Harvard University Press, Cambridge, Mass., 1959). Hampel's *Last Little Citadel* contains fascinating revelations about Conant. Oakes's *Keeping Track* describes Conant's contribution to tracking.

Dewey, John. *The School and Society.* Excerpts reprinted in *Dewey on Education: Selections* by Martin Dworkin (Teachers College Press, Columbia University, New York, 1959). I also read in Dewey's *Democracy and Education: An Introduction to the Philosophy of Education* (Macmillan, New York, 1916);

and Dewey's *The Sources of a Science of Education* (Horace Liveright, New York, 1929). Nearly every educational history I read has something to say about Dewey. Richard Hofstadter's *Anti-Intellectualism in American Life* (Knopf, New York, 1963) is especially lucid. About Dewey, I also read: *John Dewey in Perspective* by George R. Geiger (Oxford University Press, New York, 1958); *John Dewey: An Intellectual Portrait* by Sidney Hook (John Day, New York, 1939); and *John Dewey, Philosopher of Science and Freedom: A Symposium*, edited by Sidney Hook (Dial Press, New York, 1950).

Du Bois, W. E. B. *The Education of Black People*. Edited by Herbert Aptheker. University of Massachusetts Press, Amherst, 1973.

Jefferson, Thomas. Quoted in Butts, *Public Education in the United States*.

Mann, Horace. Quoted in Button et al., *History of Education*. Mann, like Dewey and Jefferson, is discussed in practically every educational history I read.

The reports from the reform movement of the 1980s are too numerous to cite. One useful analysis of the movement is contained in *Policies for America's Public Schools: Teachers, Equity, and Indicators* by Ron Haskins and Duncan Macrae (Ablex Publishing,

Norwood, N.J., 1988).

I am indebted to Sally Carlton for putting me in touch with Marla Brassard of the University of Massachusetts. I am indebted to Dr. Brassard for the observations I make about abused children in the last section of this book. Dr. Brassard also sent me several papers and put me in touch with Joan M. Featherman, who described her unpublished doctoral dissertation, *Factors Relating to the Quality of Adult Adjustment in Female Victims of Child Sexual Abuse* (University of Massachusetts, 1989). This study, of women who were sexually abused as girls, finds that most of the subjects who recovered best from the horrors of their childhoods remember adults, both from within and outside their families and very often teachers, who took an interest in them and in the process changed their lives. One fine book on the question of why some children recover well from abuse is *The Invulnerable Child*, edited by E. James Anthony and Bertram J. Cohler (Guilford Press, New York, 1987).

THORNDIKE-MAGNA hopes you have enjoyed this Large Print book. All our Large Print titles are designed for easy reading, and all our books are made to last. Other Thorndike Press or Magna Print books are available at your library, through selected bookstores, or directly from the publishers. For more information about current and upcoming titles, please call or mail your name and address to:

THORNDIKE PRESS
P.O. Box 159
Thorndike, Maine 04986
(800) 223-6121
(207) 948-2962 (in Maine and Canada call collect)

or in the United Kingdom:

MAGNA PRINT BOOKS
Long Preston, Near Skipton
North Yorkshire,
England BD23 4ND
(07294) 225

There is no obligation, of course.

happen. I want the majority to be in the A's and B's. But Clarence. I've really got to praise him. And Ashley, who I didn't think was paying *any* attention, she got a C. So did Claude." Propping up her chin with her hand, Chris gazed into her kitchen at the clock on the wall. "Oh, what am I going to do about those four who flunked? Jimmy. Well, maybe if I move his seat . . ."

It was past bedtime.

Chris's parents had always recited the rosary at night. Sometimes Chris did, too, while trying to get to sleep. Her reasons were less pious, she guessed. Chris thought of prayer as a better way of counting sheep, and of keeping her students' faces out of her bedroom. If she failed, she wouldn't sleep well, and all the next day her voice would sound to her like branches snapping.